Lecture Notes in Computer Science 10447

Commenced Publication in 1973
Founding and Former Series Editors:
Gerhard Goos, Juris Hartmanis, and Jan van Leeuwen

David Van Horn · John Hughes (Eds.)

Trends in Functional Programming

17th International Conference, TFP 2016
College Park, MD, USA, June 8–10, 2016
Revised Selected Papers

 Springer

Editors
David Van Horn
University of Maryland
College Park, MD, USA

John Hughes 🆔
Chalmers University of Technology
Gothenburg, Sweden

ISSN 0302-9743   ISSN 1611-3349   (electronic)
Lecture Notes in Computer Science
ISBN 978-3-030-14804-1   ISBN 978-3-030-14805-8   (eBook)
https://doi.org/10.1007/978-3-030-14805-8

Library of Congress Control Number: 2019932918

LNCS Sublibrary: SL1 – Theoretical Computer Science and General Issues

This Springer imprint is published by the registered company Springer Nature Switzerland AG
The registered company address is: Gewerbestrasse 11, 6330 Cham, Switzerland

Preface

This volume contains a selection of papers presented at TFP 2016, the 17th International Symposium on Trends in Functional Programming, held during June 8–10, 2016, at the University of Maryland, College Park, USA.

TFP is an international forum for researchers with interests in all aspects of functional programming, taking a broad view of current and future trends in the area. It aspires to be a lively environment for presenting the latest research results and other contributions, described in draft papers submitted prior to the symposium, and lightly peer-reviewed for relevance. In total, 19 papers were presented at the symposium, together with keynote addresses by Ron Garcia (University of British Columbia), on "Static and Dynamic Type Checking: A Synopsis," and Steve Zdancewic (University of Pennsylvania), on "Type- and Example-Driven Program Synthesis." Full versions of 18 papers were then submitted, after the symposium, for inclusion in the proceedings. Each one was reviewed anonymously by, on average, 3.7 members of the Program Committee. As a result, revised versions of ten papers were selected for inclusion in this volume. The final selection spans novel implementation methods for functional languages (three papers), type inference and verification (three papers), and functional programming techniques and applications (four papers).

We are grateful to the Program Committee members for their hard work, and to the sponsors for their generous financial support.

January 2019

David Van Horn
John Hughes

Organization

General Chair

David Van Horn   University of Maryland, USA

Program Committee Chairs

David Van Horn   University of Maryland, USA
John Hughes   Chalmers University of Technology, Sweden

Steering Committee

Peter Achten	Radboud University, Nijmegen, The Netherlands
Jurriaan Hage	University of Utrecht, The Netherlands
Kevin Hammond	University of St. Andrews, UK
Zoltán Horváth	Eötvös Loránd University of Sciences, Budapest, Hungary
John Hughes	Chalmers University of Technology, Göteborg, Sweden
Pieter Koopman	Radboud University, Nijmegen, The Netherlands
Hans-Wolfgang Loidl	Heriot-Watt University, Edinburgh, UK
Jay McCarthy	Brigham Young University, Utah, USA
Greg Michaelson	Heriot-Watt University, Edinburgh, UK
Marco T. Morazán	Seton Hall University, New York, USA
Henrik Nilsson	University of Nottingham, UK
Rex Page	University of Oklahoma, Oklahoma City, UK
Ricardo Peña	Universidad Complutense de Madrid, Spain
Manuel Serrano	Inria Sophia-Antipolis, France
Phil Trinder	Glasgow University, UK
David A. Turner	University of Kent and Middlesex University, UK
Marko van Eekelen	Open University of the Netherlands and Radboud University, Nijmegen, The Netherlands
Viktória Zsók	Eötvös Loránd University of Sciences, Budapest, Hungary

Program Committee

Amal Ahmed	Northeastern University, USA
Nada Amin	École Polytechnique Fédérale de Lausanne, Switzerland
Kenichi Asai	Ochanomizu University, Japan
Małgorzata Biernacka	University of Wrocław, Poland
Laura Castro	University of A Coruña, Spain
Ravi Chugh	University of Chicago, USA

Silvia Ghilezan	University of Novi Sad, Serbia
Clemens Grelck	University of Amsterdam, The Netherlands
Suresh Jagannathan	Purdue University, USA
Pieter Koopman	Radboud University, Nijmegen, The Netherlands
Geoffrey Mainland	Drexel University, USA
Chris Martens	University of California, Santa Cruz, USA
Jay McCarthy	University of Massachusetts, Lowell, USA
Heather Miller	École Polytechnique Fédérale de Lausanne, Switzerland
Manuel Serrano	Inria, Sophia-Antipolis, France
Scott Smith	Johns Hopkins University, USA
Éric Tanter	University of Chile, Chile
Niki Vazou	University of California, San Diego, USA
Stephanie Weirich	University of Pennsylvania, USA

Sponsors

Contents

Implementation Techniques

Space-Efficient Latent Contracts

Michael Greenberg[✉]

Pomona College, Claremont, CA, USA
michael@cs.pomona.edu

Abstract. Standard higher-order contract monitoring breaks tail recursion and leads to space leaks that can change a program's asymptotic complexity; space-efficiency restores tail recursion and bounds the amount of space used by contracts. Space-efficient contract monitoring for contracts enforcing simple type disciplines (a/k/a gradual typing) is well studied. Prior work establishes a space-efficient semantics for manifest contracts without dependency [10]; we adapt that work to a latent calculus with dependency. We guarantee space efficiency when no dependency is used; we cannot *generally* guarantee space efficiency when dependency is used, but instead offer a framework for making such programs space efficient on a case-by-case basis.

1 Introduction

Findler and Felleisen [6] brought design-by-contract [16] into the higher-order world, allowing programmers to write pre- and post-conditions on functions to be checked at runtime. Pre- and post-conditions are easy in first-order languages, where it's very clear who is to blame when a contract is violated: if the pre-condition fails, blame the caller; if the post-condition fails, blame the callee. In higher-order languages, however, it's harder to tell who calls whom! Who should be to blame when a pre-condition on a higher-order function fails? For example, consider the following contract:

$$(\mathsf{pred}(\lambda x{:}\mathsf{Int}.\ x > 0) \mapsto \mathsf{pred}(\lambda y{:}\mathsf{Int}.\ y \geq 0)) \mapsto \mathsf{pred}(\lambda z{:}\mathsf{Int}.\ z \bmod 2 = 0)$$

This contract applies to a function (call it f, with type $(\mathsf{Int}{\rightarrow}\mathsf{Int}){\rightarrow}\mathsf{Int}$) that takes another function (call it g, with type $\mathsf{Int}{\rightarrow}\mathsf{Int}$) as input. The contract says that g will only be called with positives and only return naturals; f must return an even number. If f returns an odd number, f is to blame; if g returns a negative number, then it, too is to blame. But what if g is *called* with a non-positive number, say, -1? Who is to blame then? Findler and Felleisen's insight was that even in a higher-order setting, there are only two parties to blame. Here, g was given to f, so any bad values given to g here are due to some nefarious action on f's part—blame f! That is, the higher-order case generalizes pre- and post-conditions so that the negative positions of a contract all blame the caller while the positive positions all blame the callee.

© Springer Nature Switzerland AG 2019
D. Van Horn and J. Hughes (Eds.): TFP 2016, LNCS 10447, pp. 3–23, 2019.
https://doi.org/10.1007/978-3-030-14805-8_1

Dependent contracts—where the codomain contract can refer to the function's argument—are particularly useful. For example, the square root function, sqrt, satisfies the contract: x:pred(λy:Real. $y \geq 0$) $\mapsto$ pred(λz:Real. abs $(x - z *$ $z) < \epsilon$) That is, sqrt takes a non-negative real, x, and returns a non-negative real z that's within ϵ of the square root of x. (The dependent variable x is bound in the codomain; the variable y is local to the domain predicate.)

1.1 Contracts Leak Space

While implementations of contracts have proven quite successful (particularly so in Racket [8,18]), there is a problem: contracts leak space. Why?

The default implementation of contracts works by wrapping a function in a *function proxy*. For example, to check that $f = \lambda x$:Int. $x + 1$ satisfies the contract $C = $ pred(λz:Int. $z \bmod 2 = 0$) $\mapsto$ pred(λz:Int. $z \bmod 2 = 0$), we monitor the function by wrapping it in a function proxy $\mathsf{mon}^l(C, f)$. When this proxy is called with an input v, we first check that v satisfies C's domain contract (i.e., that v is even), then we run f on v to get some result v', and then check that v' satisfies C's codomain contract (that the result is even). Here the contract will always fail blaming l: one of v and v' will always be odd.

Contracts leak space in two ways. First, there is no bound on the number of function proxies that can appear on a given function. More grievously, contracts break tail recursion. To demonstrate the issue with tail calls, we'll use the simplest example of mutual recursion: detecting parity.

$$\begin{aligned} \text{let odd} \quad &= \lambda x\text{:Int. if } (x = 0) \text{ false (even } (x - 1)) \\ \text{and even} &= \lambda x\text{:Int. if } (x = 0) \text{ true (odd } (x - 1)) \end{aligned}$$

Functional programmers will expect this program to run in constant space, because it is *tail recursive*. Adding a contract breaks the tail recursion. If we add a contract to odd and call odd 5, what contract checks accumulate (Fig. 1)?[1] Notice how the checks accumulate in the codomain? Even though the mutually recursive calls to even and odd are syntactically tail calls, we can't bound the number of codomain checks that occur. That is, we can't bound the size of the stack, and tail recursion is broken! Even though there's only one function proxy on odd, our contracts create a space leak.

1.2 Overview and Contributions

Space efficiency for gradual types [23] (a/k/a contracts constrained to type tests) is well studied [9,13,14,22,24]; Greenberg [10] developed a space-efficient semantics for general, non-dependent contracts. He used a manifest calculus, conflating contracts and types; however, contracts are typically implemented in latent calculi, where contracts are distinct from whatever types may exist. Greenberg "believe[s] it would be easy to design a latent version of eidetic λ_H, following

---

[1] Readers may observe that the contract betrays a deeper knowledge of numbers than the functions themselves. We offer this example as minimal, not naturally occurring.

$$\begin{aligned}
\text{let odd} \;&= \text{mon}^{l_{\text{odd}}}(x{:}\text{pred}(\lambda x{:}\text{Int.}\; x \geq 0) \mapsto \text{pred}(\lambda b{:}\text{Bool.}\; b \,\text{or}\, (x \bmod 2 = 0)), \\
&\qquad \lambda x{:}\text{Int. if } (x = 0) \text{ false } (\text{even } (x - 1))) \\
\text{and even} \;&= \lambda x{:}\text{Int. if } (x = 0) \text{ true } (\text{odd } (x - 1))
\end{aligned}$$

$$\begin{aligned}
&\text{odd } 5 \\
\longrightarrow^*_C \;& \text{mon}^{l_{\text{odd}}}(\text{pred}_{[x \mapsto 5]}(\dots), \text{even } 4) \\
\longrightarrow^*_C \;& \text{mon}^{l_{\text{odd}}}(\text{pred}_{[x \mapsto 5]}(\dots), \text{mon}^{l_{\text{odd}}}(\text{pred}_{[x \mapsto 3]}(\dots), \\
&\quad \text{odd } \text{mon}^{l_{\text{odd}}}(\text{pred}(\lambda x{:}\text{Int.}\; x \geq 0), 3))) \\
\longrightarrow^*_C \;& \text{mon}^{l_{\text{odd}}}(\text{pred}_{[x \mapsto 5]}(\dots), \text{mon}^{l_{\text{odd}}}(\text{pred}_{[x \mapsto 3]}(\dots), \text{even } 2)) \\
\longrightarrow^*_C \;& \text{mon}^{l_{\text{odd}}}(\text{pred}_{[x \mapsto 5]}(\dots), \text{mon}^{l_{\text{odd}}}(\text{pred}_{[x \mapsto 3]}(\dots), \text{mon}^{l_{\text{odd}}}(\text{pred}_{[x \mapsto 1]}(\dots), \\
&\quad \text{odd } \text{mon}^{l_{\text{odd}}}(\text{pred}(\lambda x{:}\text{Int.}\; x \geq 0), 1)))) \\
\longrightarrow^*_C \;& \text{mon}^{l_{\text{odd}}}(\text{pred}_{[x \mapsto 5]}(\dots), \text{mon}^{l_{\text{odd}}}(\text{pred}_{[x \mapsto 3]}(\dots), \text{mon}^{l_{\text{odd}}}(\text{pred}_{[x \mapsto 1]}(\dots), \text{even } 0)))
\end{aligned}$$

Fig. 1. Contracts break tail recursion

the translations in Greenberg, Pierce, and Weirich (GPW)" [11]; in this paper, we show that belief to be well founded by giving a space-efficient semantics for a (dependent!) variant of contract PCF (CPCF) [3,4].

The rest of this paper discusses a formulation of contracts that enjoys sound space efficiency; that is, where we slightly change the implementation of contracts so that (a) programs are observationally equivalent to the standard semantics, but (b) contracts consume a bounded amount of space. In this paper, we've omitted some of the more detailed examples and motivation—we refer curious readers to Greenberg [10], though we intend the paper to be self-contained.

We follow Greenberg's general structure, defining two forms of dependent CPCF: CPCF$_C$ is the *classic* semantics; CPCF$_E$ follows the space-efficient eidetic semantics. We are able to prove space efficiency without dependency, bounding the amount of space consumed by contracts; we are unable to prove space efficiency in general with dependency, but instead offer a framework that allows for dependent contracts to be *made* space efficient.

We offer two primary contributions: adapting Greenberg's work to a latent calculus and extending the possibility of space efficiency to dependent contracts.

There are some other, smaller, contributions as well. First, adding in nontermination moves beyond Greenberg's strongly normalizing calculi, showing that the POPL 2015 paper's result isn't an artifact of strong normalization (where we can, in theory, bound the size of the any term's evaluation in advance, not just contracts). Second, the simpler type system here makes it clear which type system invariants are necessary for space-efficiency and which are bookkeeping for proving that the more complicated manifest type system is sound. Third, by separating contracts and types, we can give tighter space bounds. Finally, we explore how space efficiency can be attained in dependent contracts. While we can't give a guarantee for dependent contracts, we show that it's possible to achieve and discuss different ways to do so.

Types	B	$::=$	$\mathsf{Bool}\mid\mathsf{Int}\mid\ \ldots$
	T	$::=$	$B\mid T_1{\to}T_2$
Terms	e	$::=$	$x\mid k\mid e_1\,op\,e_2\mid e_1\,e_2\mid\lambda x{:}T.\,e\mid\mu(x{:}T).\,e\mid\mathsf{if}\,e_1\,e_2\ e_3\mid$
			$\mathsf{err}^l\mid\mathsf{mon}^l(C,e)\mid\mathsf{mon}(c,e)$
	op	$::=$	$\mathsf{add1}\mid\mathsf{sub1}\mid\ \ldots$
	k	$::=$	$\mathsf{true}\mid\mathsf{false}\mid0\mid1\mid\ \ldots$
	w	$::=$	$v\mid\mathsf{err}^l$
	v	$::=$	$k\mid\lambda x{:}T.\,e\mid\mathsf{mon}^l(x{:}C_1\mapsto C_2,v)\mid\mathsf{mon}(x{:}c_1\mapsto c_2,\lambda x{:}T.\,e)$
	C	$::=$	$\mathsf{pred}_\sigma(e)\mid x{:}C_1\mapsto C_2$
	c	$::=$	$r\mid x{:}c_1\mapsto c_2$
	r	$::=$	$\mathsf{nil}\mid\mathsf{pred}^l_\sigma(e);r$

Fig. 2. Syntax of classic and space-efficient CPCF

2   Classic and Space-Efficient Contract PCF

We present classic and space-efficient CPCF as separate calculi sharing syntax and some typing rules (Figs. 2 and 3), and a single, parameterized operational semantics with some rules held completely in common (omitted to save space) and others specialized to each system (Fig. 4). The formal presentation is modal, with two modes: C for classic and E for space-efficient. While much is shared between the two modes—types, T; the core syntax of expressions, e; most of the typing rules—we use colors to highlight parts that belong to only one system. Classic CPCF is typeset in salmon while space-efficient CPCF is in periwinkle.

2.1   Contract PCF (CPCF)

Plain CPCF is an extension of Plotkin's 1977 PCF [17], developed first by Dimoulas and Felleisen [3,4] (our syntax is in Fig. 2). It is a simply typed language with recursion. The typing rules are straightforward (Fig. 3). The operational semantics for the generic fragment also uses conventional rules (omitted to save space). Dimoulas and Felleisen use evaluation contexts to offer a concise description of their system; we write out our relation in full, giving congruence rules (E*L, E*R, EIF) and error propagating rules (E*RAISE) explicitly—we will need to restrict congruence for casts, and our methods are more transparent written with explicit congruence rules than using the subtly nested evaluation contexts of Herman et al. [13,14].

Contracts are CPCF's distinguishing feature. Contracts, C, are installed via monitors, written $\mathsf{mon}^l(C,e)$; such a monitor says "ensure that e satisfies the contract C; if not, the blame lies with label l". Monitors only apply to appropriate types (TMON). There are two kinds of contracts in CPCF: *predicate contracts* over base type, written $\mathsf{pred}_\sigma(e)$, and *function contracts*, written $x{:}C_1\mapsto C_2$.

Predicate contracts $\mathsf{pred}_\sigma(e)$ have two parts: a predicate on base types, e, which identifies which values satisfy the contract; and a closing substitution σ which keeps track of values substituted into the contract. For example, if ι is the identity substitution mapping variables to themselves:

- $\mathsf{pred}_\iota(\lambda x{:}\mathsf{Int}.\ x > 0)$ identifies the positives;
- $\mathsf{pred}_\iota(\lambda x{:}\mathsf{Int}.\ x > y)$ identifies numbers greater than an unspecified number y; and,
- $\mathsf{pred}_{[y\mapsto 47]}(\lambda x{:}\mathsf{Int}.\ x > y)$ identifies numbers greater than 47.

When the closing substitution σ is the identity mapping ι, we write $\mathsf{pred}(e)$ instead of $\mathsf{pred}_\iota(e)$. In CPCF$_\mathsf{C}$, closing substitutions will map each variable to either (a) itself or (b) a value. Substitution into contracts is a non-issue without dependency: each contract is just closed. Having introduced dependency, we use explicit closing substitutions rather than direct substitution for three reasons: first, it simplifies our space efficiency proof for simple contracts (Sect. 4.1); second, explicitness lets us distinguish the contract $\mathsf{pred}_{[x\mapsto 0]}(\lambda x{:}\mathsf{Int}.\ x = 0)$ from $\mathsf{pred}_{[x\mapsto 0]}(\lambda x{:}\mathsf{Int}.\ 0 = 0)$; third, it emphasizes that contracts are just another form of closure. Predicates are solely over *base types*, not functions.

Function contracts $x{:}C_1 \mapsto C_2$ are satisfied by functions satisfying their parts: functions whose inputs all satisfy C_1 and whose outputs all satisfy C_2. Function contracts are dependent: the codomain contract C_2 can refer back to the input to the function. For example, the contract $x{:}\mathsf{pred}(\lambda z{:}\mathsf{Int}.\ z > 0) \mapsto \mathsf{pred}(\lambda y{:}\mathsf{Int}.\ y > x)$ is satisfied by increasing functions on the positives. Note that x is bound in the codomain, but z is not.[2] When function contracts aren't dependent, we omit the binder at the front, e.g., $\mathsf{pred}(\lambda x{:}\mathsf{Int}.\ x > 0) \mapsto \mathsf{pred}(\lambda x{:}\mathsf{Int}.\ x > 0)$ means operators on positives. We check that contracts are satisfied at runtime.

We use explicit, delayed substitutions to keep track of which values are substituted into predicate contracts. To help with our proof of space efficiency, we don't track variables that don't appear in the predicate:

$$\mathsf{pred}_\sigma(e)[v/x] = \begin{cases} \mathsf{pred}_{\sigma[x\mapsto v]}(e) & x \in \mathsf{fv}(\sigma(e)) \\ \mathsf{pred}_\sigma(e) & \text{otherwise} \end{cases}$$

Alpha equivalence allows us to give fresh names to variables in the domain of σ by consistently renaming those variables inside of the predicate e. Only holding on to substitutions that close up free variables in e is a way of modeling closures. A dependent predicate closes over some finite number of variables; a compiled representation would generate a closure with a corresponding number of slots in the closing environment. Restricting substitutions to exactly those variables appearing free in the predicate serves another purpose: we can easily recover space-efficiency bounds for programs without dependent contracts (Sect. 4.1).

2.2   Classic Contract PCF (CPCF$_\mathsf{C}$)

Classic CPCF gives a straightforward semantics to contracts (Fig. 4), largely following the seminal work by Findler and Felleisen [6]. To check a predicate contract, we simply test it (EMONPRED), returning either the value or an appropriately labeled error. Function contracts are deferred: $\mathsf{mon}^l(x{:}C_1 \mapsto C_2, v)$ is a

---

[2] Concrete syntax for such predicates can be written much more nicely, but we ignore such concerns here.

Typing rules $\boxed{\Gamma \vdash e : T}$

$$\frac{x{:}T \in \Gamma}{\Gamma \vdash x : T} \ \text{TVar} \qquad \frac{}{\Gamma \vdash k : \text{ty}(k)} \ \text{TConst} \qquad \frac{}{\Gamma \vdash \text{err}^l : T} \ \text{TBlame}$$

$$\frac{\Gamma, x{:}T_1 \vdash e_{12} : T_2}{\Gamma \vdash \lambda x{:}T_1.\ e_{12} : T_1{\to}T_2} \ \text{TAbs} \qquad \frac{\Gamma, x{:}T \vdash e : T}{\Gamma \vdash \mu(x{:}T).\ e : T} \ \text{TRec}$$

$$\frac{\begin{array}{c}\text{ty}(op) = T_1{\to}T_2{\to}T \\ \Gamma \vdash e_1 : T_1 \quad \Gamma \vdash e_2 : T_2\end{array}}{\Gamma \vdash e_1\ op\ e_2 : T} \ \text{TOp} \qquad \frac{\Gamma \vdash e_1 : T_1{\to}T_2 \quad \Gamma \vdash e_2 : T_1}{\Gamma \vdash e_1\ e_2 : T_2} \ \text{TApp}$$

$$\frac{\Gamma \vdash e_1 : \text{Bool} \quad \Gamma \vdash e_2 : T \quad \Gamma \vdash e_3 : T}{\Gamma \vdash \text{if}\ e_1\ e_2\ e_3 : T} \ \text{TIf}$$

$$\frac{\Gamma \vdash e : T \quad \Gamma \vdash C : T}{\Gamma \vdash \text{mon}^l(C, e) : T} \ \text{TMon} \qquad \frac{\Gamma \vdash e : T \quad \Gamma \vdash c : T}{\Gamma \vdash \text{mon}(c, e) : T} \ \text{TMonC}$$

Contract typing $\boxed{\Gamma \vdash C : T}$ $\boxed{\Gamma \vdash c : T}$

$$\frac{\Gamma, \Gamma' \vdash e : B{\to}\text{Bool} \quad \Gamma' \vdash \sigma}{\Gamma \vdash \text{pred}_\sigma(e) : B} \ \text{TPred} \qquad \frac{\Gamma \vdash C_1 : T_1 \quad \Gamma, x{:}T_1 \vdash C_2 : T_2}{\Gamma \vdash x{:}C_1 \mapsto C_2 : T_1{\to}T_2} \ \text{TFun}$$

$$\frac{}{\Gamma \vdash \text{nil} : B} \ \text{TCNil} \qquad \frac{\Gamma \vdash \text{pred}_\sigma(e) : B \quad \Gamma \vdash r : B}{\Gamma \vdash \text{pred}_\sigma^l(e); r : B} \ \text{TCPred}$$

$$\frac{\Gamma \vdash c_1 : T_1 \quad \Gamma, x{:}T_1 \vdash c_2 : T_2}{\Gamma \vdash x{:}c_1 \mapsto c_2 : T_1{\to}T_2} \ \text{TCFun}$$

Closing substitutions $\boxed{\Gamma \vdash \sigma}$

$$\frac{}{\emptyset \vdash \iota} \ \text{TId} \qquad \frac{\Gamma \vdash \sigma \quad x{:}T \vdash v : T}{\Gamma, x{:}T \vdash \sigma[x \mapsto v]} \ \text{TMap}$$

Fig. 3. Typing rules of classic and space-efficient CPCF

value, called a *function proxy*. When a function proxy is applied, it unwraps the proxy, monitoring the argument with the domain contract, running the function, and then monitoring the return value with the codomain contract (EMonApp).

$$\frac{}{\mathsf{mon}^l(\mathsf{pred}_\sigma(e_1), v_2) \longrightarrow_\mathsf{C} \text{if } (\sigma(e_1) \ v_2) \ v_2 \ \mathsf{err}^l} \quad \text{EMonPred}$$

$$\frac{}{\mathsf{mon}^l(x{:}C_1 \mapsto C_2, v_1) \ v_2 \longrightarrow_\mathsf{C} \mathsf{mon}^l(C_2[v_2/x], v_1 \ \mathsf{mon}^l(C_1, v_2))} \quad \text{EMonApp}$$

$$\frac{e \longrightarrow_\mathsf{C} e'}{\mathsf{mon}^l(C, e) \longrightarrow_\mathsf{C} \mathsf{mon}^l(C, e')} \quad \text{EMon} \qquad \frac{}{\mathsf{mon}^l(C, \mathsf{err}^{l'}) \longrightarrow_\mathsf{C} \mathsf{err}^{l'}} \quad \text{EMonRaise}$$

$$\frac{}{\mathsf{mon}^l(C, e) \longrightarrow_\mathsf{E} \mathsf{mon}(\mathsf{label}^l(C), e)} \quad \text{EMonLabel}$$

$$\frac{}{\mathsf{mon}(\mathsf{nil}, v_1) \longrightarrow_\mathsf{E} v_1} \quad \text{EMonCNil}$$

$$\frac{}{\mathsf{mon}(\mathsf{pred}_\sigma^l(e); r, v_1) \longrightarrow_\mathsf{E} \text{if } (\sigma(e) \ v_1) \ \mathsf{mon}(r, v_1) \ \mathsf{err}^l} \quad \text{EMonCPred}$$

$$\frac{}{\mathsf{mon}(x{:}c_1 \mapsto c_2, v_1) \ v_2 \longrightarrow_\mathsf{E} \mathsf{mon}(c_2[v_2/x], v_1 \ \mathsf{mon}(c_1, v_2))} \quad \text{EMonCApp}$$

$$\frac{e \neq \mathsf{mon}(c', e'') \quad e \longrightarrow_\mathsf{E} e'}{\mathsf{mon}(c, e) \longrightarrow_\mathsf{E} \mathsf{mon}(c, e')} \quad \text{EMonC} \qquad \frac{}{\mathsf{mon}(c, \mathsf{err}^l) \longrightarrow_\mathsf{E} \mathsf{err}^l} \quad \text{EMonCRaise}$$

$$\frac{}{\mathsf{mon}(c_2, \mathsf{mon}(c_1, e)) \longrightarrow_\mathsf{E} \mathsf{mon}(\mathsf{join}(c_1, c_2), e)} \quad \text{EMonCJoin}$$

Fig. 4. Operational semantics of classic and space-efficient CPCF

Our semantics may seem to be *lax*, where no monitor is applied to dependent uses of the argument in the codomain monitor [11]. In fact, it is agnostic: we could be *picky* by requiring that function contract monitors $\mathsf{mon}^l(x{:}C_1 \mapsto C_2, e)$ have the substitution $[x \mapsto \mathsf{mon}^l(C_1, x)]$ throughout C_2; we could be *indy* by having $[x \mapsto \mathsf{mon}^{l'}(C_1, x)]$ throughout C_2 [4]. We default to a lax rule to make our proof of soundness easier, but we'll have as a corollary that classic and space-efficient semantics yield the same result regardless of what the closing substitutions do in the codomain (Sect. 3).

Standard congruence rules allow for evaluation inside of monitors (EMon) and the propagation of errors (EMonRaise).

2.3 Space-Efficient Contract PCF (CPCF$_\mathsf{E}$)

How can we recover tail calls in CPCF? CPCF$_\mathsf{C}$ will happily wrap arbitrarily many function proxies around a value, and there's no bound on the number of codomain contract checks that can accumulate. The key idea is *joining* contracts. We'll make two changes to the language: we'll bound function proxies so each function has at most one, and we'll bound stacks to avoid redundant checking.

$$\text{label}^l(\text{pred}_\sigma(e_1)) = \text{pred}_\sigma^l(e_1)$$
$$\text{label}^l(x{:}C_1 \mapsto C_2) = x{:}\text{label}^l(C_1) \mapsto \text{label}^l(C_2)$$

$$\text{join}(\text{nil}, r_2) = r_2$$
$$\text{join}(\text{pred}_\sigma^l(e); r_1, r_2) = \text{pred}_\sigma^l(e); \text{drop}(\text{join}(r_1, r_2), \text{pred}_\sigma(e))$$
$$\text{join}(x{:}c_{11} \mapsto c_{12}, x{:}c_{21} \mapsto c_{22}) = x{:}\text{join}(c_{21}, c_{11}) \mapsto \text{join}(\text{wrap}(c_{12}, x, c_{22}), c_{22})$$

$$\text{drop}(\text{nil}, \text{pred}_\sigma(e)) = \text{nil}$$
$$\text{drop}(\text{pred}_{\sigma_2}^l(e_2); r, \text{pred}_{\sigma_1}(e_1)) =$$
$$\begin{cases} \text{drop}(r, \text{pred}_{\sigma_2}(e_2)) & \text{pred}_{\sigma_1}(e_1) \supset \text{pred}_{\sigma_2}(e_2) \\ \text{pred}_{\sigma_2}^l(e_2); \text{drop}(r, \text{pred}_{\sigma_1}(e_1)) & \text{pred}_{\sigma_1}(e_1) \not\supset \text{pred}_{\sigma_2}(e_2) \end{cases}$$

$$\text{wrap}(\text{pred}_\sigma^l(e), x, c) = \begin{cases} \text{pred}_\sigma^l(e) & x \notin \text{fv}(\sigma(e)) \\ \text{pred}_{\sigma[x \mapsto \text{mon}(\text{join}(c',c),e)]}^l(e) & \sigma(x) = \text{mon}(c', e) \\ \text{pred}_{\sigma[x \mapsto \text{mon}(c,\sigma(x))]}^l(e) & \text{otherwise} \end{cases}$$
$$\text{wrap}(\text{nil}, x, c) = \text{nil}$$
$$\text{wrap}(\text{pred}_\sigma^l(e); r, x, c) = \text{wrap}(\text{pred}_\sigma^l(e), x, c); \text{wrap}(r, x, c)$$
$$\text{wrap}(y{:}c_1 \mapsto c_2, x, c) = y{:}\text{wrap}(c_1, x, c) \mapsto \text{wrap}(c_2, x, c)$$

Fig. 5. Contract labeling and predicate stack management

We ultimately show that contracts without dependency use constant space, but that the story for dependent functions is more complex (Sect. 4).

Fortuitously, our notion of join solves both of our problems, working identically for both simple and dependent contracts. To ensure a function value can have only one proxy, we change the semantics of monitoring: when monitoring a proxied value, we join the new monitor and the old one. To bound the size of stacks contract checks, we join pending contracts to avoid redundancy.

The join operation works on *labeled contracts*, which (a) move the label from the monitor into the contract and (b) allow us to keep track of many predicates at once (Fig. 5). Concretely, labeled contracts use the metavariable c (as opposed to C), comprising function contracts as usual ($x{:}c_1 \mapsto c_2$) and *predicate stacks*, r (Fig. 2). A predicate stack r is a list of *labeled predicates* $\text{pred}^l(e)$, where nil is the empty stack.

The join operation takes two labeled contracts and combines them, eliminating redundant contracts as it goes. To join a new and an old predicate stack, we keep new contracts and eliminate redundant old ones; only more "recent" contracts are kept. Joining functions works contravariantly, being careful to maintain correct substitution behavior using wrap.

Finally, we establish what we mean by "redundant" using *predicate implication*: when does one contract imply another?

Definition 1 (Predicate implication). *Let* $\text{pred}_{\sigma_1}(e_1) \supset \text{pred}_{\sigma_2}(e_2)$ *be a relation on predicates such that:*

(Reflexivity) If $\emptyset \vdash \mathsf{pred}_\sigma(e) : B$ then $\mathsf{pred}_\sigma(e) \supset \mathsf{pred}_\sigma(e)$.

(Transitivity) If $\mathsf{pred}_{\sigma_1}(e_1) \supset \mathsf{pred}_{\sigma_2}(e_2)$ and $\mathsf{pred}_{\sigma_2}(e_2) \supset \mathsf{pred}_{\sigma_3}(e_3)$, then $\mathsf{pred}_{\sigma_1}(e_1) \supset \mathsf{pred}_{\sigma_3}(e_3)$.

(Substitutivity) When $\Gamma_{i1}, x{:}T', \Gamma_{i2} \vdash \mathsf{pred}_{\sigma_i}(e_i) : T$ and $\emptyset \vdash v : T'$, if $\mathsf{pred}_{\sigma_1}(e_1) \supset \mathsf{pred}_{\sigma_2}(e_2)$ then $\mathsf{pred}_{\sigma_1}(e_1)[v/x] \supset \mathsf{pred}_{\sigma_2}(e_2)[v/x]$.

(Adequacy) If $\emptyset \vdash \mathsf{pred}_{\sigma_i}(e_i) : T$ and $\mathsf{pred}_{\sigma_1}(e_1) \supset \mathsf{pred}_{\sigma_2}(e_2)$ then $\forall k \in \mathcal{K}_B$. $\sigma_1(e_1)\ k \longrightarrow_m$ true *implies* $\sigma_2(e_2)\ k \longrightarrow_m$ true.

(Decidability) For all $\emptyset \vdash \mathsf{pred}_{\sigma_1}(e_1) : B$ and $\emptyset \vdash \mathsf{pred}_{\sigma_2}(e_2) : B$, it is decidable whether $\mathsf{pred}_{\sigma_1}(e_1) \supset \mathsf{pred}_{\sigma_2}(e_2)$ or $\mathsf{pred}_{\sigma_1}(e_1) \not\supset \mathsf{pred}_{\sigma_2}(e_2)$.

The entire development of space-efficiency is parameterized over this implication relation, $\supset$, characterizing when one first-order contract subsumes another. We write $\not\supset$ for the negation of $\supset$. The $\supset$ relation is a *total pre-order* (a/k/a a *preference relation*)—it would be a total order, but it may not necessarily enjoy anti-symmetry. For example, we could have $\mathsf{pred}_\iota(\lambda x{:}\mathsf{Int}.\ x \geq 0) \supset \mathsf{pred}_\iota(\lambda x{:}\mathsf{Int}.\ x + 1 > 0)$ and vice versa, even though the two predicates aren't equal. You can also view $\supset$ as a total order *up-to contextual equivalence*.

There is at least one workable implication relation: syntactic equality. We say $\mathsf{pred}_{\sigma_1}(e_1) \supset \mathsf{pred}_{\sigma_2}(e_2)$ iff $e_1 = e_2$ and $\sigma_1 = \sigma_2$. Since we've been careful to store only those values that are actually referenced in the closure of the predicate, the steps to determine these equalities are finite and computable at runtime. For example, suppose we wish to show that $\mathsf{pred}_{[y\mapsto47]}(\lambda x{:}\mathsf{Int}.\ x > y) \supset \mathsf{pred}_{[y\mapsto47]}(\lambda x{:}\mathsf{Int}.\ x > y)$. The code part—the predicate $\lambda x{:}\mathsf{Int}.\ x > y$— is the same; an implementation might observe that the function pointers are equal. The environment has only one slot, for y, with the value 47 in it; an implementation might compare the two environments slot-by-slot.

Substitution in the Codomain: Lax, Picky, and Indy.

We extend Greenberg's notion of join to account for dependency with a new function, wrap. Greenberg, Pierce, and Weirich identified two variants of latent contracts in the literature, differing in their treatment of the dependent substitution of arguments in the codomain: *picky*, where we monitor the value substituted in the codomain with the domain contract; and *lax*, where the actual parameter value substituted into the codomain is unmonitored [11]. There is a third variant, *indy*, which applies a monitor to the argument value but uses a different blame label [4]. These different models of substitution all exhibit different behavior for *abusive* contracts, where the codomain contract violates the domain contract.

There is another source of substitutions in the codomain: multiple function proxies. How do the monitors unfold when we have two function proxies? In the classic lax semantics, we find (leaving the domain check unevaluated):

$$\mathsf{mon}(x{:}c_{11} \mapsto c_{12}, \mathsf{mon}(x{:}c_{21} \mapsto c_{22}, f))\ v$$
$$\longrightarrow_c \mathsf{mon}(c_{12}[v/x], \mathsf{mon}(x{:}c_{21} \mapsto c_{22}, f)\ \mathsf{mon}(c_{11}, v))$$
$$\longrightarrow_c \mathsf{mon}(c_{12}[v/x], \mathsf{mon}(c_{22}[\mathsf{mon}(c_{11}, v)/x], f\ \mathsf{mon}(c_{21}, \mathsf{mon}(c_{11}, v))))$$

Even though we're using the lax semantics, we substitute contracts into the codomain. For the space-efficient semantics to be sound, it must behave *exactly*

$C_1 = f{:}(\mathsf{pred}(\lambda x{:}\mathsf{Int}.\ x > 0) \mapsto \mathsf{pred}(\lambda x{:}\mathsf{Int}.\ x > 0)) \mapsto \mathsf{pred}(\lambda x{:}\mathsf{Int}.\ x > 0)$

$C_2 = f{:}(\mathsf{pred}(\lambda x{:}\mathsf{Int}.\ \mathsf{true}) \mapsto \mathsf{pred}(\lambda x{:}\mathsf{Int}.\ \mathsf{true})) \mapsto \mathsf{pred}(\lambda x{:}\mathsf{Int}.\ f\ 0 = 0)$

$$\mathsf{mon}^{l_1}(C_1, \mathsf{mon}^{l_2}(C_2, \lambda f{:}(\mathsf{Int}{\to}\mathsf{Int}).\ f\ 5))\ (\lambda x{:}\mathsf{Int}.\ x)$$
$$\longrightarrow_{\mathsf{C}}\ \mathsf{mon}^{l_1}(C_{12}[(\lambda x{:}\mathsf{Int}.\ x)/f],$$
$$\mathsf{mon}^{l_2}(C_2, \lambda f{:}(\mathsf{Int}{\to}\mathsf{Int}).\ f\ 5)\ \mathsf{mon}^{l_1}(C_{11}, (\lambda x{:}\mathsf{Int}.\ x)))$$
$$\longrightarrow_{\mathsf{C}}^*\ \mathsf{mon}^{l_1}(C_{12}[(\lambda x{:}\mathsf{Int}.\ x)/f], \mathsf{mon}^{l_2}(C_{22}[\mathsf{mon}^{l_1}(C_{11}, \lambda x{:}\mathsf{Int}.\ x)/f], 5))$$
$$\longrightarrow_{\mathsf{C}}\ \mathsf{mon}^{l_1}(C_{12}[(\lambda x{:}\mathsf{Int}.\ x)/f],$$
$$\mathsf{if}\ ((\lambda x{:}\mathsf{Int}.\ \mathsf{mon}^{l_1}(C_{11}, \lambda x{:}\mathsf{Int}.\ x)\ 0 = 0)\ 5)\ 5\ \ \mathsf{err}^{l_2})$$
$$\longrightarrow_{\mathsf{C}}\ \mathsf{mon}^{l_1}(C_{12}[(\lambda x{:}\mathsf{Int}.\ x)/f], \mathsf{if}\ (\mathsf{mon}^{l_1}(C_{11}, \lambda x{:}\mathsf{Int}.\ x)\ 0 = 0)\ 5\ \ \mathsf{err}^{l_2})$$
$$\longrightarrow_{\mathsf{C}}^*\ \mathsf{err}^{l_2}$$

Fig. 6. Abusive function proxies in $\mathrm{CPCF_C}$

like the classic semantics: no matter what joins happen, $\mathrm{CPCF_E}$ must replicate the contract substitutions done in $\mathrm{CPCF_C}$. We can construct an abusive contract in $\mathrm{CPCF_C}$—even though it has lax semantics—by having the inner function proxy abuse the outer one (Fig. 6). Why was blame raised? Because c_2's codomain contract *abused* c_1's domain contract. Even though $\mathrm{CPCF_C}$ has a lax semantics, wrapping multiple function proxies leads to monitoring domains from one contract in the codomain of another—a situation ripe for abuse.

Space-efficiency means joining contracts, so how can we emulate this classic-semantics substitution behavior? We use the wrap function, forcing a substitution when two function contracts are joined. By keeping track of these substitutions at every join, any joins that happen in the future will be working on contracts which already have appropriate substitutions.

$\mathrm{CPCF_E}$ uses *labeled contracts* (Fig. 2); substitution for labeled predicate contracts is explicit and delayed, as for ordinary contracts:

$$\mathsf{pred}^l_\sigma(e)[v/x] = \begin{cases} \mathsf{pred}^l_{\sigma[x \mapsto v]}(e) & x \in \mathrm{fv}(\sigma(e)) \\ \mathsf{pred}^l_\sigma(e) & \text{otherwise} \end{cases}$$
$$\mathsf{nil}[v/x] = \mathsf{nil}$$
$$(\mathsf{pred}^l_\sigma(e); r)[v/x] = \mathsf{pred}^l_\sigma(e)[v/x]; r[v/x]$$

We do *not* do any joining when a substitution occurs (but see Sect. 6). In $\mathrm{CPCF_E}$, closing substitutions map each variable to (a) itself ($[x \mapsto x]$), (b) a monitor on itself ($[x \mapsto \mathsf{mon}(c, x)]$), or (c) a value. We add an evaluation rule taking ordinary contract monitors $\mathsf{mon}^l(C, e)$ to labeled-contract monitors $\mathsf{mon}(c, e)$ by means of the labeling function label (EMONLABEL).

Space-efficiency comes by restricting congruence to only apply when there are abutting monitors (cf. EMONC here in $\mathrm{CPCF_E}$ to EMON in $\mathrm{CPCF_C}$). When two monitors collide, we *join* them (EMONCJOIN). Checking function contracts is as usual (EMONCAPP is the same as EMONAPP, only the latter works over labeled contracts); checking predicate stacks proceeds straightforwardly predicate-by-predicate (EMONCNIL and EMONCPRED).

3 Soundness for Space Efficiency

CPCF$_C$ and CPCF$_E$ are operationally equivalent, even though their cast semantics differ. We can make this connection formal by proving that every CPCF term either: (a) diverges in both CPCF$_C$ and CPCF$_E$ or (b) reduces to equivalent terms in both CPCF$_C$ and CPCF$_E$.

One minor technicality: some of the forms in our language are necessary only for runtime or only appear in one of the two calculi. We characterize *source programs* as those which omit runtime terms.

Definition 2 (Source program). *A well typed source program does not use* TBLAME *or* TMONC *(and so* TCNIL, TCPRED, *and* TCFUN *cannot be used).*

Greenberg identified the key property for proving soundness of a space efficient semantics: to be sound, the space-efficient semantics must recover a notion of congruence for checking.

Lemma 3 (Monitor congruence (single step)). *If $\emptyset \vdash e_1 : T$ and $\emptyset \vdash c : T$ and $e_1 \longrightarrow_E e_2$, then $\mathsf{mon}(c, e_1) \longrightarrow_E^* w$ iff $\mathsf{mon}(c, e_2) \longrightarrow_E^* w$.*

Proof. By cases on the step taken to find $e_1 \longrightarrow_E e_2$. In the easy case, there's no joining of coercions and the same rule can apply in both derivations. In the more interesting case, two contract monitors join. In either case, it suffices to show that the terms are ultimately confluent, since determinism will do the rest.

It is particularly satisfying that the key property for showing soundness of space efficiency can be proved independently of the inefficient semantics. Implementors can work entirely in the context of the space-efficient semantics, knowing that congruence ensures soundness. We show the observational equivalence of CPCF$_C$ and CPCF$_E$ by logical relations (Fig. 7), which gives us contextual equivalence—the strongest equivalence we could ask for.

Lemma 4 (Similar contracts are logically related). *If $\Gamma \vdash C_1 \sim C_2 : T$ and $\Gamma \vdash v_1 \simeq v_2 : T$ then $\Gamma \vdash \mathsf{mon}^l(C_1, v_1) \simeq \mathsf{mon}^l(C_2, v_2) : T$.*

Proof. By induction on the type index of the invariant relation $\Gamma \vdash C_1 \sim C_2 : T$.

Lemma 5 (Unwinding). *If $\emptyset \vdash \mu(x{:}T).\ e\ :\ T$, then $\mu(x{:}T).\ e \longrightarrow_m^* w$ iff there exists an n such that unrolling the fixpoint only n times converges to the same value, i.e., $e[\mu(x{:}T).\ \ldots\ e[\mu(x{:}T).\ e/x]\ \ldots /x] \longrightarrow_m^* w$.*

Theorem 6 (CPCF$_C$ and CPCF$_E$ terms are logically related).

1. *If $\Gamma \vdash e : T$ as a source program then $\Gamma \vdash e \simeq e : T$.*
2. *If $\Gamma \vdash C : T$ as a source program then $\Gamma \vdash C \sim C : T$.*

Proof. By mutual induction on the typing relations.

Result rules $\boxed{e_1 \sim e_2 : T}$

$$k \sim k : B \iff \mathsf{ty}(k) = B$$
$$v_{11} \sim v_{21} : T_1 \to T_2 \iff \forall e_{12} \sim e_{22} : T_1.\ v_{11}\ e_{12} \simeq v_{21}\ e_{22} : T_2$$
$$\mathsf{err}^l \sim \mathsf{err}^l : T$$

Term rules $\boxed{e_1 \simeq e_2 : T}$

$$e_1 \simeq e_2 : T \iff (e_1 \text{ diverges} \wedge e_2 \text{ diverges}) \vee (e_1 \longrightarrow_{\mathsf{C}}^* w_1 \wedge e_2 \longrightarrow_{\mathsf{E}}^* w_2 \wedge w_1 \sim w_2 : T)$$

Contract rules (invariant relation) $\boxed{\Gamma \vdash C_1 \sim C_2 : T}$

$$\Gamma \vdash \mathsf{pred}_{\sigma_1}(e_1) \sim \mathsf{pred}_{\sigma_2}(e_2) : B \iff \Gamma \vdash \sigma_1\ (e_1) \simeq \sigma_2(e_2) : B \to \mathsf{Bool}$$
$$\Gamma \vdash x{:}C_{11} \mapsto C_{12} \sim x{:}C_{21} \mapsto C_{22} : T_1 \to T_2 \iff$$
$$\Gamma \vdash C_{11} \sim C_{21} : T_1 \wedge \Gamma, x{:}T_1 \vdash C_{12} \sim C_{22} : T_2$$

Closing substitutions and open terms $\boxed{\Gamma \models \delta}$ $\boxed{\Gamma \vdash e_1 \simeq e_2 : T}$

$$\Gamma \models \delta \iff \forall x \in \mathrm{dom}(\Gamma).\ \delta_1(x) \sim \delta_2(x) : \Gamma(x)$$
$$\Gamma \vdash e_1 \simeq e_2 : T \iff \forall \Gamma \models \delta.\ \delta_1(e_1) \simeq \delta_2(e_2) : T$$

Fig. 7. Logical relation between classic and space-efficient CPCF

4 Bounds for Space Efficiency

We have seen that CPCF$_\mathsf{E}$ behaves the same as CPCF$_\mathsf{C}$ (Theorem 6), but is CPCF$_\mathsf{E}$ actually space efficient? For programs that don't use dependency, yes! With dependency, the story is more complicated.

4.1 The Simple Case

Greenberg showed that for *simple* contracts—without dependency—we can put a bounds on space [10]. We can recover his result in our more general framework. Observe that a given source program e starts with a finite number of predicate contracts in it. As e runs, no new predicates appear (because dependent substitutions have no effect), but predicates may accumulate in stacks. In the worst case, a predicate stack could contain every predicate contract from the original program e exactly once... but no more than that, because joins remove redundancy! Function contracts are also bounded: e starts out with function contracts of a certain height, and evaluation can only shrink that height. The leaves of function contracts are labeled with predicate stacks, so the largest contract we could ever see is of maximum height with maximal predicate stacks at every leaf. As the program runs, abutting monitors are joined, giving us a bound on the total number of monitors in a program (one per non-monitor AST node).

  We can make these ideas formal by first defining what we mean by "all the predicates in a program", and then showing that evaluation doesn't introduce predicates (Lemma 9). We let $\mathsf{preds}(e)$ be the set of predicates in a term, where a predicate is represented as a pair of term and a closing substitution.

Predicate extraction | $\mathsf{preds}(e), \mathsf{preds}(C), \mathsf{preds}(c) : \mathcal{P}(e \times (\mathit{Var} \rightharpoonup e))$ |

$$\mathsf{preds}(x) = \emptyset$$
$$\mathsf{preds}(k) = \emptyset$$
$$\mathsf{preds}(\lambda x{:}T.\ e) = \mathsf{preds}(e)$$
$$\mathsf{preds}(\mathsf{mon}^l(C, e)) = \mathsf{preds}(C) \cup \mathsf{preds}(e)$$
$$\mathsf{preds}(\mathsf{mon}(c, e)) = \mathsf{preds}(c) \cup \mathsf{preds}(e)$$
$$\mathsf{preds}(e_1\ e_2) = \mathsf{preds}(e_1) \cup \mathsf{preds}(e_2)$$
$$\mathsf{preds}(e_1\ op\ e_2) = \mathsf{preds}(e_1) \cup \mathsf{preds}(e_2)$$
$$\mathsf{preds}(\mathsf{if}\ e_1\ e_2\ e_3) =$$
$$\mathsf{preds}(e_1) \cup \mathsf{preds}(e_2) \cup \mathsf{preds}(e_3)$$
$$\mathsf{preds}(\mathsf{err}^l) = \emptyset$$

$$\mathsf{preds}(\mathsf{pred}_\sigma(e)) =$$
$$\{(e, \sigma)\} \cup \mathsf{preds}(e) \cup \bigcup\nolimits_{[x \mapsto v] \in \sigma} \mathsf{preds}(v)$$
$$\mathsf{preds}(x{:}C_1 \mapsto C_2) = \mathsf{preds}(C_1) \cup \mathsf{preds}(C_2)$$

$$\mathsf{preds}(\mathsf{nil}) = \emptyset$$
$$\mathsf{preds}(\mathsf{pred}_\sigma^l(e); r) = \{(e, \sigma)\} \cup \mathsf{preds}(e) \cup$$
$$\bigcup\nolimits_{[x \mapsto e'] \in \sigma} \mathsf{preds}(e') \cup \mathsf{preds}(r)$$
$$\mathsf{preds}(x{:}c_1 \mapsto c_2) = \mathsf{preds}(c_1) \cup \mathsf{preds}(c_2)$$

Contract size | $P_B : \mathbb{N}$ | | $S_B : \mathbb{N}$ | | $\mathsf{size}(C) : \mathbb{N}$ |

$$P_B = |\{e \in \mathsf{preds}(e) \mid \Gamma \vdash \mathsf{pred}_\sigma(e) : B\}| \qquad S_B = L \cdot P_B \cdot \log_2 P_B$$

$$\mathsf{size}(\mathsf{pred}_\sigma(e)) = S_B \text{ when } \emptyset \vdash \mathsf{pred}_\sigma(e) : B \qquad \mathsf{size}(x{:}C_1 \mapsto C_2) = \mathsf{size}(C_1) + \mathsf{size}(C_2)$$

Fig. 8. Predicate extraction and contract size

We say program e *uses simple contracts* when all predicates in e are closed and every predicate stack has no redundancies. As such a program reduces, no new contracts appear (and contracts may disappear).

Lemma 7. $\mathsf{preds}(e[e'/x]) \subseteq \mathsf{preds}(e) \cup \mathsf{preds}(e')$.

Proof. By induction on e. If e is a predicate contract, it has no free variables (by assumption), so the substitution doesn't hold on to anything.

Lemma 8. *If $\emptyset \vdash c_1 : T$ and $\emptyset \vdash c_2 : T$ then $\mathsf{preds}(\mathsf{join}(c_1, c_2)) \subseteq \mathsf{preds}(c_1) \cup \mathsf{preds}(c_2)$.*

Proof. By induction on c_1, ignoring wrap's substitution by Lemma 7.

Lemma 9 (Reduction is non-increasing in simple predicates). *If $\emptyset \vdash e : T$ and $e \longrightarrow_m e'$ then $\mathsf{preds}(e') \subseteq \mathsf{preds}(e)$.*

Proof. By induction on the step taken.

To compute the concrete bounds, we define P_B as the number of distinct predicates at the base type B. We can represent a predicate stack at type B in S_B bits, where L is the number of bits needed to represent a blame label. A given well typed contract $\emptyset \vdash C : T$ can then be represented in $\mathsf{size}(C)$ bits, where each predicate stacks are represented is S_B bits and function types are represented as trees of predicate stacks. Finally, since reduction is non-increasing (Lemma 9), we can bound the amount of space used by any contract by looking at the source program, e: we can represent all contracts in our program in at most $s = \max_{C \in e} \mathsf{size}(C)$ space—constant for a fixed source program.

Readers familiar with Greenberg's paper (and earlier work, like Herman et al. [13]) will notice that our bounds are more precise, tracking the number of holes in contracts per type ($\mathsf{size}(C)$) rather than simply computing the largest conceivable type ($2^{\mathsf{height}(T)}$).

4.2   The Dependent Case

In the dependent case, we can't *generally* bound the number of contracts by the size of contracts used in the program. Consider the following term, where $n \in \mathbb{N}$:

$$\begin{aligned}
&\mathsf{let}\ \mathsf{downTo} = \mu(f{:}\mathsf{Int}{\rightarrow}\mathsf{Int}).\\
&\quad \mathsf{mon}^l(x{:}\mathsf{pred}(\lambda x{:}\mathsf{Int}.\ x \geq 0) \mapsto \mathsf{pred}(\lambda y{:}\mathsf{Int}.\ x \geq y),\\
&\quad\quad \lambda x{:}\mathsf{Int}.\ \mathsf{if}\ (x = 0)\ 0\ (f\ (x - 1)))\ \mathsf{in}\\
&\quad \mathsf{downTo}\ n
\end{aligned}$$

How many different contracts will appear in a run of this program? As downTo runs, we'll see n different forms of the predicate $\mathsf{pred}^l_{\sigma_i}(\lambda y{:}\mathsf{Int}.\ x \geq y)$. We'll have one $\sigma_n = [x \mapsto n]$ on the first call, $\sigma_{n-1} = [x \mapsto n - 1]$ on the second call, and so on. But n's magnitude doesn't affect our measure of the size of source program's contracts. The number of distinct contracts that appear will be effectively unbounded.

In the simple case, we get bounds automatically, using the smallest possible implication relation—syntactic equality. In the dependent case, it's up to the programmer to identify implications that recover space efficiency. We can recover space efficiency for downTo by saying $\mathsf{pred}_{\sigma_1}(\lambda y{:}\mathsf{Int}.\ x \geq y) \supset \mathsf{pred}_{\sigma_2}(\lambda y{:}\mathsf{Int}.\ x \geq y)$ iff $\sigma_1(x) \leq \sigma_2(x)$. Then the codomain checks from recursive calls will be able to join:

$$\begin{aligned}
\mathsf{downTo}\ n &\longrightarrow^*_{\mathsf{E}} \mathsf{mon}^l(\mathsf{pred}_{[x \mapsto n]}(\ldots), \ldots)\\
&\longrightarrow^*_{\mathsf{E}} \mathsf{mon}^l(\mathsf{pred}_{[x \mapsto n]}(\ldots), \mathsf{mon}^l(\mathsf{pred}_{[x \mapsto n - 1]}(\ldots), \ldots))\\
&\longrightarrow^*_{\mathsf{E}} \mathsf{mon}^l(\mathsf{pred}_{[x \mapsto n - 1]}(\ldots), \ldots)
\end{aligned}$$

Why are we able to recover space efficiency in this case? Because we can come up with an easily decidable implication rule for our specific predicates matching how our function checks narrower and narrower properties as it recurses.

Recall the mutually recursive even/odd example (Fig. 1). We can make this example space-efficient by adding the implication that:

$$\mathsf{pred}_{\sigma_1}(\lambda b{:}\mathsf{Bool}.\ b\ \mathsf{or}\ (x\ \mathsf{mod}\ 2 = 0)) \supset \mathsf{pred}_{\sigma_2}(\lambda b{:}\mathsf{Bool}.\ b\ \mathsf{or}\ (x\ \mathsf{mod}\ 2 = 0))$$

iff $\sigma_1(x) + 2 = \sigma_2(x)$. Suppose we put contracts on both even and odd:

let odd $=$ mon$^{l_{\text{odd}}}(x{:}\mathsf{pred}(\lambda x{:}\mathsf{Int}.\ x \geq 0) \mapsto \mathsf{pred}(\lambda b{:}\mathsf{Bool}.\ b \text{ or } (x \bmod 2 = 0)),$
$$\lambda x{:}\mathsf{Int}.\ \text{if } (x = 0) \text{ false } (\text{even } (x - 1)))$$

and even $=$
mon$^{l_{\text{even}}}(x{:}\mathsf{pred}(\lambda x{:}\mathsf{Int}.\ x \geq 0) \mapsto \mathsf{pred}(\lambda b{:}\mathsf{Bool}.\ b \text{ or } ((x + 1) \bmod 2 = 0)),$
$$\lambda x{:}\mathsf{Int}.\ \text{if } (x = 0) \text{ true } (\text{odd } (x - 1)))$$

Now our trace of contracts won't be homogeneous; eliding domain contracts:

$$\text{odd } 5 \longrightarrow^*_C \text{mon}^{l_{\text{odd}}}(\mathsf{pred}_{[x \mapsto 5]}(\dots), \text{even } 4)$$
$$\longrightarrow^*_C \text{mon}^{l_{\text{odd}}}(\mathsf{pred}_{[x \mapsto 5]}(\dots), \text{mon}^{l_{\text{even}}}(\mathsf{pred}_{[x \mapsto 4]}(\dots),$$
$$\text{mon}^{l_{\text{odd}}}(\mathsf{pred}_{[x \mapsto 3]}(\dots), \text{mon}^{l_{\text{even}}}(\mathsf{pred}_{[x \mapsto 2]}(\dots),$$
$$\text{mon}^{l_{\text{odd}}}(\mathsf{pred}_{[x \mapsto 1]}(\dots), \text{even } 0)))))$$

To make these checks space efficient, we'd need several implications; we write odd$_p$ for $\lambda b{:}\mathsf{Bool}.\ b$ or $(x \bmod 2 = 0)$ and even$_p$ for $\lambda b{:}\mathsf{Bool}.\ b$ or $((x + 1) \bmod 2 = 0)$. The following table gives conditions on the implication relation for the row predicate to imply the column predicate:

$\supset$	$\mathsf{pred}_{\sigma_2}(\text{odd}_p)$	$\mathsf{pred}_{\sigma_2}(\text{even}_p)$
$\mathsf{pred}_{\sigma_1}(\text{odd}_p)$	$\sigma_1(x) + 2 = \sigma_2(x)$	$\sigma_1(x) + 1 = \sigma_2(x)$
$\mathsf{pred}_{\sigma_1}(\text{even}_p)$	$\sigma_1(x) + 1 = \sigma_2(x)$	$\sigma_1(x) + 2 = \sigma_2(x)$

Having all four of these implications allows us to eliminate any pair of checks generated by the recursive calls in odd and even, reducing the codomain checking to constant space—here, just one check. We could define a different implication relation, where, say, $\mathsf{pred}_{\sigma_1}(\text{odd}_p) \supset \mathsf{pred}_{\sigma_2}(\text{odd}_p)$ iff $\sigma_1(x) \bmod 2 = \sigma_2(x) \bmod 2$. Such an implication would apply more generally than those in the table above.

As usual, there is a trade-off between time and space. It's possible to write contracts where the necessary implication relation for space efficiency amounts to checking both contracts. Consider the following tail-recursive factorial function:

let any $= \lambda z{:}\mathsf{Int}.\ \text{true}$
let fact $= \mu(f{:}\mathsf{Int}{\to}\mathsf{Int}{\to}\mathsf{Int}).$
$$\text{mon}^l(x{:}\mathsf{pred}(\text{any}) \mapsto acc{:}\mathsf{pred}(\text{any}) \mapsto \mathsf{pred}(\lambda y{:}\mathsf{Int}.\ x \geq 0),$$
$$\lambda x{:}\mathsf{Int}.\ \lambda acc{:}\mathsf{Int}.\ \text{if } (x = 0) \ acc \ (f \ (x - 1) \ (x * acc)))$$

This contract isn't *wrong*, just strange: if you call fact with a negative number, the program diverges and you indeed won't get a value back out (contracts enforce partial correctness). A call of fact 3 yields monitors that check, from outside to inside, that $3 \geq 0$ and $2 \geq 0$ and $1 \geq 0$ and $0 \geq 0$. When should we say that $\mathsf{pred}_{\sigma_1}(\lambda y{:}\mathsf{Int}.\ x \geq 0) \supset \mathsf{pred}_{\sigma_1}(\lambda y{:}\mathsf{Int}.\ x \geq 0)$? We could check that $\sigma_1(x) \geq \sigma_2(x)$... but the time cost is just like checking the original contract.

5   Where Should the Implication Relation Come from?

The simplest option is to punt: derive the implication relation as the reflexive transitive closure of a programmer's rules. A programmer might specify how several different predicates interrelate as follows:

```
1 y : Int {x1 >= y} implies y : Int {x2 >= y} when x1 <= x2
2 y : Int {x1 >  y} implies y : Int {x2 >= y} when x1 <= x2 + 1
3 y : Int {x1 >  y} implies y : Int {x2 >  y} when x1 <= x2
```

A default collection of such implications might come with the language; library programmers should be able to write their own, as well. But it is probably unwise to allow programmers to write arbitrary implications: what if they're wrong? A good implementation would only accept verified implications, using a theorem prover or an SMT solver to avoid bogus implications.

Rather than having programmers write their own implications, we could try to *automatically* derive the implications. Given a program, a fixed number of predicates occur, even if an unbounded number of predicate/closing substitution pairings might occur at runtime. Collect all possible predicates from the source program, and consider each pair of predicates over the same base type, $\mathsf{pred}(e_1)$ and $\mathsf{pred}(e_2)$ such that $\Gamma \vdash e_i : B \rightarrow \mathsf{Bool}$. We can derive from the typing derivation the shapes of the respective closing substitutions, σ_1 and σ_2. What are the conditions on σ_1 and σ_2 such that $\mathsf{pred}_{\sigma_1}(e_1) \supset \mathsf{pred}_{\sigma_2}(e_2)$? We are looking for a property $P(\sigma_1, \sigma_2)$ such that:

$$\forall k \in \mathcal{K}_B, \ P(\sigma_1, \sigma_2) \wedge \sigma_1(e_1) \ k \ \longrightarrow_{\mathsf{E}}^{*} \ \mathsf{true} \Rightarrow \sigma_2(e_2) \ k \ \longrightarrow_{\mathsf{E}}^{*} \ \mathsf{true}$$

Ideally, P is also efficiently decidable—at least more efficiently than deciding both predicates. The problem of finding P can be reduced to that of finding the weakest precondition for the safety of the following function:

```
1 fun x : B =>
2   let y0 = v10, ..., yn = v1n  (* σ1's bindings *)
3       z0 = v20, ..., zn = v2m  (* σ2's bindings *) in
4   if e1 x then (if e2 x then () else error) else ()
```

Since P would be the *weakest* precondition, we would know that we had found the most general condition for the implication relation. Whether or not the most general condition is the *best* condition depends on context. We should also consider a cost model for P; programmers may want to occasionally trade space for time, not bothering to join predicates that would be expensive to test.

Finding implication conditions resembles liquid type inference [15,19,27]: programmers get a small control knob (which expressions can go in P) and then an SMT solver does the rest. The settings are different, though: liquid types are about verifying programs, while we're executing checks at runtime.

5.1   Implementation

Implementation issues abound. How should the free variables in terms be represented? What kind of refactorings and optimizations can the compiler do, and how might they interfere with the set of contracts that appear in a program? When is the right moment in compilation to fix the implication relation? More generally, what's the design space of closure representations and calling conventions for languages with contracts?

6   Extensions

Generalizing our space-efficient semantics to sums and products does not seem particularly hard: we'd need contracts with corresponding shapes, and the join operation would push through such shapes. Recursive types and datatypes are more interesting [21]. Findler et al.'s lazy contract checking keeps contracts from changing the asymptotic time complexity of the program [7]; we may be able to adapt their work to avoid changes in asymptotic space complexity, as well.

The predicates here range over base types, but we could also allow predicates over other types. If we allow predicates over higher types, how should the adequacy constraint on predicate implication (Definition 1) change?

Impredicative polymorphism in the style of System F would require even more technical changes. The introduction of type variables would make our reasoning about names and binders trickier. In order to support predicates over type variables, we'd need to allow predicates over higher types—and so our notion of adequacy of $\supset$ would change. In order to support predicates over quantified types, we'd need to change adequacy again. Adequacy would end up looking like the logical relation used to show relational parametricity: when would we have $\forall \alpha. T_1 \supset \forall \alpha. T_2$? If we substitute T_1' for α on the left and T_2' for α on the right (and T_1' and T_2' are somehow related), then $T_1[T_1'/\alpha] \supset T_2[T_2'/\alpha]$. Not only would the technicalities be tricky, implementations would need to be careful to manage closure representations correctly (e.g., what happens if polymorphic code differs for boxed and unboxed types?).

We don't treat blame as an interesting algebraic structure—it's enough for our proofs to show that we always produce the same answer. Changing our calculus to have a more interesting notion of blame, like *indy* semantics [4] or involutive blame labels [28,29], would be a matter of pushing a shallow change in the semantics through the proofs.

Finally, it would make sense to have substitution on predicate stacks perform joins, saying $(\mathsf{pred}_\sigma^l(e); r)[v/x] = \mathsf{join}(\mathsf{pred}_\sigma^l(e)[v/x]; \mathsf{nil}, r[v/x])$, so that substituting a value into a predicate stack checks for newly revealed redundancies. We haven't proved that this change would be sound, which would require changes to both type and space-efficiency soundness.

7   Related Work

For the technique of space efficiency itself, we refer the reader to Greenberg [10] for a full description of related work. We have striven to use Greenberg's notation exactly, but we made some changes in adapting to dependent contracts: the cons operator for predicate stacks is a semi-colon, to avoid ambiguity; there were formerly two things named join, but one has been folded into the other; and our predicates have closing substitutions to account for dependency. We place one more requirement on the implication relation than Greenberg did: monotonicity under substitution, which we call *substitutivity*. Substitutions weren't an issue in his non-dependent system, but we must require that if a join can happen without having a value for x, then the same join happens when we know x's value.

CPCF was first introduced in several papers by Dimoulas et al. in [3,4], and has later been the subject of studies of blame for dependent function contracts [5] and static analysis [26]. Our exact behavioral equivalence means we could use results from Tobin-Hochstadt et al.'s static analysis in terms of $\mathrm{CPCF_C}$ to optimize space efficient programs in $\mathrm{CPCF_E}$. More interestingly, the predicate implication relation $\supset$ seems to be doing some of the work that their static analysis does, so there may be a deeper relationship.

Thiemann introduces a manifest calculus where the compiler optimizes casts for time efficiency: a theorem prover uses the "delta" between types to synthesize more efficient checks [25]. His deltas and our predicate implication relation are similar. He uses a separate logical language for predicates and restricts dependency (codomains can only depend on base values, avoiding abusive contracts).

Sekiyama et al. [20] also use delayed substitutions in their polymorphic manifest contract calculus, but for different technical reasons. While delayed substitutions resemble explicit substitutions [1] or explicit bindings [2,12], we use delayed substitutions more selectively and to resolve issues with dependency.

The manifest type system in Greenberg's work is somewhat disappointing compared to the type system given here. Greenberg works much harder than we do to prove a stronger type soundness theorem... but that theorem isn't enough to help materially in proving the soundness of space efficiency. Developing the approach to dependency used here was much easier in a latent calculus, though several bugs along the way would have been caught early by a stronger type system. Type system complexity trade-offs of this sort are an old story.

7.1   Racket's Implementation

If contracts leak space, how is it that they are used so effectively throughout PLT Racket? Racket is designed to avoid using contracts in leaky ways. In Racket, contracts tend to go on module boundaries. Calls inside of a module then don't trigger contract checks—including recursive calls, like in the even/odd example. Racket *will* monitor recursive calls across module boundaries, and these checks can indeed lead to space leaks. In our terms, Racket tends to implement contract checks on recursive functions as follows:

$$\mathsf{downTo} = \mathsf{mon}^l(x{:}\mathsf{pred}(\lambda x{:}\mathsf{Int}.\ x \geq 0) \mapsto \mathsf{pred}(\lambda y{:}\mathsf{Int}.\ x \geq y),$$
$$\mu(f{:}\mathsf{Int}{\rightarrow}\mathsf{Int}).\ \lambda x{:}\mathsf{Int}.\ \mathsf{if}\ (x = 0)\ 0\ (f\ (x - 1)))$$

Note that calling downTo n will merely check that the final result is less than n—none of the intermediate values. Our version of downTo above puts the contract *inside* the recursive knot, forcing checks every time (Sect. 4.2).

Racket also offers a less thorough form of space efficiency. We can construct a program where Racket will avoid redundant checks, but wrapping the underlying function with the same contract twice leads to a space leak (Fig. 9).[3]

---

[3] Robby Findler, personal correspondence, 2016-05-19.

```
1  (define (count-em-integer? x)
2    (printf "checking ~s\n" x)
3    (integer? x))
4  (letrec
5    ([f (contract (-> any/c count-em-integer?)
6          (lambda (x) (if (zero? x) x (f (- x 1))))
7          'pos 'neg)])
8    (f 3))
```

Fig. 9. Space-efficiency in Racket

Finally, contracts are first-class in Racket. Computing new contracts at runtime breaks our framing of space-efficiency: if we can't predetermine which contracts arise at runtime, we can't fix an implication relation in advance. We hope that CPCF$_E$ is close enough to Racket's internal model to provide insight into how to achieve space efficiency for at least some contracts in Racket.

8   Conclusion

We have translated Greenberg's original result [10] from a manifest calculus [11] to a latent one [3,4]. In so doing, we have: offered a simpler explanation of the original result; isolated the parts of the type system required for space bounds; and, extended the original result, by covering more features (dependency and nontermination) and more precisely bounding non-dependent programs.

Acknowledgments. The existence of this paper is due to comments from Sam Tobin-Hochstadt and David Van Horn that I chose to interpret as encouragement. Robby Findler provided the Racket example and helped correct and clarify a draft; Sam Tobin-Hochstadt also offered corrections and suggestions. The reviews offered helpful comments, too.

References

1. Abadi, M., Cardelli, L., Curien, P.L., Lévy, J.J.: Explicit substitutions. J. Funct. Program. (JFP) **1**(4), 375–416 (1991)
2. Ahmed, A., Findler, R.B., Siek, J., Wadler, P.: Blame for all. In: Principles of Programming Languages (POPL) (2011)
3. Dimoulas, C., Felleisen, M.: On contract satisfaction in a higher-order world. TOPLAS **33**(5), 16:1–16:29 (2011)
4. Dimoulas, C., Findler, R.B., Flanagan, C., Felleisen, M.: Correct blame for contracts: no more scapegoating. In: Principles of Programming Languages (POPL) (2011)
5. Dimoulas, C., Tobin-Hochstadt, S., Felleisen, M.: Complete monitors for behavioral contracts. In: Seidl, H. (ed.) ESOP 2012. LNCS, vol. 7211, pp. 214–233. Springer, Heidelberg (2012). https://doi.org/10.1007/978-3-642-28869-2_11

6. Findler, R.B., Felleisen, M.: Contracts for higher-order functions. In: International Conference on Functional Programming (ICFP) (2002)
7. Findler, R.B., Guo, S., Rogers, A.: Lazy contract checking for immutable data structures. In: Chitil, O., Horváth, Z., Zsók, V. (eds.) IFL 2007. LNCS, vol. 5083, pp. 111–128. Springer, Heidelberg (2008). https://doi.org/10.1007/978-3-540-85373-2_7
8. Flatt, M., PLT: Reference: Racket. Technical report, PLT-TR-2010-1, PLT Design Inc. (2010). http://racket-lang.org/tr1/
9. Garcia, R.: Calculating threesomes, with blame. In: International Conference on Functional Programming (ICFP) (2013)
10. Greenberg, M.: Space-efficient manifest contracts. In: Principles of Programming Languages (POPL) (2015)
11. Greenberg, M., Pierce, B.C., Weirich, S.: Contracts made manifest. In: Principles of Programming Languages (POPL) (2010)
12. Grossman, D., Morrisett, G., Zdancewic, S.: Syntactic type abstraction. TOPLAS **22**(6), 1037–1080 (2000)
13. Herman, D., Tomb, A., Flanagan, C.: Space-efficient gradual typing. In: Trends in Functional Programming (TFP), pp. 404–419, April 2007
14. Herman, D., Tomb, A., Flanagan, C.: Space-efficient gradual typing. High. Order Symbol. Comput. **23**(2), 167–189 (2010)
15. Jhala, R.: Refinement types for Haskell. In: Programming Languages Meets Program Verification (PLPV), p. 27. ACM, New York (2014)
16. Meyer, B.: Eiffel: The Language. Prentice-Hall Inc., Upper Saddle River (1992)
17. Plotkin, G.: LCF considered as a programming language. Theoret. Comput. Sci. **5**(3), 223–255 (1977)
18. Racket contract system (2013)
19. Rondon, P.M., Kawaguchi, M., Jhala, R.: Liquid types. In: Programming Language Design and Implementation (PLDI) (2008)
20. Sekiyama, T., Igarashi, A., Greenberg, M.: Polymorphic manifest contracts, revised and resolved. TOPLAS (2016, accepted in September; to appear)
21. Sekiyama, T., Nishida, Y., Igarashi, A.: Manifest contracts for datatypes. In: Principles of Programming Languages (POPL), pp. 195–207. ACM, New York (2015)
22. Siek, J., Thiemann, P., Wadler, P.: Blame, coercion, and threesomes: together again for the first time. In: Programming Language Design and Implementation (PLDI) (2015)
23. Siek, J.G., Taha, W.: Gradual typing for functional languages. In: Scheme and Functional Programming Workshop, September 2006
24. Siek, J.G., Wadler, P.: Threesomes, with and without blame. In: Principles of Programming Languages (POPL), pp. 365–376. ACM, New York (2010)
25. Thiemann, P.: A delta for hybrid type checking. In: Lindley, S., McBride, C., Trinder, P., Sannella, D. (eds.) A List of Successes That Can Change the World. LNCS, vol. 9600, pp. 411–432. Springer, Cham (2016). https://doi.org/10.1007/978-3-319-30936-1_22
26. Tobin-Hochstadt, S., Van Horn, D.: Higher-order symbolic execution via contracts. In: OOPSLA, pp. 537–554. ACM, New York (2012)
27. Vazou, N., Rondon, P.M., Jhala, R.: Abstract refinement types. In: Felleisen, M., Gardner, P. (eds.) ESOP 2013. LNCS, vol. 7792, pp. 209–228. Springer, Heidelberg (2013). https://doi.org/10.1007/978-3-642-37036-6_13

28. Wadler, P.: A complement to blame. In: Ball, T., Bodik, R., Krishnamurthi, S., Lerner, B.S., Morrisett, G. (eds.) SNAPL. LIPIcs, vol. 32, pp. 309–320. Schloss Dagstuhl-Leibniz-Zentrum fuer Informatik (2015)
29. Wadler, P., Findler, R.B.: Well-typed programs can't be blamed. In: Castagna, G. (ed.) ESOP 2009. LNCS, vol. 5502, pp. 1–16. Springer, Heidelberg (2009). https://doi.org/10.1007/978-3-642-00590-9_1

Cactus Environment Machine
Shared Environment Call-by-Need

George Stelle[1,2(✉)], Darko Stefanovic[1], Stephen L. Olivier[2], and Stephanie Forrest[1]

[1] University of New Mexico, Albuquerque, USA
{stelleg,darko,forrest}@cs.unm.edu
[2] Sandia National Laboratories, Albuquerque, USA
slolivi@sandia.gov

Abstract. Existing machines for lazy evaluation use a *flat* representation of environments, storing the terms associated with free variables in an array. Combined with a heap, this structure supports the shared intermediate results required by lazy evaluation. We propose and describe an alternative approach that uses a *shared* environment to minimize the overhead of delayed computations. We show how a shared environment can act as both an environment and a mechanism for sharing results. To formalize this approach, we introduce a calculus that makes the shared environment explicit, as well as a machine to implement the calculus, the *Cactus Environment Machine*. A simple compiler implements the machine and is used to run experiments for assessing performance. The results show reasonable performance and suggest that incorporating this approach into real-world compilers could yield performance benefits in some scenarios.

1 Introduction

Call-by-need evaluation is a formalization of the idea that work should be delayed until needed, and performed only once. Existing implementations of call-by-need take care in *packaging* a delayed computation, or *thunk*, by building a closure with an array that contains the bindings of all free variables [7,24]. The overhead induced by this operation is well known, and is one reason existing implementations avoid thunks wherever possible [18]. The key insight of our Cactus Environment ($\mathscr{CE}$) Machine is that this overhead can be minimized by only recording a location in a shared environment.

As an example, consider the application $f\ e$. In existing call-by-need implementations, e.g., the STG machine [24], a closure with a flat environment will be constructed for e. Doing so incurs a time and memory cost proportional to the number of free variables of e.[1] We minimize this packaging cost by recording a location in a shared environment, which requires only two machine words (and two instructions) for the thunk: one for the code pointer, and one for the environment pointer. One way to think about the approach is that it is *lazier* about lazy evaluation: in the case that e is unneeded, the work to package it in a thunk is entirely wasted. In the spirit of lazy evaluation, we attempt to minimize this potentially unnecessary work.

The main contributions of the paper are:

---

[1] In some implementations, these are lambda-lifted to be formal parameters, but the principle is the same.

© Springer Nature Switzerland AG 2019
D. Van Horn and J. Hughes (Eds.): TFP 2016, LNCS 10447, pp. 24–43, 2019.
https://doi.org/10.1007/978-3-030-14805-8_2

- A big-step calculus and small-step abstract machine that formalize the notion of a shared environment for call-by-need evaluation using an explicitly shared environment (Sect. 4).
- A simple implementation of the abstract machine that compiles to x86 assembly with a preliminary evaluation that shows performance comparable to existing implementations (Sects. 6 and 7).

Section 2 reviews relevant background material, and Sect. 3 discusses the current landscape of environment representations, highlighting the opportunity for combining shared environments with lazy evaluation. We then provide some intuition for why this might be combination might be desirable, and formalize the connection between call-by-need evaluation and shared environments in a calculus (Sect. 4). Section 5 uses the calculus to derive a novel abstract machine, the $\mathscr{CE}$ machine, explains how $\mathscr{CE}$ uses the shared environment in a natural way to implement lazy evaluation, and gives its formal semantics. We then describe a straightforward implementation of $\mathscr{CE}$ in Sect. 6, extended with machine literals and primitive operations, and compiling directly to native code. We evaluate the implementation in Sect. 7, showing that it is capable of performing comparably to existing implementations despite lacking several common optimizations, and we discuss the results. We discuss related work, the limitations of our approach, and some ideas for future work in Sect. 8, and conclude the paper in Sect. 9.

2 Background and Motivation

This section provides relevant background for the $\mathscr{CE}$ machine, outlining lambda calculus, evaluation strategies, and Curien's calculus of closures.

2.1 Preliminaries

We begin with the simple lambda calculus [5]:

$$t ::= x \mid \lambda x.t \mid t\,t$$

where x is a variable, $\lambda x.t$ is an abstraction, and $t\,t$ is an application. We also use lambda calculus with deBruijn indices, which replaces variables with a natural number indexing into the binding lambdas. This calculus is given by the syntax:

$$t ::= i \mid \lambda t \mid t\,t$$

where $i \in \mathbb{N}$. In both cases, we use the standard Barendregt syntax conventions, namely that applications are left associative and the bodies of abstractions extend as far as possible to the right [5]. A *value* in lambda calculus refers to an abstraction. We are concerned only with evaluation to weak head normal form (WHNF), which terminates on an abstraction without entering its body.

In mechanical evaluation of expressions, it would be too inefficient to perform explicit substitution. To solve this, the standard approach uses closures [6,8,20,24].

Closures combine a term with an environment, which binds the free variables of the term to closures.

As the formal basis for closures we use Curien's calculus of closures [8], Fig. 1. It is a formalization of closures with an environment represented as a list of closures, indexed by deBruijn indices. We will occasionally modify this calculus by replacing the deBruijn indices with variables for readability, in which case variables are looked up in the environment instead of indexed, e.g., $t[x = c, y = c']$) [5]. We also add superscript and subscript markers to denote unique syntax elements, e.g., $t', t_1 \in$ Term.

Syntax

$$t ::= i \mid \lambda t \mid t\, t \qquad\qquad \text{(Term)}$$
$$i \in \mathbb{N} \qquad\qquad \text{(Variable)}$$
$$c ::= t[\rho] \qquad\qquad \text{(Closure)}$$
$$\rho ::= \bullet \mid c \cdot \rho \qquad\qquad \text{(Environment)}$$

Semantics

$$\frac{t_1[\rho] \overset{*}{\to}_L \lambda t_2[\rho']}{t_1 t_3[\rho] \to_L t_2[t_3[\rho] \cdot \rho']} \qquad\qquad \text{(LEval)}$$

$$i[c_0 \cdot c_1 \cdot ... c_i \cdot \rho] \to_L c_i \qquad\qquad \text{(LVar)}$$

Fig. 1. Curien's call-by-name calculus of closures [8]

2.2 Evaluation Strategies

There are three standard evaluation strategies for lambda calculus: call-by-value, call-by-need, and call-by-name. Call-by-value evaluates every argument to a value, whereas call-by-need and call-by-name only evaluate an argument if it is needed. If an argument is needed more than once, call-by-name re-computes the value, whereas call-by-need memoizes the value, so it is computed at most once. Thus, call-by-need attempts to embody the best of both worlds—never repeat work (call-by-value), and never perform unnecessary work (call-by-name). These are intuitively good properties to have, and we illustrate the correctness of such an intuition with the following example, modified from [10]:

$$\overbrace{c_m(c_m(\cdots(c_m}^{m} \text{ id id})\cdots)\text{id})\ true\ id\ bottom$$

where $c_n = \lambda s.\lambda z.s\,(\overbrace{s \cdots (s}^{n}\, z)\cdots)$, $true = \lambda t.\lambda f.t$, $id = \lambda x.x$, and $bottom = (\lambda x.x\, x)\lambda x.x\, x$. Call-by-value never terminates, call-by-name takes exponential time, and call-by-need takes only polynomial time [10]. Of course, this is a contrived example, but it illustrates desirable properties of call-by-need.

In practice, however, there are significant issues with call-by-need evaluation. We focus on the following: *Delaying a computation is slower than performing it immediately.* This issue is well known [18,24], and has become part of the motivation for *strictness analysis* [23,32], which transforms non-strict evaluation to strict when possible.

2.3   Existing Call-by-Need Machines

Diehl et al. [11] review the call-by-need literature in detail. Here we summarize the most relevant points.

The best known machine for lazy evaluation is the Spineless Tagless G-Machine (STG machine), which underlies the Glasgow Haskell Compiler (GHC). STG uses flat environments that can be allocated on the stack, the heap, or some combination [24].

Two other influential lazy evaluation machines relevant to the $\mathscr{CE}$ machine are the call-by-need Krivine machines [14,19,28], and the three-instruction machine (TIM) [13]. Krivine machines started as an approach to call-by-name evaluation, and were later extended to call-by-need [10,14,19,28]. The $\mathscr{CE}$ modifies the lazy Krivine machine to capture the environment sharing given by the cactus environment. The TIM is an implementation of call-by-need and call-by-name [13]. It involves, as the name suggests, three machine instructions, TAKE, PUSH, and ENTER. In Sect. 6, we follow Sestoft [28] and re-appropriate these instructions for the $\mathscr{CE}$ machine.

There has also been recent interest in *heapless* abstract machines for lazy evaluation. Danvy et al. [9] and Garcia et al. [27] independently derived similar machines from the call-by-need lambda calculus [4]. These are interesting approaches, but it is not yet clear how these machines could be implemented efficiently.

3   Environment Representations

As mentioned in Sect. 2, environments bind free variables to closures. There is significant flexibility in how they can be represented. In this section we review this design space in the context of existing work, both for call by value and call by need.[2]

There are two common approaches to environment representation: *flat* environments and *shared* environments (also known as linked environments) [2,29]. A flat environment is one in which each closure has its own record of the terms its free variables are bound to. A shared environment is one in which parts of that record can be shared among multiple closures [2,29]. For example, consider the following term:

$$(\lambda x.(\lambda y.t)(\lambda z.t_1))t_2$$

Assuming the term t has both x and y as free variables, we must evaluate it in the environment binding both x and y. Similarly, assuming t_1 contains both z and x as free

---

[2] Some work refers to this space as *closure* representation rather than *environment* representation [2,29]. Because the term part of the closure is simply a code pointer and the interesting design choices are in the environment, we refer to the topic as environment representation.

variables, we must evaluate it in an environment containing bindings for both x and z. Thus, we can represent the closures for evaluating t and t_1 as

$$t[x = t_2[\bullet], y = c]$$

and

$$t_1[x = t_2[\bullet], z = c_1]$$

respectively, where $\bullet$ is the empty environment. These are examples of *flat* environments, where each closure comes with its own record of all of its free variables. Because of the nested scope of the given term, x is bound to the same closure in the two environments. Thus, we can also create a shared, linked environment, represented by the following diagram:

Now each of the environments is represented by a linked list, with the binding of x shared between them. This is an example of a *shared* environment [2]. This shared, linked structure dates back to the first machine for evaluating expressions, Landin's SECD machine [20].

The drawbacks and advantages of each approach are well known. With a flat environment, variable lookup can be performed with a simple offset [1,24]. On the other hand, significant duplication can occur, as we will discuss in Sect. 3.1. With a shared environment, that duplication is removed, but at the cost of possible link traversal upon dereference.

As with most topics in compilers and abstract machines, the design space is actually more complex. For example, Appel and Jim show a wide range of hybrids [2] between the two, and Appel and Shao [29] show an optimized hybrid that aims to achieve the benefits of both approaches. And as shown in the next section, choice of evaluation strategy further complicates the picture.

3.1 Existing Call-by-Need Environments

Existing call by need machines use flat environments with a heap of closures [7,13, 18,24]. These environments may contain some combination of primitive values and pointers into the heap (p below). The pointers and heap implement the memoization of results required for call by need. Returning to the earlier example, $(\lambda x.(\lambda y.t)(\lambda z.t_1))t_2$, we can view a simplified execution state for this approach when entering t as follows:

Closure

$$t[x = p_0, y = p_1]$$

Heap

$$p_0 \mapsto t_2[\bullet]$$
$$p_1 \mapsto \lambda z.t_1[x = p_0]$$

Consider $t_2[\bullet]$, the closure at p_0. If it is not in WHNF (this sort of unevaluated closure is called a *thunk* [17,25]), then if it is entered in either the evaluation of t or t_1, the resulting value will overwrite the closure at p_0. The result of the computation is then shared with all other instances of x in t and t_1. In the case that terms have a large number of shared variables, environment duplication can be expensive. Compile-time transformation [25] (tupling arguments) helps, but we show that the machine can avoid duplication completely.

Depending on t, either or both of the closures created for its free variables may not be evaluated. Therefore, it is possible that the work of creating the environment for that thunk will be wasted. This waste is well known, and existing approaches address it by avoiding thunks as much as possible [18,24]. Unfortunately, in cases like the above example, thunks are necessary. We aim to minimize the cost of creating such thunks.

Thunks are special in another way. Recall that one advantage of flat environments is quick variable lookups. In a lazy language, this advantage is reduced because *a thunk can only be entered once*. After it is entered, it is overwritten with a value, so the next time that heap location is entered it is entered with a value and a different environment. Thus, the work to ensure that the variable lookup is fast is used only once. This is in contrast to a call by value language, in which every closure is constructed for a value, and can be entered an arbitrary number of times.

A more subtle drawback of the flat environment representation is that environments can vary in size, and thus a value in WHNF can be too large to fit in the space allocated for the thunk it is replacing. This problem is discussed in [24], where the proposed solution is to put the value closure in a fresh location in the heap where there is sufficient room. The original thunk location is then replaced with an indirection to the value at the freshly allocated location. These indirections are removed during garbage collection, but do impose some cost, both in runtime efficiency and implementation complexity [24].

We have thus far ignored a number of details with regard to current implementations. For example, the STG machine can split the flat environment, so that part is allocated on the stack and part on the heap. The TIM allocates its flat environments separately from its closures so that each closure is a code pointer, environment pointer pair [13] while the STG machine keeps environment and code co-located [24]. Still, the basic design principle holds: a flat environment for each closure allows quick variable indexing, but with an initial overhead.

To summarize, the flat environment representation in a call by need language implies that whenever a term might be needed, the necessary environment is constructed from the current environment. This operation can be expensive, and it is wasted if the variable is never entered. In this work, we aim to minimize this potentially unnecessary overhead.

Figure 2 depicts the design space relevant to this paper. There are existing call by value machines with both flat and shared environments, and call by need machines with flat environments. As far as we are aware, we are the first to use a shared environment to implement lazy evaluation.

It is worth noting that there has been work on lazy machines that effectively use linked environments, which could potentially be implemented as a shared environment, e.g., Sestoft's work on Krivine machines [28], but none make the realization that the shared environment can be used to implement sharing of results, which is the primary contribution of this paper.

	Flat Environment	Shared Environment
Call by need	STG [24], TIM [13], GRIN [7]	$\mathscr{CE}$ Machine (this paper)
Call by value	ZAM [21], SML/NJ [3]	ZAM, SECD [20], SML/NJ

Fig. 2. Evaluation strategy and environment structure design space. Each acronym refers to an existing implementation. Some implementations use multiple environment representations.

4   Cactus Environment Calculus

This section shows how the shared environment approach can be applied to call-by-need evaluation. We start with a calculus that abstracts away environment representation, Curien's calculus of closures, and we show how it can be modified to force sharing. See Curien's call-by-name calculus of closures in Fig. 1.[3]

The LEval rule pushes a closure onto the environment, and the LVar rule indexes into the environment, entering the corresponding closure. We show in this section that by removing ambiguity about how the environments are represented, and forcing them to be represented in a *cactus stack* [30], we can define our novel call-by-need calculus.

To start, consider again the example from Sect. 3, this time with deBruijn indices: $(\lambda(\lambda t)\ (\lambda t_1))t_2$. The terms t and t_1, when evaluated in the closure calculus, would have the following environments, respectively:

$$c \cdot t_2[\bullet] \cdot \bullet$$
$$c_1 \cdot t_2[\bullet] \cdot \bullet$$

Again, the second closure is identical in each environment. And again, we can represent these environments with a shared environment, this time keeping call-by-need evaluation in mind:

---

[3] Curien calls it a "lazy" evaluator, and there is some ambiguity with the term lazy, but we use the term only to mean call-by-need. We also remove the condition checking that $i < m$ because we are only concerned with evaluation of closed terms.

This inverted tree structure seen earlier with the leaves pointing toward the root is called a *cactus stack* (sometimes called a spaghetti stack or saguaro stack) [15,16]. In this particular cactus stack, every node defines an environment as the sequence of closures in the path to the root. If $t_2[\bullet]$ is a thunk, and is updated in place with the value after its first reference, then both environments would contain the resulting value. This is exactly the kind of sharing that is required by call-by-need, and thus we can use this structure to build a call-by-need evaluator. This is the essence of the cactus environment calculus and the cactus environment ($\mathscr{CE}$) machine.

Curien's calculus of closures does not differentiate between flat and shared environment representations, and indeed, no calculus that we are aware of has had the need to. Therefore, we must derive a calculus of closures, forcing the environment to be shared. Because we can hold the closure directly in the environment, we choose to replace the standard heap of closures with a *heap of environments*. To enforce sharing, we extend Curien's calculus of closures to explicity include the heap of environments, which we refer to as a *cactus environment*.

See Fig. 3 for the syntax and semantics of the cactus calculus. Recall that we are only concerned with evaluation of closed terms. The initial closed term t is placed in a $(t[0], \varepsilon[0 \mapsto \bullet])$ tuple, and evaluation terminates on a value. We use some shorthand to make heap notation more palatable, for both the big-step semantics presented here and the small step semantics presented in the next section. $\mu(l, i) = l' \mapsto c \cdot l''$ denotes that looking up the i'th element in the linked environment structure starting at l results in location l', where closure c and continuing environment l'' reside. $\mu(l) = c \cdot l'$ is the statement that $l \mapsto c \cdot l' \in \mu$, and $\mu(u \mapsto c \cdot l')$ is μ with location u updated to map to $c \cdot e$. We define two different semantics, one for call-by-name and one for call-by-need, which makes the connection to Curien's call-by-name calculus more straightfoward. The rule for application (MEval and NEval) is identical for both semantics: each evaluates the left hand side to a function, then binds the variable in the cactus environment, extending the current environment.

The only difference between this semantics and Curien's is that if we need to extend an environment multiple times, the semantics *requires* sharing it among the extensions. This makes no real difference for call-by-name, but it is needed for the sharing of results in the NVar rule. The explicit environment sharing ensures that the closure that is overwritten with a value is shared correctly.

4.1 Correctness

Ariola et al. define the standard call-by-need semantics in [4]. To show correctness, we show that there is a strong bisimulation between $\to_N$ and their operational semantics, $\Downarrow$ (Fig. 4).

Theorem 1. (Strong Bisimulation)

$$\to_N \sim \Downarrow$$

We start with a *flattening* relation between a configuration for $\Downarrow$ and a configuration for $\to_N$. The deBruijn indexed terms and the standard terms are both converted to terms

Syntax

$$t ::= i \mid \lambda t \mid t\, t \qquad \text{(Term)}$$
$$i \in \mathbb{N} \qquad \text{(Variable)}$$
$$c ::= t[l] \qquad \text{(Closure)}$$
$$v ::= \lambda t[l] \qquad \text{(Value)}$$
$$\mu ::= \varepsilon \mid \mu[l \mapsto \rho] \qquad \text{(Heap)}$$
$$\rho ::= \bullet \mid c \cdot l \qquad \text{(Environment)}$$
$$l, f \in \mathbb{N} \qquad \text{(Location)}$$
$$s ::= (c, \mu) \qquad \text{(State)}$$

Call-by-Name Semantics

$$\frac{(t[l], \mu) \xrightarrow{*}_M (\lambda t_2[l'], \mu') \quad f \notin \mathrm{dom}(\mu')}{(t\, t_3[l], \mu) \to_M (t_2[f], \mu'[f \mapsto t_3[l] \cdot l'])} \qquad \text{(MEval)}$$

$$\frac{\mu(l, i) = l' \mapsto c \cdot l''}{(i[l], \mu) \to_M (c, \mu)} \qquad \text{(MVar)}$$

Call-by-Need Semantics

$$\frac{(t[l], \mu) \xrightarrow{*}_N (\lambda t_2[l'], \mu') \quad f \notin \mathrm{dom}(\mu')}{(t\, t_3[l], \mu) \to_N (t_2[f], \mu'[f \mapsto t_3[l] \cdot l'])} \qquad \text{(NEval)}$$

$$\frac{\mu(l, i) = l' \mapsto c \cdot l'' \quad (c, \mu) \xrightarrow{*}_N (v, \mu')}{(i[l], \mu) \to_N (v, \mu'(l' \mapsto v \cdot l''))} \qquad \text{(NVar)}$$

Fig. 3. Cactus calculus syntax and semantics.

$$\Phi, \Psi, \Upsilon ::= x_1 \mapsto t_1, \ldots, x_n \mapsto t_n \qquad \text{(Heap)}$$

$$\frac{\langle \Phi \rangle t \Downarrow \langle \Psi \rangle \lambda x.t'}{\langle \Phi, x \mapsto t, \Upsilon \rangle x \Downarrow \langle \Psi, x \mapsto \lambda x.t', \Upsilon \rangle \lambda x.t'} \qquad \text{(Id)}$$

$$\frac{}{\langle \Phi \rangle \lambda x.t \Downarrow \langle \Phi \rangle \lambda x.t} \qquad \text{(Abs)}$$

$$\frac{\langle \Phi \rangle t_l \Downarrow \langle \Psi \rangle \lambda x.t_n \quad \langle \Psi, x' \mapsto t_m \rangle [x'/x] t_n \Downarrow \langle \Upsilon \rangle \lambda y.t'}{\langle \Phi \rangle t_l\, t_m \Downarrow \langle \Upsilon \rangle \lambda y.t'} \qquad \text{(App)}$$

Fig. 4. Ariola et. al's operational semantics

that use deBruijn indices for local variables and direct heap locations for free variables. The flattening relation holds only when both terms are closed under their corresponding heaps. It holds trivially for the special case of initializing each configuration with a standard term and its corresponding deBruijn-indexed term, respectively. The proof proceeds by induction on the step relation for each direction of the bisimulation.

5 $\mathscr{CE}$ Machine

Using the calculus of cactus environments defined in the previous section, we derive an abstract machine: the $\mathscr{CE}$ machine. The syntax and semantics are defined in Fig. 5.

Syntax

$$
\begin{array}{llr}
s ::= \langle c, \sigma, \mu \rangle & & \text{(State)} \\
t ::= i \mid \lambda t \mid t\, t & & \text{(Term)} \\
i \in \mathbb{N} & & \text{(Variable)} \\
c ::= t[l] & & \text{(Closure)} \\
v ::= \lambda t[l] & & \text{(Value)} \\
\mu ::= \varepsilon \mid \mu[l \mapsto \rho] & & \text{(Heap)} \\
\rho ::= \bullet \mid c \cdot l & & \text{(Environment)} \\
\sigma ::= \square \mid \sigma\, c \mid \sigma\, u & & \text{(Context)} \\
l, u, f \in \mathbb{N} & & \text{(Location)}
\end{array}
$$

Semantics

$$
\begin{array}{lr}
\langle v, \sigma\, u, \mu \rangle \rightarrow_{\mathscr{CE}} \langle v, \sigma, \mu(u \mapsto v \cdot l) \rangle \text{ where } c \cdot l = \mu(u) & \text{(Upd)} \\
\langle \lambda t[l], \sigma\, c, \mu \rangle \rightarrow_{\mathscr{CE}} \langle t[f], \sigma, \mu[f \mapsto c \cdot l] \rangle\, f \notin \text{dom}(\mu) & \text{(Lam)} \\
\langle t\, t'[l], \sigma, \mu \rangle \rightarrow_{\mathscr{CE}} \langle t[l], \sigma\, t'[l], \mu \rangle & \text{(App)} \\
\langle 0[l], \sigma, \mu \rangle \rightarrow_{\mathscr{CE}} \langle c, \sigma\, l, \mu \rangle \text{ where } c \cdot l' = \mu(l) & \text{(Var1)} \\
\langle i[l], \sigma, \mu \rangle \rightarrow_{\mathscr{CE}} \langle (i-1)[l'], \sigma, \mu \rangle \text{ where } c \cdot l' = \mu(l) & \text{(Var2)}
\end{array}
$$

Fig. 5. Syntax and semantics of the $\mathscr{CE}$ machine.

The machine operates as a small-step implementation of the calculus, extended only with a context to implement the updates from the NVar subderivation ($\sigma\, u$) and the operands from the NEval subderivation ($\sigma\, c$). Much like the calculus, a term t is inserted into an initial state $\langle t[0], \sigma, \varepsilon[0 \mapsto \bullet] \rangle$. On the update rule, the current closure is a value, and there is an update marker as the outermost context. This implies that a variable was entered and that the current closure represents the corresponding value for that variable. Thus, we update the location u that the variable entered, replacing whatever term was entered with the current closure. The Lam rule takes an argument off the context and binds it to a variable, allocating a fresh heap location for the bound variable. This ensures that every instance of the variable will point to this location, and thus the bound term will be evaluated at most once. The App rule simply pushes an argument term in the current environment. The Var1 rule enters the closure pointed to by the environment location, while the Var2 rule traverses the cactus environment to locate the correct closure.

To get some intuition for the $\mathscr{CE}$ machine and how it works, consider Fig. 6, evaluation of the term $(\lambda a.(\lambda b.b\,a)\lambda c.c\,a)\,((\lambda i.i)\lambda j.j)$, which is $(\lambda(\lambda 0\,1)\,\lambda 0\,1)\,((\lambda 0)\,\lambda 0)$ with deBruijn indices.

$$\langle(\lambda(\lambda 0\,1)\,\lambda 0\,1)\,((\lambda 0)\,\lambda 0)[0],\Box,\varepsilon[0\mapsto\bullet]\rangle$$

$\rightarrow_{\mathscr{CE}} \langle\lambda(\lambda 0\,1)\,\lambda 0\,1[0],\Box(\lambda 0)\,\lambda 0[0],\varepsilon[0\mapsto\bullet]\rangle$

$\rightarrow_{\mathscr{CE}} \langle(\lambda 0\,1)\,\lambda 0\,1[1],\Box,\varepsilon[0\mapsto\bullet][1\mapsto(\lambda 0)\,\lambda 0[0]\cdot 0]\rangle$

$\rightarrow_{\mathscr{CE}} \langle\lambda 0\,1[1],\Box\lambda 0\,1[1],\varepsilon[0\mapsto\bullet][1\mapsto(\lambda 0)\,\lambda 0[0]\cdot 0]\rangle$

$\rightarrow_{\mathscr{CE}} \langle 0\,1[2],\Box,\varepsilon[0\mapsto\bullet][1\mapsto(\lambda 0)\,\lambda 0[0]\cdot 0][2\mapsto\lambda 0\,1[1]\cdot 1]\rangle$

$\rightarrow_{\mathscr{CE}} \langle 0[2],\Box 1[2],\varepsilon[0\mapsto\bullet][1\mapsto(\lambda 0)\,\lambda 0[0]\cdot 0][2\mapsto\lambda 0\,1[1]\cdot 1]\rangle$

$\rightarrow_{\mathscr{CE}} \langle\lambda 0\,1[1],\Box 1[2]2,\varepsilon[0\mapsto\bullet][1\mapsto(\lambda 0)\,\lambda 0[0]\cdot 0][2\mapsto\lambda 0\,1[1]\cdot 1]\rangle$

$\rightarrow_{\mathscr{CE}} \langle\lambda 0\,1[1],\Box 1[2],\varepsilon[0\mapsto\bullet][1\mapsto(\lambda 0)\,\lambda 0[0]\cdot 0][2\mapsto\lambda 0\,1[1]\cdot 1]\rangle$

$\rightarrow_{\mathscr{CE}} \langle 0\,1[3],\Box,\varepsilon[0\mapsto\bullet][1\mapsto(\lambda 0)\,\lambda 0[0]\cdot 0][2\mapsto\lambda 0\,1[1]\cdot 1][3\mapsto 1[2]\cdot 1]\rangle$

$\rightarrow_{\mathscr{CE}} \langle 0[3],\Box 1[3],\varepsilon[0\mapsto\bullet][1\mapsto(\lambda 0)\,\lambda 0[0]\cdot 0][2\mapsto\lambda 0\,1[1]\cdot 1][3\mapsto 1[2]\cdot 1]\rangle$

$\rightarrow_{\mathscr{CE}} \langle 1[2],\Box 1[3]3,\varepsilon[0\mapsto\bullet][1\mapsto(\lambda 0)\,\lambda 0[0]\cdot 0][2\mapsto\lambda 0\,1[1]\cdot 1][3\mapsto 1[2]\cdot 1]\rangle$

$\rightarrow_{\mathscr{CE}} \langle 0[1],\Box 1[3]3,\varepsilon[0\mapsto\bullet][1\mapsto(\lambda 0)\,\lambda 0[0]\cdot 0][2\mapsto\lambda 0\,1[1]\cdot 1][3\mapsto 1[2]\cdot 1]\rangle$

$\rightarrow_{\mathscr{CE}} \langle(\lambda 0)\,\lambda 0[0],\Box 1[3]31,\varepsilon[0\mapsto\bullet][1\mapsto(\lambda 0)\,\lambda 0[0]\cdot 0][2\mapsto\lambda 0\,1[1]\cdot 1][3\mapsto 1[2]\cdot 1]\rangle$

$\rightarrow_{\mathscr{CE}} \langle\lambda 0[0],\Box 1[3]31\lambda 0[0],\varepsilon[0\mapsto\bullet][1\mapsto(\lambda 0)\,\lambda 0[0]\cdot 0][2\mapsto\lambda 0\,1[1]\cdot 1][3\mapsto 1[2]\cdot 1]\rangle$

$\rightarrow_{\mathscr{CE}} \langle 0[4],\Box 1[3]31,\varepsilon[0\mapsto\bullet][1\mapsto(\lambda 0)\,\lambda 0[0]\cdot 0][2\mapsto\lambda 0\,1[1]\cdot 1][3\mapsto 1[2]\cdot 1][4\mapsto\lambda 0[0]\cdot 0]\rangle$

$\rightarrow_{\mathscr{CE}} \langle\lambda 0[0],\Box 1[3]314,\varepsilon[0\mapsto\bullet][1\mapsto(\lambda 0)\,\lambda 0[0]\cdot 0][2\mapsto\lambda 0\,1[1]\cdot 1][3\mapsto 1[2]\cdot 1][4\mapsto\lambda 0[0]\cdot 0]\rangle$

$\rightarrow_{\mathscr{CE}} \langle\lambda 0[0],\Box 1[3]31,\varepsilon[0\mapsto\bullet][1\mapsto(\lambda 0)\,\lambda 0[0]\cdot 0][2\mapsto\lambda 0\,1[1]\cdot 1][3\mapsto 1[2]\cdot 1][4\mapsto\lambda 0[0]\cdot 0]\rangle$

$\rightarrow_{\mathscr{CE}} \langle\lambda 0[0],\Box 1[3]3,\varepsilon[0\mapsto\bullet][1\mapsto\lambda 0[0]\cdot 0][2\mapsto\lambda 0\,1[1]\cdot 1][3\mapsto 1[2]\cdot 1][4\mapsto\lambda 0[0]\cdot 0]\rangle$

$\rightarrow_{\mathscr{CE}} \langle\lambda 0[0],\Box 1[3],\varepsilon[0\mapsto\bullet][1\mapsto\lambda 0[0]\cdot 0][2\mapsto\lambda 0\,1[1]\cdot 1][3\mapsto\lambda 0[0]\cdot 1][4\mapsto\lambda 0[0]\cdot 0]\rangle$

$\rightarrow_{\mathscr{CE}} \langle 0[5],\Box,\varepsilon[0\mapsto\bullet][1\mapsto\lambda 0[0]\cdot 0][2\mapsto\lambda 0\,1[1]\cdot 1][3\mapsto\lambda 0[0]\cdot 1][4\mapsto\lambda 0[0]\cdot 0][5\mapsto 1[3]\cdot 0]\rangle$

$\rightarrow_{\mathscr{CE}} \langle 1[3],\Box 5,\varepsilon[0\mapsto\bullet][1\mapsto\lambda 0[0]\cdot 0][2\mapsto\lambda 0\,1[1]\cdot 1][3\mapsto\lambda 0[0]\cdot 1][4\mapsto\lambda 0[0]\cdot 0][5\mapsto 1[3]\cdot 0]\rangle$

$\rightarrow_{\mathscr{CE}} \langle 0[1],\Box 5,\varepsilon[0\mapsto\bullet][1\mapsto\lambda 0[0]\cdot 0][2\mapsto\lambda 0\,1[1]\cdot 1][3\mapsto\lambda 0[0]\cdot 1][4\mapsto\lambda 0[0]\cdot 0][5\mapsto 1[3]\cdot 0]\rangle$

$\rightarrow_{\mathscr{CE}} \langle\lambda 0[0],\Box 51,\varepsilon[0\mapsto\bullet][1\mapsto\lambda 0[0]\cdot 0][2\mapsto\lambda 0\,1[1]\cdot 1][3\mapsto\lambda 0[0]\cdot 1][4\mapsto\lambda 0[0]\cdot 0][5\mapsto 1[3]\cdot 0]\rangle$

$\rightarrow_{\mathscr{CE}} \langle\lambda 0[0],\Box 5,\varepsilon[0\mapsto\bullet][1\mapsto\lambda 0[0]\cdot 0][2\mapsto\lambda 0\,1[1]\cdot 1][3\mapsto\lambda 0[0]\cdot 1][4\mapsto\lambda 0[0]\cdot 0][5\mapsto 1[3]\cdot 0]\rangle$

$\rightarrow_{\mathscr{CE}} \langle\lambda 0[0],\Box,\varepsilon[0\mapsto\bullet][1\mapsto\lambda 0[0]\cdot 0][2\mapsto\lambda 0\,1[1]\cdot 1][3\mapsto\lambda 0[0]\cdot 1][4\mapsto\lambda 0[0]\cdot 0][5\mapsto\lambda 0[0]\cdot 0]\rangle$

Fig. 6. $\mathscr{CE}$ machine example. Evaluation of $(\lambda(\lambda 0\,1)\,\lambda 0\,1)\,((\lambda 0)\,\lambda 0)$

5.1 Correctness

We prove that the reflexive transitive closure of the $\mathscr{CE}$ machine step relation evaluates to a value and heap and empty context iff $\rightarrow_N$ evaluates to the same value and heap.

Theorem 2. (Equivalence)

$$(c, \mu) \to_N (v, \mu') \;\leftrightarrow\; \langle c, \Box, \mu \rangle \xrightarrow{*}_{\mathscr{CE}} \langle v, \Box, \mu' \rangle$$

By induction on the $\to_N$ step relation for one direction, and induction on the reflexive transitive closure of the $\to_{\mathscr{CE}}$ step relation for the other.

6   Implementation

This section describes how the $\mathscr{CE}$ machine can be mapped directly to x64 insructions. Specifically, we re-define the three instructions given by the TIM [13]: TAKE, ENTER, and PUSH, and implement them with x64 assembly. We also describe several design decisions, as well as some optimizations. All implementation and benchmark code is available at http://cs.unm.edu/~stelleg/cem-tfp2016.tar.gz.

Each closure is represented as a ⟨code pointer, environment pointer⟩ tuple. The Context is implemented as a stack, with updates represented as a ⟨null pointer, environment pointer⟩ tuple to differentiate them from closure arguments. The Heap, or cactus environment, is implemented as a heap containing ⟨closure, environment pointer⟩ structs. As a result, each cell in the heap takes 3 machine words.

6.1   Compilation

The three instructions are given below, with descriptions of their behavior.

- TAKE: Pops a context item off the stack. If the item is an update u, the instruction updates the location u with the current closure. If it is an argument c, the instruction binds the closure c to the fresh location in the cactus environment.
- ENTER i: Enters the closure defined by variable index i, the current environment pointer, and the current cactus environment.
- PUSH m: Pushes the code location m along with the current environment pointer.

Each of these instructions corresponds directly to a corresponding lambda term: abstraction compiles to TAKE, application to PUSH, and variables to ENTER. Each is compiled using a direct implementation of the transition functions of the $\mathscr{CE}$ machine. The mapping from lambda terms can be seen in Fig. 7, which defines the compiler. Unlike the TIM, our version of TAKE doesn't have an arity; we compile a sequence of lambdas as a sequence of TAKE instructions. While we have not compared performance of the two approaches directly, we suspect that n inlined TAKE instructions should be roughly as fast as a TAKE n instruction. Similarly, the ENTER i instruction can be implemented either as a loop or unrolled, depending on i, and more performance comparisons are needed to determine the trade-off between code size and speed.

We compile to x64 assembly. Each of the three instructions is mapped onto x64 instructions with a macro. The PUSH instruction is particularly simple, consisting of only two x64 instructions (two pushes, one for the code pointer and one for the environment pointer). This is actually an important point: *thunk creation is only two hardware instructions, regardless of environment size.*

$$C[\![t\,t']\!] = \text{PUSH } label_{C[\![t']\!]} : C[\![t]\!] \mathbin{+\!\!+} C[\![t']\!]$$

$$C[\![\lambda t]\!] = \text{TAKE} : C[\![t]\!]$$

$$C[\![i]\!] = \text{ENTER } i$$

Fig. 7. $\mathscr{CE}$ machine compilation scheme. C compiles a sequence of instructions from a term. The *label* represents a code label: each instruction is given a unique label. The : operator denotes prepending an item to a sequence and $\mathbin{+\!\!+}$ denotes concatenating two sequences.

6.2   Machine Literals and Primitive Operations

Following Sestoft [28], we extend the $\mathscr{CE}$ machine to include machine literals and primitive operations. Figure 8 shows the parts of syntax and semantics that are new or modified.

Syntax

$$
\begin{aligned}
t ::= \; & i \mid \lambda t \mid t\,t \mid n \mid op & \text{(Term)} \\
n \in \; & \mathbb{I} & \text{(Integer)} \\
op ::= \; & + \mid - \mid * \mid / \mid = \mid > \mid < & \text{(PrimOp)} \\
v ::= \; & \lambda t[l] \mid n[l] & \text{(Value)}
\end{aligned}
$$

Integer and Primop Semantics

$$
\begin{aligned}
\langle n[l], \sigma\, c, \mu, k \rangle &\rightarrow_{\mathscr{CE}} \langle c, \sigma\, n[l], \mu, k \rangle & \text{(Int)} \\
\langle op[l], \sigma\, n'\, n, \mu, k \rangle &\rightarrow_{\mathscr{CE}} \langle op(n',n)[l], \sigma, \mu, k \rangle & \text{(Op)}
\end{aligned}
$$

Fig. 8. Extensions to the syntax and semantics of the $\mathscr{CE}$ machine.

6.3   Omitted Extensions

Our implementation omits a few other standard extensions. Here we address some of these omissions.

Data types are a common extension that we omit [7,24]. We take the approach of Sestoft [28] that these can be efficiently implemented with pure lambda terms. For example, consider a list data type (in Haskell syntax): `data List a = Cons a (List a) | Nil`. This can be represented in pure lambda terms with $Cons = \lambda h.\lambda t.\lambda c.\lambda n.c\,h\,t$ and $Nil = \lambda c.\lambda n.n$.

Let bindings are another term commonly included in functional language compilers, even in the internal representation [7,24]. Non-recursive let is syntactic sugar for a lambda binding and application, and we treat it as such. This approach helps ensure that we can of compile arbitrary lambda terms, while some approaches require pre-processing [13,28].

Recursive let bindings are a third omission. Here we follow Rozas [26]: If it can be represented in pure lambda terms, it should be. Thus, we implement recursion using the standard Y combinator. In the case of mutual recursion, we use the Y combinator in conjunction with a church tuple of the mutually recursive functions. Without the appropriate optimizations [26], this approach has high overhead, as we discuss in Sect. 7.1.

6.4 Optimizations

The $\mathscr{CE}$ implementation described in the previous section is completely unoptimized. For example, no effort is expended to discover global functions to avoid costly jumps to pointers in the heap [24]. Indeed, every variable reference will look up the code pointer in the shared environment and jump to it. There is also no implementation of control flow analysis as used by Rozas to optimize away the Y combinator. Thus, every recursive call exhibits the large overhead involved in re-calculating the fixed point of the function.

We do, however, implement two basic optimizations, primarily to reduce the load on the heap:

– POP: A TAKE instruction can be converted to a POP instruction that throws away the operand on the top of the stack if there are no variables bound to the λ term in question. For example, the function $\lambda x.\lambda y.x$ can be implemented with TAKE, POP, ENTER 0.
– ENTERVAL: An ENTER instruction, when entering a closure that is already a value, should not push an update marker onto the stack. This shortcut prevents unnecessary writes to the stack and heap [14,24,28].

6.5 Garbage Collection

We have implemented a simple mark and sweep garbage collector with the property that it does not require two spaces because constant-sized closures in the heap allow a linked-list representation for the free cells. Indeed, while the abstract machine from Sect. 5 increments a free heap counter, the actual implementation uses the next free cell in the linked list.

Because the focus of this paper is not on the performance of garbage collection, we ensure the benchmarks in Sect. 7 are not dominated by GC time.

7 Performance Evaluation

This section reports experiments that assess the strengths and weaknesses of the $\mathscr{CE}$ machine. We evaluate using benchmarks from the nofib benchmark suite. Because we have implemented only machine integers, and must translate the examples by hand, we use a subset of the nofib suite that excludes floating point values and arrays. A list of the benchmarks used and a brief description is given in Fig. 9.

- **exp3:** A Peano arithmetic benchmark. Computes 3^8 and prints the result.
- **queens:** Computes the number of solutions to the nqueens problem for an n by n board.
- **primes:** A simple primes sieve that computes the nth prime.
- **digits-of-e1:** A calculation of the first n digits of e using continued fractions.
- **digits-of-e2:** Another calculation of the first n digits of e using an infinite series.
- **fib:** Naively computes the nth Fibonacci number.
- **fannkuch:** Counts the number of reverses of a subset of a list.
- **tak:** A synthetic benchmark involving basic recursion.

Fig. 9. Description of benchmarks

We compare the $\mathscr{CE}$ machine with two existing implementations:

- GHC: The Glasgow Haskell compiler. A high performance, optimizing compiler based on the STG machine [24].
- UHC: The Utrecht Haskell compiler. An optimizing compiler based on the GRIN machine [7, 12].

We use GHC version 7.10.3 and UHC version 1.1.9.3. We compile with $-O0$ and $-O3$, and show the results for both. Where possible, we pre-allocate a heap of 1 GB to avoid measuring the performance of GC implementations. The tests were run on an Intel(R) Xeon(R) CPU E5-4650L at 2.60 GHz, running Linux version 3.16.

7.1 Results

Figure 10 gives the benchmark results. In general, we are outperformed by GHC, sometimes significantly, and we outperform UHC. We spend the remainder of the section analyzing these performance differences.

	$\mathscr{CE}$	GHC -O0	UHC -O0	GHC -O3	UHC -O3
exp3 8	1.530	1.176	3.318	1.038	2.286
tak 16 8 0	0.366	0.146	1.510	0.006	1.416
primes 1500	0.256	0.272	1.518	0.230	1.532
queens 9	0.206	0.050	0.600	0.012	0.598
fib 35	2.234	0.872	10.000	0.110	8.342
digits-of-e1 1000	3.576	1.274	21.938	0.118	22.010
digits-of-e2 1000	0.404	0.792	3.430	0.372	3.278
fannkuch 8	0.560	0.084	2.184	0.048	2.196

Fig. 10. Machine literals benchmark results. Measurement is wall clock time, units are seconds. Times averaged over 5 runs.

There are many optimizations built into the abstract machine underlying GHC, but profiling indicates that three in particular lead to much of the performance disparity:

- **Register allocation:** The $\mathscr{CE}$ machine has no register allocator. In contrast, by passing arguments to functions in registers, GHC avoids much heap thrashing.
- **Unpacked literals:** This allows GHC to keep machine literals without tags in registers for tight loops. In contrast, the $\mathscr{CE}$ machine operates entirely on the stack, and has a code pointer associated with every machine literal.
- **Y combinator:** Because recursion in the $\mathscr{CE}$ machine is implemented with a Y combinator, it performs poorly. This could be alleviated with CFA-based techniques, similar to those used in [26].

Lack of register allocation is the primary current limitation of the $\mathscr{CE}$ machine. The STG machine pulls the free variables into registers, allowing tight loops with everything kept in registers. However, it is less clear how to effectively allocate registers in a fully shared environment setting. That said, we believe being lazier about register allocation, e.g., not loading values into registers that may not be used, could have some performance benefits.

To isolate the effect of register allocation and unpacked machine literals, we replace machine integers with Church numerals in a compatible subset of the evaluation programs. Figure 11 shows the performance results with this modification, which are much improved, with the $\mathscr{CE}$ machine occasionally even outperforming optimized GHC.

	$\mathscr{CE}$	GHC -O0	UHC -O0	GHC -O3	UHC -O3
tak 14 7 0	1.610	2.428	7.936	1.016	7.782
primes 32	0.846	1.494	4.778	0.666	5.290
queens 8	0.242	0.374	1.510	0.154	1.508
fib 23	0.626	0.940	5.026	0.468	5.336
digits-of-e2 6	0.138	1.478	5.056	0.670	5.534
fannkuch 7	0.142	0.124	0.796	0.040	0.808

Fig. 11. Church numeral benchmark results. Measurement is wall clock time, units are seconds. Times averaged over 5 runs.

Next, we consider the disparity due to the Y-combinator, by running a simple exponentiation example with Church numerals, calculating $3^8 - 3^8 = 0$. In this case, the $\mathscr{CE}$ machine significantly outperform both GHC and UHC, as seen in Fig. 12.

	$\mathscr{CE}$	GHC -O0	UHC -O0	GHC -O3	UHC -O3
pow 3 8	0.564	1.994	4.912	0.906	4.932

Fig. 12. Church numeral exponentiation benchmark results. Measurement is wall clock time, units are seconds. Times averaged over 5 runs.

These results give us confidence that by adding the optimizations mentioned above, among others, the $\mathscr{CE}$ machine has the potential to be the basis of a real-world compiler. We discuss how some of these optimizations can be applied to the $\mathscr{CE}$ machine in Sect. 8.

7.2   The Cost of the Cactus

Recall that variable lookup is linear in the index of the variable, following pointers until the index is zero. As one might guess, the lookup cost is high. For example, for the queens benchmark without any optimizations, variable lookup took roughly 80–90% of the $\mathscr{CE}$ machine runtime, as measured by profiling. Much of that cost was for lookups of known combinators, however, so for the benchmarks above we added the inlining mentioned in the previous section. Still, even with this simple optimization, variable lookup takes roughly 50% of execution time. There is some variation across benchmarks, but this is a rough approximation for the average cost. We discuss how this cost could be addressed in future work in Sect. 8.

8   Discussion and Related Work

Some related work was discussed earlier to provide background and context. Here, we briefly and explicitly compare our approach with earlier work. We also discuss areas for future work.

8.1   Closure Representation

Appel and Shao [29] and Appel and Jim [2] both cover the design space for closure representation, and develop an approach called *safely linked closures*. It uses flat closures when there is no duplication, and links in a way that preserves liveness, to prevent violation of the *safe for space complexity* (SSC) rule [1]. While we do not address SSC or garbage collection in general, understanding the relationship between SSC and shared environment call-by-need is an interesting area for future work. In particular, hot environments with no sharing could benefit greatly from replacing shared structure with flat.

8.2   Eval/Apply vs. Push/Enter

Marlow and Peyton Jones describe two approaches to the implementation of function application: eval/apply, where the function is evaluated and then passed the necessary arguments, and push/enter, where the arguments are pushed onto the stack and the function code is entered [22]. They conclude that despite push/enter being a standard approach to lazy machines, eval/apply performs better. While our current approach uses push/enter, investigating whether eval/apply could be usefully implemented for a shared environment machine like the $\mathscr{CE}$ machine is an interesting avenue for future work.

8.3   Collapsed Markers

Friedman et al. show how a machine can be designed to prevent multiple adjacent update markers being pushed onto the stack [14]. This property is desirable because multiple adjacent update markers are always updated with the same value. They give examples showing that in some cases, these redundant update markers can cause an otherwise constant-space stack to grow unbounded. They implement an optimization that collapses update markers by adding a layer of indirection between heap locations and closures. We propose a similar approach, but without the performance hit caused by an extra layer of indirection. Upon a variable dereference the $\mathscr{CE}$ machine checks if the top of the stack is an update. If it is, instead of pushing a redundant update marker onto the stack, it replaces the closure in the heap at the desired location with an update marker. Then, the variable dereference rule checks for an update marker upon dereference, and will update accordingly. We have begun to implement this optimization, but leave the full implementation and description for future work.

8.4 Register Allocation

One advantage of flat environments is that register allocation is straightforward [1, 24, 31]. It is less obvious how to do register allocation with the $\mathscr{CE}$ machine. We speculate that it should be possible to do a sufficient job, particularly in the cases that matter most, e.g. unboxed machine literals, though certainly not easy.

One possible approach that could work well with our shared environment approach would be to only load strict free variables into registers. That is to say, some environment variables may not be used, and only the ones we know will be used should be loaded into registers, while the rest should be loaded on demand.

8.5 Verification

A signal property of our implementation is its simplicity, which makes it an attractive target for a verified compiler. Because it avoids complexities required for flat environment implementations, e.g., black hole updates, basing a verified compiler on this machine is another exciting area for future work.

9 Conclusion

Lazy evaluation has long suffered from high overhead when delaying computations. While strictness analysis helps to alleviate this issue, there are and there always will be cases it cannot catch. Existing implementations choose to pay an up-front cost of constructing a flat environment to ensure efficient variable lookup if a delayed computation is used. When a delayed computation is never used, this overhead is wasted. In this paper we have presented a novel approach that minimizes this overhead. We have achieved this overhead minimization by taking an old idea, shared environments, and using them in a novel way. By leveraging the structure inherent in a shared environment to share results of computation, we have avoided some of the overheads involved in delaying a computation.

We conclude by summarizing the key points of this paper. First, a shared environment, explicitly represented as a cactus stack, is a natural way to share the results of computation as required by lazy evaluation. Second, this approach is in a sense *lazier* about lazy evaluation than existing implementations because it avoids some unnecessary packaging. Third, this approach can be formalized in both big-step and small-step semantics. Lastly, the abstract machine can be implemented as a compiler in a straightforward way, yielding performance comparable to existing implementations.

Acknowledgments. This material is based upon work supported by the National Science Foundation under grant CCF-1422840, NSF (1518878,1444871), DARPA (FA8750-15-C-0118), AFRL (FA8750-15-2-0075), the Sandia National Laboratories Academic Alliance, and the Santa Fe Institute. Sandia National Laboratories is a multi-program laboratory managed and operated by Sandia Corporation, a wholly owned subsidiary of Lockheed Martin Corporation, for the U.S. Department of Energy's National Nuclear Security Administration under contract DE-AC04-94AL85000.

References

1. Appel, A.W.: Compiling with Continuations. Cambridge University Press, Cambridge (1992)
2. Appel, A.W., Jim, T.: Optimizing closure environment representations. Technical report (1988)
3. Appel, A.W., MacQueen, D.B.: Standard ML of New Jersey. In: Maluszyński, J., Wirsing, M. (eds.) PLILP 1991. LNCS, vol. 528, pp. 1–13. Springer, Heidelberg (1991). https://doi.org/10.1007/3-540-54444-5_83
4. Ariola, Z.M., Maraist, J., Odersky, M., Felleisen, M., Wadler, P.: A call-by-need lambda calculus. In: Proceedings of the 22nd ACM SIGPLAN-SIGACT Symposium on Principles of Programming Languages, pp. 233–246 (1995)
5. Barendregt, H.P.: The Lambda Calculus. North-Holland Amsterdam, Amsterdam (1984)
6. Biernacka, M., Danvy, O.: A concrete framework for environment machines. ACM Trans. Comput. Log. **9**(1), 6 (2007)
7. Boquist, U., Johnsson, T.: The GRIN project: a highly optimising back end for lazy functional languages. In: Kluge, W. (ed.) IFL 1996. LNCS, vol. 1268, pp. 58–84. Springer, Heidelberg (1997). https://doi.org/10.1007/3-540-63237-9_19
8. Curien, P.L.: An abstract framework for environment machines. Theor. Comput. Sci. **82**(2), 389–402 (1991)
9. Danvy, O., Millikin, K., Munk, J., Zerny, I.: On inter-deriving small-step and big-step semantics: a case study for storeless call-by-need evaluation. Theor. Comput. Sci. **435**, 21–42 (2012)
10. Danvy, O., Zerny, I.: A synthetic operational account of call-by-need evaluation. In: Proceedings of the 15th Symposium on Principles and Practice of Declarative Programming, pp. 97–108 (2013)
11. Diehl, S., Hartel, P., Sestoft, P.: Abstract machines for programming language implementation. Futur. Gener. Comput. Syst. **16**(7), 739–751 (2000)
12. Dijkstra, A., Fokker, J., Swierstra, S.D.: The architecture of the Utrecht Haskell compiler. In: Proceedings of the 2nd ACM SIGPLAN Symposium on Haskell, pp. 93–104 (2009)
13. Fairbairn, J., Wray, S.: TIM: a simple, lazy abstract machine to execute supercombinators. In: Functional Programming Languages and Computer Architecture, pp. 34–45 (1987)
14. Friedman, D., Ghuloum, A., Siek, J., Winebarger, O.: Improving the lazy Krivine machine. High.-Order Symb. Comput. **20**, 271–293 (2007)
15. Hauck, E., Dent, B.A.: Burroughs' B6500/B7500 stack mechanism. In: Proceedings of the 30 April–2 May 1968, Spring Joint Computer Conference, pp. 245–251 (1968)
16. Ichbiah, J.: Rationale for the Design of the ADA Programming Language. Cambridge University Press, Cambridge (1991)
17. Ingerman, P.Z.: A way of compiling procedure statements with some comments on procedure declarations. Commun. ACM **4**(1), 55–58 (1961)
18. Johnsson, T.: Efficient compilation of lazy evaluation. In: Proceedings of the 1984 SIGPLAN Symposium on Compiler Construction, pp. 58–69 (1984)

19. Krivine, J.: A call-by-name lambda-calculus machine. High.-Order Symb. Comput. **20**(3), 199–207 (2007)
20. Landin, P.J.: The mechanical evaluation of expressions. Comput. J. **6**(4), 308–320 (1964)
21. Leroy, X.: The ZINC experiment: an economical implementation of the ML language. Technical report 117, INRIA (1990)
22. Marlow, S., Jones, S.P.: Making a fast curry: push/enter vs. eval/apply for higher-order languages. J. Funct. Program. **16**(4–5), 415–449 (2006)
23. Mycroft, A.: Abstract interpretation and optimising transformations for applicative programs. Ph.D. thesis (1982)
24. Peyton Jones, S.L.: Implementing lazy functional languages on stock hardware: the spineless tagless G-machine. J. Funct. Program. **2**(2), 127–202 (1992)
25. Peyton Jones, S.L., Lester, D.R.: Implementing Functional Languages. Prentice-Hall, Inc., Upper Saddle River (1992)
26. Rozas, G.J.: Taming the Y operator. In: ACM SIGPLAN Lisp Pointers, vol. 1, pp. 226–234 (1992)
27. Sabry, A., Lumsdaine, A., Garcia, R.: Lazy evaluation and delimited control. Log. Methods Comput. Sci. **6**, 153–164 (2010)
28. Sestoft, P.: Deriving a lazy abstract machine. J. Funct. Program. **7**(3), 231–264 (1997)
29. Shao, Z., Appel, A.W.: Space-efficient closure representations. In: Proceedings of the 1994 ACM Conference on Lisp and Functional Programming (1994)
30. Stenstrom, P.: VLSI support for a cactus stack oriented memory organization. In: Proceedings of the Twenty-First Annual Hawaii International Conference on System Sciences, Volume I. Architecture Track, vol. 1, pp. 211–220 (1988)
31. Terei, D.A., Chakravarty, M.M.: An LLVM backend for GHC. In: Proceedings of the Third ACM Haskell Symposium on Haskell, Haskell 2010, pp. 109–120 (2010)
32. Wadler, P., Hughes, R.J.M.: Projections for strictness analysis. In: Functional Programming Languages and Computer Architecture, pp. 385–407 (1987)

Improving Sequential Performance of Erlang Based on a Meta-tracing Just-In-Time Compiler

Ruochen Huang, Hidehiko Masuhara$^{(\boxtimes)}$, and Tomoyuki Aotani

Tokyo Institute of Technology, Tokyo 152-8552, Japan
hrc706@gmail.com, masuhara@acm.org, aotani@c.titech.ac.jp

Abstract. In widely-used actor-based programming languages, such as Erlang, sequential execution performance is as important as scalability of concurrency. In order to improve sequential performance of Erlang, we develop Pyrlang, an Erlang virtual machine with a just-in-time (JIT) compiler by applying an existing meta-tracing JIT compiler. In this paper, we overview our implementation and present the optimization techniques for Erlang programs, most of which heavily rely on function recursion. Our preliminary evaluation showed approximately 38% speedup over the standard Erlang interpreter.

Keywords: Meta-tracing · JIT · Erlang · BEAM

1 Introduction

Erlang [4] is a dynamically-typed, functional and concurrent programming language based on the actor model [1]. It is widely used for practical applications that require distribution, concurrency and availability. The application area ranges from telecommunication, banking, electric commerce to instant messaging [2], and recently expanding to server side like Cowboy[1], Chicago Boss[2], and MochiWeb[3].

We consider that sequential execution performance in Erlang is as important as scalability of concurrency. In this regard, the two mainstream implementations of Erlang, namely the BEAM virtual machine (or BEAM in short) [3] and the HiPE compiler (or HiPE in short) [13], are either less efficient or less portable. BEAM is a bytecode interpreter, and guarantees bytecode level portability across different platforms. Its sequential execution is however slow due to the interpreter-based execution[4]. HiPE is a static native code compiler, and

---

[1] https://github.com/ninenines/cowboy.

[2] https://github.com/ChicagoBoss/ChicagoBoss.

[3] https://github.com/mochi/mochiweb.

[4] According to the Computer Language Benchmarks Game (http://benchmarksgame. alioth.debian.org/), BEAM is slower than C by the factors of 4–95 with 10 benchmark programs.

© Springer Nature Switzerland AG 2019
D. Van Horn and J. Hughes (Eds.): TFP 2016, LNCS 10447, pp. 44–58, 2019.
https://doi.org/10.1007/978-3-030-14805-8_3

is faster than BEAM[5]. However, despite of the performance improvement, the compiled code using HiPE loses the compatibility, which means we cannot use it cross-platform. Moreover, users cannot re-compile libraries without source-code into native code using HiPE.

Alternatively, we propose Pyrlang, a virtual machine for the BEAM bytecode with a just-in-time (JIT) compiler. We use the RPython's meta-tracing JIT compiler [5] as a back-end. Although the back-end is primarily designed for imperative programming languages like Python (as known as the PyPy project), Pyrlang achieved approximately 38% speedup over BEAM.

Contributions. The contributions of the paper can be explained from the two viewpoints: as an alternative implementation of Erlang, and as an application of a meta-tracing JIT compiler to a mostly-functional language.

As an alternative implementation of Erlang, Pyrlang demonstrates a potential of JIT compilation for Erlang[6]. Even though our initial implementation was the result of a few month's work, the performance was comparable to an existing static Erlang compiler. This suggests that, by reusing a quality back-end, we could provide Erlang a JIT compiler with a number of modern optimizations.

From a viewpoint of tracing JIT compilers, Pyrlang is equipped with a new more strict tracing JIT policy, which focus on detecting more frequently executed path under conditional branch. In our research, we found that a naive application of a tracing JIT compiler suffers overheads when the compiler chooses less frequent paths. We showed that a new tracing policy reduces the overheads by the factor of 2.9% on average.

Organization of the Paper. The paper is organized as follows. Section 2 introduces the instruction set of BEAM as well as an overview of a meta-tracing JIT compiler. Section 3 describes the key design decisions in Pyrlang. Section 4 proposes an optimization technique for improving performance of functions with recursive calls. Section 5 evaluates the performance of Pyrlang by comparing against the existing Erlang implementations. Section 6 discusses related work. Section 7 concludes the paper with discussing future work.

2   Background

2.1   Erlang and BEAM Bytecode

The mainstream Erlang implementation compiles an Erlang program to bytecode, and executes on BEAM. We here briefly explain the architecture of the bytecode language by using a few examples.

---

[5] Though HiPE is known to exhibit largely different performance improvements depending on the types of application programs [12], it speeds up by the factors from 1.8 to 3.5 according to the benchmark results in a literature [15] and our experiments.

[6] Other than BEAM and HiPE, there are a few attempts to support JIT compilation for Erlang, which we discuss in the later section of the paper.

BEAM is a bytecode-based register machine, whose instruction set includes register transfers (e.g., move), conditional jumps (e.g., is_eq_exact and is_lt_exact), arithmetic operations (expressed as calls to built-in functions like "gc_bif erlang:+/2"), and function calls (e.g., call and call_only). There are three sets of registers, namely X, Y and F, which are denoted as $x(i)$, $y(i)$ and $f(i)$, respectively. The X and F registers store values of any types other than floating point numbers, and values of floating point values, respectively. They are used for passing parameters to and returning results from functions, and can also be used as caller-saved temporary variables. The Y registers are callee-saved, and can be used for storing local variables in a function body. There are instructions to save (allocate_zero) and restore (deallocate) Y registers.

```
; function  my_module : add /2
L2:          ;  x(0)  :=  x(0)  +  x(1)
             gc_bif2  erlang:+/2  x(0)  x(1)  x(0)
             return
             . . .
L5:          move  #3  x(0)
             move  #5  x(1)
             call  L2
             . . .
```

Fig. 1. An add function and its invocation in BEAM bytecode

```
; function  fact : fact /2
L2:          ;  if  x(0)==0,  jump  to  L3
             is_eq_exact  L3,  x(0),  #0
             ;  x(0)  :=  x(1)
             move  x(1),  x(0)
             return
L3:          ;  x(2)  :=  x(0)  −  1
             gc_bif2  erlang:−/2,  x(0),  #1,  x(2)
             ;  x(1)  :=  x(0)  *  x(1)
             gc_bif2  erlang:*/2,  x(0),  x(1),  x(1)
             move  x(2),  x(0)
             call_only  L2  ;  tail  call
```

Fig. 2. A tail-recursive factorial function in BEAM bytecode

Figures 1, 2 and 3 show three simple functions in BEAM bytecode.

Figure 1 shows a function that adds two parameters (from L2) and a code fragment that calls the function with parameters 3 and 5 (from L5). The function expects parameters in registers $x(0)$ and $x(1)$, and returns a result by storing it in $x(0)$. The instruction immediately after L2 (gc_bif2 erlang:+/2) is a built-in function that stores the sum of two registers into a register. To invoke a function,

```
; function  fact : fact /1
L2:         ;  if  x(0)==0,  jump  to  L3
            is_eq_exact  L3,  x(0),  #0
            move  #1,  x(0)  ;  x(0)  :=  1
            return
L3:         allocate_zero  1,  1  ; save  Y  registers
            ;  x(1)  :=  x(0)  −  #1
            gc_bif2  erlang :−/2,  x(0),  #1,  x(1)
            move  x(0),  y(0);  save  x(0)  to  y(0)
            move  x(1),  x(0)
            call  1,  L2                ; non−tail  call
            ;  x(0)  :=  y(0)  *  x(0)
            gc_bif2  erlang :*/2,  y(0),  x(0),  x(0)
            deallocate  1  ; restore  Y  registers
            return
```

Fig. 3. A non-tail recursive factorial function in BEAM bytecode

the caller sets parameters on X registers, and then executes the call instruction. As can be seen in the code, the caller and the callee share the X registers.

Figure 2 shows a factorial function written in a tail recursive manner, where the second parameter accumulates the product of numbers computed so far. The first instruction from L2 (is_eq_exact) compares two parameters and jumps if they are the same. The last instruction of the function (call_only) is a tail-call. Note that BEAM uses different instructions for tail (call_only) and non-tail calls (call).

Figure 3 shows a non-tail recursive factorial function. Since the function multiplies the result from a recursive call by the given argument, it saves the argument $(x(0))$ into a callee-saved register $(y(0))$ before the recursive invocation. The block from L3 saves and restores the Y registers at the beginning and the end of the block, respectively.

2.2   Meta-tracing JIT Compiler

A meta-tracing JIT compiler [5,7] monitors an execution of an interpreter of a target language, and generates optimized native code for a frequently executed instruction sequence (called a *hot trace*) of the *subject* program (which is the Erlang program in our work). Though it can be seen as an application of a tracing JIT compiler to an interpreter program, annotations specialized to interpreters optimizations make it possible to generate compiled code of the subject program, rather than compiled code of the interpreter. As a result, the technique enables to build a JIT compiler of a language by writing an interpreter of that language with proper annotations. In the case of Pyrlang, we use a meta-tracing JIT compiler for interpreters written in RPython, a subset of Python. In other words, we write a BEAM bytecode interpreter in RPython.

Meta-tracing JIT compilers basically have the same mechanism as tracing JIT compilers. We therefore explain the mechanisms of tracing JIT compilers first, and then the notions specific to meta-tracing JIT compilers.

A tracing JIT compiler works by (1) detecting a frequently executed instruction (called *a JIT merge point*) in an execution of a program, which is usually a backward jump instruction, (2) then recording a series of executed instructions from the merge point (which we call a *trace*), and (3) compiling the trace to optimized code. When the control reaches the merge point again, the optimized code runs instead of the original one. Since a trace is a straightline code fragment spanning over multiple functions, the compiler effectively achieves aggressive inlining with low-level optimizations like constant propagation.

When the counter of a JIT merge point hits a threshold, the compiler records a trace, which is a series of executed instructions, until the control comes back to the same JIT merge point. The compiler converts the trace into native code by applying optimizations like the constant propagation. When a conditional branch remains in a trace, it is converted to a *guard*, which checks the condition and jumps back to the original program when the condition code holds differently from the recorded trace.

Meta-tracing JIT compilers are tracing JIT compilers that optimize an *interpreter program* (which is the interpreter written by RPython in our case). Their mechanisms for monitoring and tracing an execution of the subject program are the same as the one in general tracing JIT compilers, except for the notion of program locations. While general tracing JIT compilers select a trace from the loops in the interpreter program, meta-tracing JIT compilers do so from the loops in an subject program. To do so, they recognize the *program counter* variable (denoted as pc hereafter) in the interpreter, and assign a different execution frequency counter to different pc values. With this extension, the compilers detect frequently executed instruction in the subject program, and record the interpreter's execution until it evaluates the same instruction in the subject program.

In the rest of the paper, we simply refer JIT merge points as locations in subject programs. Except that the program locations are indirectly recognized through variables in the interpreter, the readers can understand the subsequent discussion in the paper as if we are working with a dedicated tracing JIT compiler for BEAM.

3   Implementation Overview

This section overviews the design of Pyrlang's JIT compiler, which is embodied as a BEAM bytecode interpreter written in RPython. We first show the representation of data structures in the interpreter, and then describes the design of the dispatch loop (i.e., the interpreter's main loop).

3.1   Data Representation

Instructions and Literal Values. We represent a BEAM bytecode program as an RPython array of instruction objects. An instruction object is an RPython object that contains operands in its fields. Literal values are stored in literal tables, whose indices are used in the operands.

We made the following design decisions in order to let the JIT compiler perform obvious operations at compile time. (1) We separately manage the literal table for integers, and the table for other types. This will eliminate dynamic type checking for integer literals. (2) We mark the instruction array and all fields of instruction objects as "immutable." This will eliminate operations for fetching instructions and operands from the generated code.

Atoms. We represent an atom by an index of a global atom table, which contains the identifiers of dynamically created atoms. This will make the equality test between atoms constant time.

X and F Registers. We use two RPython lists for X and F registers, respectively. We also mark those lists *virtualizable*[7], which is an optimization hint in RPython. This hint encourages the compiler to perform scalar replacement of marked objects, so that they do not need to be allocated, as a result fields reads/writes can be treated as pure data dependencies and their data are ideally kept in registers only.

Y Registers and Stack Frame. We represent Y registers and the stack frame as a pair of resizable lists with stack pointers. The first list serves as a stack of Y registers whose indices are shifted by its stack pointer. The stack pointer is adjusted by the allocate_zero and deallocate instructions. The second list serves as a stack of return addresses. The runtime initially constructs those two lists with fixed lengths, yet re-allocates a new lists with twice length of the current one when the stack pointer reaches to the end of either list.

Our representation differs from a linked-list of frames, which is found in typical implementations of interpreters. The rationales behind our representation are as follows. (1) We use single list a fixed-length (yet resizable) list for avoiding allocation overheads of frames that were required at every function invocation in the linked-list representation. (2) We separately manage the local variables and the return addresses so as to give static types to the return addresses.

3.2   Dispatch Loop

The core of the BEAM bytecode interpreter is a single loop called *the dispatch loop*, which fetches a bytecode instruction at the program counter, and jumps to the *handler* code that corresponds to the instruction. A handler performs

---

[7] https://pypy.readthedocs.org/en/release-2.4.x/jit/virtualizable.html.

operations of the respective instruction, such as moving values between registers, performing arithmetic operations, and changing the value of the program counter.

The design of the dispatch loop is similar to typical bytecode interpreters, except for the following three Pyrlang specific points. (1) We use a local variable for managing the program counter, which is crucial for the JIT compiler to eliminate accesses to the program counter. (2) The handler for call_only merely changes the program counter value as the instruction is for tail calls, which effectively realizes tail call elimination. (3) The dispatch loop yields its execution for realizing the green threading. To do so, the loop has a yield counter, and the handlers of some instructions (those can become an end of a trace) terminates the dispatch loop when the counter is decremented to zero.

4 Finer-Grained Path Profiling

4.1 The False Path Problem

A tracing JIT compiler sometimes chooses an execution path as a compilation target, even if it is not frequently executed. We call this problem *the false path problem*, as an analogy to the false loop problem [10].

One of the causes of the false path problem is mismatch between profiling and compilation. A tracing JIT compiler selects the first execution path executed from a merge point whose execution counter exceeds a threshold. When there are conditional branches after the merge point, the selected path can be different from the one that is frequently executed.

When a false path is selected and compiled, it puts a considerable amount of performance penalty on the frequently executed paths that share the same merge point. This is because the execution from the merge point has to follow the compiled false path, and then frequently fails; i.e., a conditional branch goes to a different target from the compiled path. Upon a failure, the runtime needs to reconstruct an intermediate interpreter state.

4.2 An Naive Profiling Policy for Functions

A naive profiling policy for functional programs can cause the false path problem. Let us illustrate this by using a simple concrete program after we introduced a naive profiling policy.

For functional programs where loops are realized by recursive function calls, a naive profiling policy places merge points at the beginnings of functions. In fact, we used this policy in our first implementation, which we refer as *pyrlang-naive* in the rest of the paper. Technically, pyrlang-naive actually marks call (non-tail function invocation), call_only (tail function invocation), and return as JIT merge points. Since we have tail call elimination as introduced in Sect. 3, tail recursions in Pyrlang are similar with typical loops in an imperative language, as a tracing JIT compiler expects.

```
; function  cd : cd /1
L2 :
            is_eq_exact  L3,  x(0),  #1    A
            move  #10,  x(0)     } B
            call_only  L2
L3 :
            gc_bif2  erlang:−/2,  x(0),  #1,  x(0)  } C
            call_only  L2
```

Fig. 4. A countdown function which restarts itself from 10

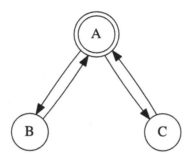

Fig. 5. Control flow graph of the count-down function. (The alphabets in the nodes correspond to the basic blocks in Fig. 4. The doubly-circled node denotes the JIT merge point.)

Figures 4 and 5 show a countdown function in the BEAM bytecode with its control flow graph. The function infinitely repeats counting numbers from 10 to 1. While imperative languages realize the computation double nested loops, functional languages typically realize it a recursive function with a conditional branch as can be seen in the control flow graph. In this case, node B is executed one out of ten iterations.

The two loops, namely A–B–A and A–C–A in the control flow graph, share the single JIT merge point, namely A. This means that the compiler has 10% of chance to select the less frequently path (i.e., A–B–A). Then, the subsequent executions from A use the compiled trace for the path A–B–A, and fail 9 out of 10 cases.

4.3 Pattern Matching Tracing

We propose an improved policy for tracing called *pattern matching tracing*. The basic idea is to place JIT merge points on the destinations of conditional branches, instead of the beginnings of functions so as to distinguish different paths as different traces. For the countdown function, we place JIT merge points on the target nodes of conditional branches, namely B and C as in the control-flow graph shown in Fig. 6.

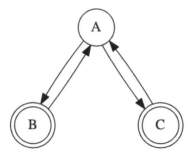

Fig. 6. Control flow graph of the countdown function for pattern matching tracing

With this policy, the compiler will select more frequently executed paths because the merge points are placed in all branch targets. In the example, the merge point C will hit the threshold before B will, and the path starting from the next execution of C (i.e., C–A–C) will be compiled first.

We implemented this policy in the Pyrlang's dispatch loop by marking conditional branch destinations, instead of function entries, as JIT merge points.

4.4 Two State Tracing

In addition to the pattern matching tracing, we also use two state tracing policy proposed for Pycket [6]. The basic idea of two state tracing is to distinguish entries of recursive functions by the caller instruction address. We implement it by using the program counter as well as the caller's address (we refer as *caller-pc* hereafter) as the interpreted program's location.

5   Evaluation

5.1   Benchmark Environment

We evaluate the performance of Pyrlang and its optimization technique with subsets of two benchmark suites. The one is the Scheme Larceny benchmark suite[8] that is translated by the authors from Scheme to Erlang. The other is the ErLLVM benchmark suite[9], which is developed to evaluate the HiPE LLVM backend. Since the current implementation of Pyrlang supports a limited set of primitives, we excluded programs that test concurrency, binary data processing, and modules using the built-in functions that are not yet implemented in Pyrlang. Also, currently there is an unsolved bug in Pyrlang which causes the execution crashing when dealing with float datatype during context switching, so we have to excluded benchmark programs related to it like fibfp and fpsum, too.

---

[8] https://github.com/pnkfelix/larceny-pnk/tree/master/test/Benchmarking/
    CrossPlatform/src.
[9] https://github.com/cstavr/erllvm-bench/tree/master/src.

We evaluate three different versions of Pyrlang, namely (*pyrlang*) the version using pattern matching tracing, (*pyrlang-two-state*) the version using only two state tracing, which is the same as *pyrlang* except JIT merge points are placed in function entities rather than functional branch destinations, (*pyrlang-naive*) the version using only naive tracing policy, as we introduced in Sect. 4.2.

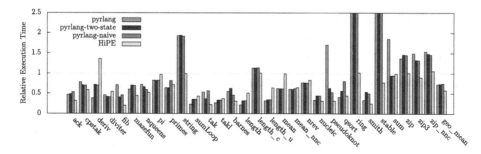

Fig. 7. Execution Times with pyrlang, pyrlang-two-state, pyrlang-naive and HiPE, relative to BEAM (the shorter is the better)

We emphasize that Pyrlang does not apply low-level optimizations such as calling convention for the x86 architecture [15], and the local type propagation [16] that are used in BEAM or HiPE. Furthermore, we use the original BEAM instruction set for the ease of implementation, unlike BEAM which internally uses superinstructions [9, Sect. 3.15] in order to reduce interpretation overheads.

All the benchmark programs are executed on a 1.87 GHz Intel Core i7 processor with 8 MB cache memory and 8 GB main memory, running GNU/Linux 14.04. The version of the BEAM runtime and HiPE is Erlang R16B03, with the highest optimization option (-o3) for HiPE. The backend of Pyrlang is RPython revision b7e79d170a32 (timestamped at 2016-01-13 04:38).

Each program is executed inside a loop, whose number of iterations is manually selected so that the loop runs for at least 5 s. The benchmark results in this section are indicated by the execution times relative to the ones with the BEAM runtime.

5.2 Overall Performance

Figure 7 shows the execution times of 30 programs in the benchmark suites, executed with the three versions of Pyrlang, HiPE and the BEAM runtime. The height of each bar shows the relative time to the execution time with BEAM. The rightmost 4 bars (geo_mean) are the geometric means.

As can be seen in Fig. 7, pyrlang-match is 38.3% faster than the BEAM, yet still 25.2% slower than HiPE. With some benchmark programs that are relatively non-trivial, such as deriv, pi, nucleic, and qsort, pyrlang-match is the fastest among 5 implementations. There is a group of the programs (*string*, *length_c*, *pseudoknot*, *ring*, *stable*, *sum*, *zip*, *zip3*, and *zip_nnc*) where Pyrlang is slower than BEAM and HiPE. We conjecture that most of the slow cases are caused by the overhead of Erlang datatype allocation. This is expected since we simply use RPython objects to implement datatypes such as lists, function closures without any further low-level optimizations. The programs *ring* and *stable* are the only two benchmark programs using green threads in our benchmark suite, which indicate room of optimization around thread implementations.

5.3   Effect of Pattern Matching Tracing

Improvements by Pattern Matching Tracing. In this section, we evaluate effectiveness of our proposed pattern matching tracing by comparing execution times of benchmark programs with three versions of Pyrlang, namely the one with pattern matching tracing (pyrlang), one with two state tracing (pyrlang-two-state) and naive tracing (pyrlang-naive). In pyrlang-naive, we mark merely 3 kinds of instructions as JIT merge points, namely call (non-tail invocation), call_only (tail invocation), and return. Also, in this version, the JIT merge points are identified by only *pc* but not by *caller-pc*, which we introduced in Sect. 4.

As we can see, pyrlang is 1.3% and 2.9% faster than pyrlang-two-state and pyrlang-naive on average, respectively.

There are programs where pyrlang is significantly slower, namely *sum* and *pseudoknot*. Sum is a program using two Erlang built-in functions, namely lists:seq and lists:sum, to generate a long Erlang list and to calculate the sum of the elements in the generated list, respectively. Pseudoknot is a program that generates pseudoknot matrix from a database of nucleotide conformations. With sum, we found Pyrlang only generates a trace for lists:sum, but not for lists:seq, which contributed to the significant performance degradation. Currently we are not clear why the lists:seq is missed, which remains as the future work to be resolved. With pseudoknot, we found a loop of a long series of conditional branches that serves as a dispatch loop. This control structure created overly many JIT merge points with Pyrlang-match, though only a few of them are compiled. We conjecture that we can reduce the number of JIT merge points so as to improve performance.

Also, there are two programs where Pyrlang is significantly faster, namely *deriv* and *qsort*. Deriv is a program that performs symbolic derivation of mathematical expressions. Qsort is a program that performs quick-sorting of a number sequence. We observed that, in both benchmark programs, Pyrlang generated much longer traces. In deriv, the longest compiled trace corresponds to an expression of a specific shape (namely multiplication of variables). We presume that the trace is significantly effective as the program has many sub-expressions in the same shape. In Qsort, the longest compiled trace corresponds to a loop in partition function. In fact, Pyrlang records a whole execution of the partition for a short sequence. We have to point out that these two cases heavily depend on the program inputs, which might not be as effective when inputs can vary among executions. In other words, those results indicate that Pyrlang with the pattern matching tracing is quite effective when a program follows a few specific paths in a complicated control structure.

6   Related Work

PyPy [5], an alternative implementation of Python, is the primary target system of the meta-tracing JIT compiler in RPython. It is reported to be faster than an interpreter implementation (CPython) by the factor of 7.1[10] while achieving high compatibility. This suggests that the meta-tracing JIT compiler is a realistic approach to provide an efficient and highly compatible language implementation with a JIT compiler. The meta-tracing JIT compiler's design is implicitly affected by the language features of PyPy (or Python), such as a stack-based bytecode language and use of loop constructs in source programs.

Pycket [6] is an implementation of Racket runtime system based on the meta-tracing JIT compiler in RPython. Similar to Erlang, Racket is a Scheme-like functional programming language, in which user programs use recursive calls for iterations. It proposes a two-state-tracing [6], which is a light-weight solution to the false loop problem [10]. The basic idea of two-state-tracing is to record the previous abstract syntax tree node of the node in a function head, and use both previous node (1st state) and current node (2nd state) to identify a JIT merge point. It means a function head node in a control flow graph is duplicated. The pattern matching tracing extends the two-state-tracing by moving the 2nd state from a function head to a conditional jumping destination. By this approach, in addition to duplicate the function head nodes in a control flow graph, we also duplicate the nodes of conditional jumping destinations.

BEAMJIT [8] is a tracing JIT compiler implementation for Erlang. It extracts the basic handler code for each BEAM instruction from the BEAM runtime. The extracted handler code is then used to construct the content of a trace. The JIT therefore can be integrated in the BEAM runtime with high compatibility. The implementation work is quite different between our work and BEAMJIT because we already have a JIT compiler provided by RPython that almost for free, and target to build a BEAM VM using RPython that can match best to RPython JIT compiler, while BEAMJIT uses BEAM VM with full compatibility, and tries to build a JIT compiler that can match best to existing BEAM VM. BEAMJIT is reported 25% reduction in runtime in well-behaved programs.

ErLLVM [17] is a modified version of HiPE that uses LLVM as its back-end instead of the original code generator. Similar to Pyrlang, it uses an existing compiler backend, but it inherits other characteristics, like ahead-of-time compilation, from HiPE. It is reported that ErLLVM has almost the same performance as HiPE.

PyHaskell [19] is another functional programming language implementation that uses the RPython meta-tracing JIT compiler. Similar to Pyrlang, it is implemented as an interpreter of an intermediate language (called the Core language).

---

[10] According to the data from http://speed.pypy.org.

To the best of the authors' knowledge, current PyHaskell supports a few primitives, and still slower than an existing static compiler, GHC in most cases.

HappyJIT [11] is a PHP implementation that uses the RPython meta-tracing JIT compiler. Its stack representation is a pre-allocated array of RPython objects, similar to the Y registers in Pyrlang. However, HappyJIT is slower than Zend Engine for the programs mainly performing recursive function calls. As far as the authors know, HappyJIT does not have a tracing policy specialized to recursive functions.

7 Conclusions and Future Work

We proposed Pyrlang, a virtual machine for the BEAM bytecode language with a meta-tracing just-in-time (JIT) compiler. At the high-level view, we merely needed to write a BEAM interpreter in RPython in order to adapt the compiler for Erlang. We however needed to make careful decisions in the interpreter design for achieving reasonable runtime performance. We also proposed an optimization technique called the *pattern matching tracing* for performance improvement. With the technique (and the two state tracing for Pyret), the compiler can select longer traces (which usually give better performance) by distinguishing different branches in a loop.

Our current implementation runs micro-benchmark programs 38.3% faster than the standard BEAM interpreter. Though it is still slower than HiPE in some benchmark programs, we believe that a JIT compiler with our approach can achieve similar level of performance by introducing further low-level optimizations.

We also emphasize that most of the implementation decisions of Pyrlang in Sect. 3 using RPython can be also easily applied to any other functional programming language implementations, because most functional programming languages share the similar feature in common.

Pattern Matching Tracing is also a general approach to improve tracing JIT policy, it focus on determining the path selection below some conditional branches, which means it can be also applied to any other tracing JIT compiler.

Our implementation is has several points of improvements and extensions as discussed below.

Improvement of Pattern Matching Tracing: As we explained in Sect. 5.2, there are programs that are poorly optimized with the pattern matching tracing. While we identified the causes of overheads for some programs, we need to collect more cases and generalize the causes of overheads so that we can improve the strategy of trace selection.

List Optimization: Our experiments showed that Pyrlang performs more poorly than BEAM and HiPE with programs that allocate a large amount of objects (e.g., very long lists). While we are still investigating the underlying memory manager's performance in RPython, we plan to introduce well-known optimizations for functional style list processing, such as cdr-coding [14] and list unrolling [18]. We also consider to use the live variable hints in the BEAM bytecode during garbage collection.

Compatibility: There are still data types and operators that need to be implemented in Pyrlang. Those data types include bit strings and binaries. Though it is a matter of engineering, an (semi-)automated approach would be helpful to ensure compatibility.

References

1. Agha, G.: Actors: A Model of Concurrent Computation in Distributed Systems. MIT Press, Cambridge (1986)
2. Armstrong, J.: Erlang: a survey of the language and its industrial applications. In: Proceedings of the Symposium on Industrial Applications of Prolog, INAP 1996, pp. 16–18 (1996)
3. Armstrong, J.: The development of Erlang. In: Proceedings of International Conference on Functional Programming 1997, pp. 196–203. ACM (1997)
4. Armstrong, J.L., Virding, S.R.: Erlang: an experimental telephony programming language. In: Proceedings of XIII International Switching Symposium, pp. 43–48 (1980)
5. Bolz, C.F., Cuni, A., Fijalkowski, M., Rigo, A.: Tracing the meta-level: PyPy's tracing JIT compiler. In: Proceedings of the 4th workshop on the Implementation, Compilation, Optimization of Object-Oriented Languages and Programming Systems, pp. 18–25. ACM (2009)
6. Bolz, C.F., Pape, T., Siek, J., Tobin-Hochstadt, S.: Meta-tracing makes a fast Racket. In: Proceedings of Workshop on Dynamic Languages and Applications (2014)
7. Bolz, C.F., Tratt, L.: The impact of meta-tracing on VM design and implementation. Sci. Comput. Program. **98**, 408–421 (2015)
8. Drejhammar, F., Rasmusson, L.: BEAMJIT: a just-in-time compiling runtime for Erlang. In: Proceedings of the Thirteenth ACM SIGPLAN Workshop on Erlang, pp. 61–72. ACM (2014)
9. Hausman, B.: The Erlang BEAM virtual machine specification. http://www.cs-lab.org/historical_beam_instruction_set.html, October 1997. Rev. 1.2
10. Hayashizaki, H., Wu, P., Inoue, H., Serrano, M.J., Nakatani, T.: Improving the performance of trace-based systems by false loop filtering. In: Proceedings of the Sixteenth International Conference on Architectural Support for Programming Languages and Operating Systems, pp. 405–418. ACM (2012)
11. Homescu, A., Şuhan, A.: HappyJIT: a tracing JIT compiler for PHP. In: Proceedings of the 7th Symposium on Dynamic Languages, pp. 25–36. ACM (2011)
12. Johansson, E., Nyström, S.-O., Lindgren, T., Jonsson, C.: Evaluation of HiPE, an Erlang native code compiler. Technical report, 99/03, Uppsala University ASTEC (1999)
13. Johansson, E., Nyström, S.-O., Pettersson, M., Sagonas, K.: HiPE: High performance Erlang. Technical Report ASTEC 99/04, Uppsala University (1999)
14. Li, K., Hudak, P.: A new list compaction method. Softw. Pract. Exp. **16**(2), 145–163 (1986)
15. Pettersson, M., Sagonas, K., Johansson, E.: The HiPE/x86 Erlang compiler: system description and performance evaluation. In: Hu, Z., Rodríguez-Artalejo, M. (eds.) FLOPS 2002. LNCS, vol. 2441, pp. 228–244. Springer, Heidelberg (2002). https://doi.org/10.1007/3-540-45788-7_14

16. Sagonas, K., Pettersson, M., Carlsson, R., Gustafsson, P., Lindahl, T.: All you wanted to know about the HiPE compiler: (but might have been afraid to ask). In: Proceedings of the Third ACM SIGPLAN Workshop on Erlang, pp. 36–42. ACM (2003)
17. Sagonas, K., Stavrakakis, C., Tsiouris, Y.: ErLLVM: an LLVM backend for Erlang. In: Proceedings of the Eleventh ACM SIGPLAN Workshop on Erlang Workshop, pp. 21–32. ACM (2012)
18. Shao, Z., Reppy, J.H., Appel, A.W.: Unrolling lists. In: Proceedings of the ACM Conference on Lisp and Functional Programming, pp. 185–195 (1994)
19. Thomassen, E.W.: Trace-based just-in-time compiler for Haskell with RPython. Master's thesis, Norwegian University of Science and Technology Trondheim (2013)

Types and Verification

Proving Type Class Laws for Haskell

Andreas Arvidsson, Moa Johansson$^{(\boxtimes)}$, and Robin Touche

Department of Computer Science and Engineering,
Chalmers University of Technology, Gothenburg, Sweden
andreas.arvidson@gmail.com, moa.johansson@chalmers.se,
robin_touche@hotmail.com

Abstract. Type classes in Haskell are used to implement ad-hoc polymorphism, i.e. a way to ensure both to the programmer and the compiler
that a set of functions are defined for a specific data type. All instances
of such type classes are expected to behave in a certain way and satisfy
laws associated with the respective class. These are however typically
just stated in comments and as such, there is no real way to enforce that
they hold. In this paper we describe a system which allows the user to
write down type class laws which are then automatically instantiated
and sent to an inductive theorem prover when declaring a new instance
of a type class.

1 Introduction

Type classes in Haskell are used to implement ad-hoc polymorphism, or overloading [19]. They allow programmers to define functions which behave differently depending on the types of their arguments. A type-class declares a set of
(abstract) functions and their types, and any datatype declared an instance of
the class has to provide implementations for those functions. Below is the Haskell
library type class `Monoid`, which declares the three abstract functions `mempty`,
`mappend` and `mconcat`:

```
class Monoid a where
    mempty :: a
    mappend :: a -> a -> a
    mconcat :: [a] -> a
```

Usually, when we define a type-class we have some expectation on what
properties instances of this type class should satisfy when implementing the
functions specified. These are captured by *type class laws*. For monoids, any
instance is supposed to satisfy the laws below:

This paper describes work from Anders Arvidsson's and Robin Touche's joint MSc
thesis at Chalmers [1], supervised by Moa Johansson.

D. Van Horn and J. Hughes (Eds.): TFP 2016, LNCS 10447, pp. 61–74, 2019.
https://doi.org/10.1007/978-3-030-14805-8_4

```
-- Left identity
mappend mempty x = x

-- Right identity
mappend x mempty = x

-- Associativity of mappend
mappend x (mappend y z) = mappend (mappend x y) z

-- Specification of mconcat
mconcat = foldr mappend mempty
```

The last law is in fact a specification for the *default implementation* of the mconcat function, which is commonly used (unless the user wants to provide their own, optimised, implementation). The last law then becomes a trivial identity.

Example 1. The most obvious instance of Monoid is probably Lists, but we may for instance also declare the natural numbers to be monoids, with + corresponding to mappend:

```
data Nat = Zero | Succ Nat

-- Natural number addition
(+) :: Nat -> Nat -> Nat
Zero + a = a
(Succ a) + b = Succ (a + b)

-- Natural number multiplication
(*) :: Nat -> Nat -> Nat
Zero * m = Zero
(Succ n) * m = m + (n * m)

-- Make Nat an instance of the Monoid type class
instance Monoid Nat where
    mempty = Zero
    mappend = (+)
```

We could also have declared Nat a monoid in a different manner, with with * corresponding to mappend:

```
instance Monoid Nat where
    mempty = Succ Zero
    mappend = (*)
```

These instances of the Monoid class are quite simple. By just looking at them, we might convince ourselves that they behave in accordance with the type class laws for monoids, and settle for that. But what if we had a more complicated instance or had made a mistake? Unfortunately, in Haskell, type class laws are typically only stated in comments or documentation, if at all, and there is no support for checking that an instance of a type class actually behaves in accordance with the laws. Furthermore, type class laws could be used in, for example, compiler optimisations. Any violation of the laws could then cause inconsistencies between the original code and the optimised version, which is clearly undesirable.

To address these problems, Jeuring et al. developed a framework for expressing and testing type class laws in Haskell using the QuickCheck tool [3,9]. As further work, they identify the need to also provide stronger guarantees by also *proving* type class laws using an automated theorem prover. However, the type class laws typically present in Haskell programs often involve recursive functions and datatypes, which means that we might need induction to prove them. While there has been much success using SMT-solvers and first-order theorem provers for reasoning about programs, such provers, e.g. Z3 and E [6,14], typically do not support induction. Some of the difficulties with inductive proofs is that they often require auxiliary lemmas, which themselves require induction. A system built to handle these kind of problems is HipSpec [4], a state-of-the-art automated inductive theorem for Haskell. Our contributions combine the ideas from earlier work on testing type class laws with inductive theorem proving, and allow us to:

- Write down type class laws in Haskell as *abstract properties* (Sect. 3.1), including support for types with class constraints.
- Automatically instantiate these abstract properties when new instances of a type class is declared, and translate them into a intermediate language called TIP [11], suitable for passing on to automated theorem provers (Sect. 3.2).
- Send the generated conjectures to an automated inductive theorem prover for proof, or output the result as a TIP-problem file. In the experiments reported in this paper, we use the aforementioned HipSpec system for proofs (Sect. 4).

This allows us to state the type class laws abstractly only once, and automatically infer and prove the concrete properties that any new instance need to satisfy to comply with the type class laws.

2 Background: HipSpec and TIP

HipSpec allows the user to write down properties to prove in the Haskell source code, in a similar manner to how Haskell programmers routinely write QuickCheck properties. HipSpec supports a subset of the core Haskell language, with the caveat that functions are currently assumed to be terminating and values assumed to be finite. HipSpec can, if required, apply induction to the conjectures it is given, and then send the resulting proof obligations to an external theorem prover, such as Z3, E or Waldmeister [6,8,14]. The power of HipSpec comes from its *theory exploration* phase: when given a conjecture to prove, HipSpec first use its subsystem QuickSpec [5,15], which *explores* the functions occurring in the problem by automatically suggesting a set of potentially useful basic lemmas, which HipSpec then proves by induction. These can then be used in the proof of the main conjecture. However, as theory exploration happens first, HipSpec sometimes also proves some extra properties, perhaps not strictly needed. We consider this a small price for the extra power theory exploration provides.

Example 2. As a small example, consider asking HipSpec to prove that our `natAdd` function from the introduction is indeed is commutative. The Haskell file is annotated with the property we wish to prove:

```
prop_add_commute  x  y  =  x  +  y  ===  y  +  x
```

The symbol `===` denote (polymorphic) equality in HipSpec properties. Calling HipSpec on this file instantly produces the output:

```
Proved:
    (m + n)  ===  (n + m)
    (m + (n + o))  ===  (n + (m + o))
    prop_add_commute    x + y  ===  y + x
```

Notice that HipSpec has printed out two properties it discovered and proved itself during its theory exploration phase (one of which is identical to the property we stated!). Proving `prop_add_commute` is then trivial.

The TIP Language. TIP is a general format for expressing problems for inductive theorem provers based on SMT-LIB [2], extended with support for datatypes and recursive functions. The latest version of HipSpec also supports the TIP-language [11] as input in addition to Haskell. In our work, we use TIP as an intermediate language into which Haskell functions, types and properties are translated in order to facilitate passing them on to various external theorem provers.

We will not give an in depth description of the syntax of TIP here, save for a small example of the property we saw above, namely that addition is commutative:

```
(assert-not (forall ((x Nat)) (= (plus x y) (plus y x))))
```

The keyword `assert-not` is used to tell the prover which properties to attempt to prove (this is inherited from SMT-LIB, where proofs are by refutation). Similarly, the keyword `assert` is used to tell the provers which properties are to be treated as axioms.

The ambition of TIP is to provide a shared format for many inductive theorem provers, thereby making it easier to share benchmarks and compare different provers. There exists a growing number of benchmarks for inductive theorem provers written in the TIP language, and a suite of tools for translating TIP into various common input formats for automated theorem provers such as SMT-LIB and TPTP [13,17]. We make use of the TIP language when instantiating typeclass laws as described in the next section. The advantage is that this allows us to, in the future, more easily experiment with other inductive theorem proving backends, not only HipSpec. Furthermore, any inductive problems which the theorem prover cannot prove, can be added to the TIP benchmark suite to provide developers with additional challenge problems.

3 Instantiating Type Class Laws

In the previous section, we showed how HipSpec has traditionally been used, with the user annotating the source file with properties to prove. In a sense, HipSpec has been used mainly as a theorem prover, which just happened to take (a subset of) Haskell as input. In this work, we want to be able to handle more of the Haskell language, and thereby take a step towards building a more useful tool also for programmers, and not just as a theorem prover with Haskell as input.

3.1 Expressing Type Class Laws

Type class law are expressed almost as normal HipSpec properties, using much of the same syntax as in Example 2. The difference is that the type class laws use *abstract functions*, i.e. functions which need to be supplied concrete definitions for the class instances. This is reflected in the type signature of the law, which contains type variables with class constraints. These abstract laws will give rise to multiple different versions specialised for each individual instance of that class. The type-class laws can be declared at the same time as the type-class itself, and later automatically instantiated when an instance of the corresponding type-class is declared.

Example 3. Consider one of the type class laws for monoids which we have encountered before. As an abstract HipSpec property, it is defined as follows:

```
mappendAssoc :: Monoid a => a -> a -> a -> Equality a
mappendAssoc x y z =
  mappend x (mappend y z) === mappend (mappend x y) z
```

Notice that the type variable `a` is required to be a `Monoid` in the type signature. `Equality` is HipSpec's type for equational properties to prove, and is represented using `===`.

3.2 Instantiating Laws

HipSpec and TIP does currently only supports fully polymorphic type variables, i.e. type variables which have no constraints on the values they can assume. Since type class laws contain type variables with such constraints (e.g. the constraint that `a` must be a monoid in Example 3), they must be converted into specialised versions for each instance of the type class. This is rather straight-forward, and done by manipulating the GHC Core expressions resulting from compilation. For each type variable constrained by a type class, we first simply replace it with the type of all possible instances defined in the current file (if there are any).

The type class law `mappendAssoc` from Example 3 will for the `Nat` instance we saw before become automatically instantiated as shown below:

```
mappendAssoc1 :: Nat -> Nat -> Nat -> Equality Nat
mappendAssoc1 x y z =
  mappend x (mappend y z) === mappend (mappend x y) z
```

In the interest of readability of the example, we give the property in a Haskell-like syntax, rather than in GHC Core, but emphasise that this is part of an automated step in the implementation, and nothing the user will ever see as output. Notice that the type constraint `Monoid a` has disappeared.

GHC Core implements type classes by dictionary passing, i.e. when an overloaded function, like `mappend` is called, a lookup in the dictionary provides the appropriate concrete instance. For increased readability of the generated TIP-code, we inline dictionary lookups and rename them with more informative new names.

```
MonoidNatmappend x (MonoidNatmappend y z) ===
    MonoidNatmappend (MonoidNatmappend x y) z
```

The new function `MonoidNatmappend` is included in the resulting TIP file, defined as the corresponding function from Example 1 (i.e. `+` or `*`, depending on which `Monoid` instance we are considering).

3.3 Superclasses and Instances with Constraints

Sometimes, it is appropriate to include some additional information in the generated TIP problem file, other than the function definitions and instances of the type class laws. This includes, for example, assumptions that superclass laws are inherited by its subclasses and assumptions about laws that ought to hold about constrained type variables. Both cases are handled by introducing a new dummy type about which we can assert those extra facts.

Superclass Laws. Haskell type classes may be defined as subclasses of already existing type classes. For instance, the type class `Ord`, used for totally ordered datatypes, is an extension of the type class for equality, `Eq`:

```
class Eq a => Ord a where
...
```

This means that instances of `Ord` must also be instances of `Eq`, otherwise the compiler will complain. When generating instances of type class laws, we have therefore made the design decision to assume that all the superclass laws hold when attempting to prove the corresponding subclass laws. For example, this means assuming that the laws for `Eq` holds while proving the laws for a new instance of `Ord`. In other words, we assume that the `Eq` laws were already proved before, when `a` was declared an instance of `Eq`. This allows us to handle our proofs modularly, treating each type class in isolation and not having to worry about long chains of dependencies between type classes. The generated TIP file which we pass to the theorem prover must therefore include the super class laws as axioms holding for the type a. To achieve this, the type variable a is substituted by an arbitrary dummy datatype, about which we may include such assertions.

Constrained Class Instances. Another similar scenario is when the class instance itself has a constrained type variable in its declaration. This is often the case for polymorphic data types, for example `Maybe a` if declaring it an instance of `Monoid` like in the example below:

```
instance Monoid a => Monoid (Maybe a) where
    ...
```

In this case we need to take a little more care when instantiating the type class laws; we cannot simply replace the type variable a in the `Monoid a` constraint by all its possible instances, as this includes `Maybe a` itself, as well as `Maybe(Maybe(...))` and so on. Clearly this is not what's intended. Instead, we will interpret this to mean that: *Assuming* that the type a is a `Monoid`, satisfying the associated type class laws, then prove that `Maybe a` does too. Just as for superclasses, we now substitute a for a new concrete dummy type, about which we can assert the laws for monoids, and use them when proving the laws for `Maybe`.

4   Proving Type Class Laws

Once the TIP files has been generated they are automatically piped through to an inductive theorem prover. Here we use HipSpec, but some other inductive theorem prover could equally well be integrated in our architecture as long as it supports TIP as input. We have focused the experiments presented here to a number of type classes where many of the laws are a little bit harder to prove than for basic type classes (such as `Eq`) and may require induction. A longer evaluation on additional examples can be found in the MSc thesis accompanying this paper, but omitted here due to limited space [1].

The experiments presented here use a development version of the HipSpec system, which includes improvements such as native support for the TIP-format as input, and options for more informative proof output which explains the steps of the proofs. However, unlike the previous version of HipSpec (described in [4]), the new version does not, at the time of writing, fully support higher-order functions. We have therefore not yet been able to prove all laws of common type classes such as `Monoid`, `Functor` and `Monad`. Addressing this issue is ongoing work. Our tool can however output problem files in TIP-format also for type-classes containing higher-order functions.

4.1 Experimental Results

The timings in the experiments were obtained on a laptop computer with an Intel Core i7-3630QM 2.4 GHz processor and 8 GB of memory, running Arch Linux and GHC version 7.10.3. The source files for all the experiments are available online from: https://github.com/chip2n/hipspec-typeclasses/src/Evaluation/.

In the experimental results, we use the symbol ✓ to denote a successful proof, ✗ to denote prover failure for a true law, and ! to denote prover failure on a law violation, i.e. on a false instance of a law. HipSpec does not currently give counter-examples for laws that do not hold. For laws that cannot be proved, the user will have to use a separate tool like QuickCheck to check if a counter example can be found to indicate a law violation, as opposed to a true law which is beyond the provers automated capabilities. In the future, we would like to combine HipSpec with previous work on testing type class laws [9], to resolve this.

Semiring. Our first experiment comes from algebra, and is about semirings. A semiring is a set coupled with operators for addition (+) and multiplication (*), as well as identity values for both of them. As a Haskell type class, this can be expressed as:

```
class Semiring a where
    zero :: a
    one  :: a
    (+)  :: a -> a -> a
    (*)  :: a -> a -> a
```

The following eight laws are supposed to hold for semirings:

1. $(a + b) + c = a + (b + c)$
2. $0 + a = a + 0 = a$
3. $a + b = b + a$
4. $(a * b) * c = a * (b * c)$
5. $1 * a = a * 1 = a$
6. $a * (b + c) = (a * b) + (a * c)$
7. $(a + b) * c = (a * c) + (b * c)$
8. $0 * a = a * 0 = 0$

We experimented with the following four instances of semirings:

Nat: Natural numbers with addition and multiplication and identities 0 and 1.
Bool (1): Disjunction for addition and conjunction for multiplication with identities False and True
Bool (2): Conjunction for addition and disjunction for multiplication with identities True and False

Matrix2: A 2-by-2 matrix with matrix addition and multiplication and identities empty matrix and identity matrix respectively, and entries belong to another semiring[1].

Results: Semiring									
Instance	Law								Total time
	1	2	3	4	5	6	7	8	
Nat	✓	✓	✓	✓	✓	✓	✓	✓	28.2 s
Bool (1)	✓	✓	✓	✓	✓	✓	✓	✓	2.9 s
Bool (2)	✓	✓	✓	✓	✓	✓	✓	✓	2.9 s
Matrix2	✓	✓	✓	✓	✓	✗	✗	✓	29.3 s

Most of these proofs are rather easy for HipSpec, except the distributivity properties for matrices (laws 7 and 8, which hold but are not proved here). We conjecture that this is due to the fact that HipSpec has not been told anything about auxiliary functions for summations of matrix elements row/column-wise, which is required here. Notice that in the case of the natural numbers and matrices, HipSpec spends more time doing theory exploration, and inventing lemmas. For the booleans, the proofs are straight-forward and do not even need induction.

CommutativeSemiring. To demonstrate a type class which depend on a superclass, we also included a commutative semiring in our evaluation.

```
class Semiring a => CommutativeSemiring a
```

As the name suggests, a commutative semiring is a semiring with one additional law stating that * is commutative:

1. $a * b = b * a$

We tested the same instances as for semirings:

Results: CommutativeSemiring		
Instance	Law	Total time
	1	
Nat	✓	21.0 s
Bool (1)	✓	2.8 s
Bool (2)	✓	2.5 s
Matrix2	!	11.9 s

As expected, natural numbers and booleans can easily be shown to also be commutative semirings. Note that the matrix instance fails as expected; matrix multiplication is not commutative.

---

[1] The elements must belong to a semiring for the square matrix to do so.

Reversible. The next type class characterise data structures that can be reversed:

```
class Reversible a where
     reverse :: a -> a
```

It has one law, stating that **reverse** is idempotent:

| 1. *reverse (reverse xs) = xs* |

We tested the following three instances:

List (rev): Naive recursive list reverse.
List (qrev): List reverse using accumulator.
Tree: A binary tree with a mirror operation, flipping the tree left to right.

Results: Reversible

Instance	Law	Total time
	1	
List (*rev*)	✓	5.9 s
List (*qrev*)	✓	5.7 s
Tree	✓	0.9 s

All these proofs require induction, and the ones about lists also need auxiliary lemmas which HipSpec must discover and prove first. However, as there is only very few functions and laws present (unlike for semirings), this is rather fast.

Monoid. We have already encountered the Monoid type class as a running example.

| 1. *mappend mempty x = x* |
| 2. *mappend x mempty = x* |
| 3. *mappend x (mappend y z) = mappend (mappend x y) z* |

We here omit the 4th law (the default implementation for **mconcat**) which is higher-order and, as mentioned above, not yet supported in the development version of HipSpec we are using. We give the results for the remaining three laws, and do so for the datatype instances we have seen before. The **Matrix2** instance has the additional constraint of requiring its elements to also be monoids, and similarly, **Maybe a** has a constraint requiring **a** to be a monoid.

Laws 1 and 2 for monoids are rather trivial. The only instance needing slightly longer is when *mappend* is instantiated to natural number multiplication, in which law 3 needs some lemmas to be discovered and proved.

Results: Monoid				
Instance	Law			Total time
	1	2	3	
Nat (add)	✓	✓	✓	4.3 s
Nat (mul)	✓	✓	✓	27.3 s
Matrix2 (mul)	✓	✓	✓	2.3 s
List	✓	✓	✓	1.5 s
Maybe	✓	✓	✓	2.1 s

4.2   Discussion of Results and Further Work

The proof obligations resulting from the type classes above are mainly within the comfort zone of an inductive theorem prover such as HipSpec. Usually, the prover just needs a few seconds to complete the proofs, unless it has discovered many candidate lemmas during the theory exploration phase. This is the downside of using HipSpec: it sometimes eagerly spends some time proving lemmas that turn out not to be necessary for the final proof. Targeting the exploration by for example attempting to extract information from failed proofs is further work.

It is somewhat disappointing that we have not yet been able to automatically prove any higher-order laws, but hope that it is merely a matter of time until support has been added also to the new version of HipSpec. The lack of higher-order support is not inherent to the new version of HipSpec, but due to an incomplete module in HipSpec for reading in TIP files. We could have opted for using an old version of HipSpec, but it does not support TIP as an input language, and we would have had to instead produce modified copies of the original Haskell source files to give to the prover. This would likely have meant less automation of the whole proving pipeline. Furthermore, the new version of HipSpec uses the latest version of QuickSpec for lemma discovery [15], which is much faster and more powerful that the old version. We also think it is valuable to output the instantiated laws and proof obligations in the TIP format, which can more easily be shared between different theorem proving systems. This means that we are not actually bound to just a single theorem prover (HipSpec), but can quite easily connect our work also to other provers, should a better one become available. Furthermore, the user could edit the TIP file output by our tool to for example add extra facts that the prover did not discovery automatically.

HipSpec's proof output depends on which external prover it uses for proof obligations. Details of the rewriting steps can be presented to the user when Waldmeister is used [8], but we often want to use other more powerful provers such as Z3 [6]. Adding richer proof output for additional prover backends, counter-examples for laws violations and other user feedback about failed proofs is further work. This has however been partially addressed in HipSpec's sister system Hipster, which shares the same theory exploration component, but is integrated in the interactive proof assistant Isabelle/HOL [10,12] for proofs. Hipster produces snippets of Isabelle proof scripts for discovered lemmas.

HipSpec currently assumes that functions to be terminating and values are finite. There is however nothing in principle that would stop us from, for example, connecting HipSpec to a termination checker and extending it with for instance co-induction to reason about infinite structures.

5   Related Work

Zeno is an earlier inductive theorem prover for Haskell [16], which is unfortunately no longer maintained. Unlike HipSpec it had its own internal theorem prover, while HipSpec is designed around the TIP language for easier communication with different external provers used to handle proof obligations arising after applying induction. Zeno did not support theory exploration but instead conjectured lemmas based subgoals remaining in stuck proofs.

HERMIT [7] is a system for mechanising equational reasoning about Haskell programs. Properties are written as GHC rewrite rules in the Haskell source code and proven either interactively in the HERMIT shell or by writing a script which automates the process. As opposed to HipSpec, which is fully automatic and exploits external theorem provers, HERMIT is an more of an interactive proof assistant relying on the user to specify the steps of proofs. HERMIT also requires the user to supply all lemmas, and does not support any form of theory exploration like HipSpec.

LiquidHaskell is a contract-based verification framework based on refinement types [18]. Refinement types are essentially the addition of logical predicates to 'refine' the types of inputs and outputs to functions. These predicates are restricted to theories with decision procedures, which ensures contracts are written in a logic suitable for being checked by a SMT solver. LiquidHaskell is a more mature system than HipSpec, but restricted to decidable theories so it does not support automated induction and theory exploration.

6   Conclusion

This work demonstrates how automated theorem proving and functional programming can be integrated to provide benefit to programmers. We showed how type class laws can be expressed as abstract properties, then instantiated and proved when we declare a new instance of a type class. Moving type class laws from informal descriptions in the documentation to something that is actually enforced would both help programmers to a shared understanding of the purpose of the type class as well as helping them implement instances correctly.

Many Haskell programmers are today routinely writing QuickCheck properties which are automatically tested on many randomly generated values. In the future, we envisage programmers writing similar properties and laws, and using a tool similar to what's described here to not only test, but also *prove* their programs correct, with little more overhead than using QuickCheck. We believe our work is at least a small step on the way towards this ambitious goal.

References

1. Arvidsson, A., Touche, R.: Proving type class laws in Haskell. Master's thesis, Chalmers University of Technology (2016)
2. Barrett, C., Stump, A., Tinelli, C.: The SMT-LIB standard - version 2.0. In: Proceedings of the 8th International Workshop on Satisfiability Modulo Theories, Edinburgh, Scotland, July 2010
3. Claessen, K., Hughes, J.: QuickCheck: a lightweight tool for random testing of Haskell programs. In: Proceedings of ICFP, pp. 268–279 (2000)
4. Claessen, K., Johansson, M., Rosén, D., Smallbone, N.: Automating inductive proofs using theory exploration. In: Bonacina, M.P. (ed.) CADE 2013. LNCS (LNAI), vol. 7898, pp. 392–406. Springer, Heidelberg (2013). https://doi.org/10.1007/978-3-642-38574-2_27
5. Claessen, K., Smallbone, N., Hughes, J.: QUICKSPEC: guessing formal specifications using testing. In: Fraser, G., Gargantini, A. (eds.) TAP 2010. LNCS, vol. 6143, pp. 6–21. Springer, Heidelberg (2010). https://doi.org/10.1007/978-3-642-13977-2_3
6. de Moura, L., Bjørner, N.: Z3: an efficient SMT solver. In: Ramakrishnan, C.R., Rehof, J. (eds.) TACAS 2008. LNCS, vol. 4963, pp. 337–340. Springer, Heidelberg (2008). https://doi.org/10.1007/978-3-540-78800-3_24
7. Farmer, A., Sculthorpe, N., Gill, A.: Reasoning with the HERMIT: tool support for equational reasoning on GHC core programs. In: Proceedings of the 2015 ACM SIGPLAN Symposium on Haskell, Haskell 2015, pp. 23–34. ACM, New York (2015)
8. Hillenbrand, T., Buch, A., Vogt, R., Löchner, B.: Waldmeister - high-performance equational deduction. J. Autom. Reason. **18**(2), 265–270 (1997)
9. Jeuring, J., Jansson, P., Amaral, C.: Testing type class laws. In: 2012 ACM SIGPLAN Haskell Symposium, Copenhagen, pp. 49–60 (2012)
10. Johansson, M., Rosén, D., Smallbone, N., Claessen, K.: Hipster: integrating theory exploration in a proof assistant. In: Watt, S.M., Davenport, J.H., Sexton, A.P., Sojka, P., Urban, J. (eds.) CICM 2014. LNCS (LNAI), vol. 8543, pp. 108–122. Springer, Cham (2014). https://doi.org/10.1007/978-3-319-08434-3_9
11. Claessen, K., Johansson, M., Rosén, D., Smallbone, N.: TIP: tons of inductive problems. In: Kerber, M., Carette, J., Kaliszyk, C., Rabe, F., Sorge, V. (eds.) CICM 2015. LNCS (LNAI), vol. 9150, pp. 333–337. Springer, Cham (2015). https://doi.org/10.1007/978-3-319-20615-8_23
12. Nipkow, T., Paulson, L.C., Wenzel, M. (eds.): Isabelle/HOL. LNCS, vol. 2283. Springer, Heidelberg (2002). https://doi.org/10.1007/3-540-45949-9
13. Rosén, D., Smallbone, N.: TIP: tools for inductive provers. In: Davis, M., Fehnker, A., McIver, A., Voronkov, A. (eds.) LPAR 2015. LNCS, vol. 9450, pp. 219–232. Springer, Heidelberg (2015). https://doi.org/10.1007/978-3-662-48899-7_16
14. Schulz, S.: System description: E 1.8. In: McMillan, K., Middeldorp, A., Voronkov, A. (eds.) LPAR 2013. LNCS, vol. 8312, pp. 735–743. Springer, Heidelberg (2013). https://doi.org/10.1007/978-3-642-45221-5_49
15. Smallbone, N., Johansson, M., Claessen, K., Algehed, M.: Quick specifications for the busy programmer. J. Funct. Program. **27** (2017). https://doi.org/10.1017/S0956796817000090
16. Sonnex, W., Drossopoulou, S., Eisenbach, S.: Zeno: an automated prover for properties of recursive data structures. In: Flanagan, C., König, B. (eds.) TACAS 2012. LNCS, vol. 7214, pp. 407–421. Springer, Heidelberg (2012). https://doi.org/10.1007/978-3-642-28756-5_28

17. Sutcliffe, G.: The TPTP problem library and associated infrastructure: the FOF and CNF parts, v3.5.0. J. Autom. Reason. **43**(4), 337–362 (2009)
18. Vazou, N., Seidel, E.L., Jhala, R.: LiquidHaskell: experience with refinement types in the real world. SIGPLAN Not. **49**(12), 39–51 (2014)
19. Wadler, P., Blott, S.: How to make ad-hoc polymorphism less ad-hoc. In: Proceedings of the 16th ACM SIGPLAN-SIGACT Symposium on Principles of Programming Languages, POPL 1889, pp. 60–76. ACM, New York (1989)

Dynamic Flow Analysis for JavaScript

Nico Naus[1]([✉]) and Peter Thiemann[2]

[1] Utrecht University, Utrecht, The Netherlands
n.naus@uu.nl
[2] Albert-Ludwigs-Universität Freiburg, Freiburg im Breisgau, Germany
thiemann@acm.org

Abstract. Static flow analyses compute a safe approximation of a program's dataflow without executing it. Dynamic flow analyses compute a similar safe approximation by running the program on test data such that it achieves sufficient coverage.

We design and implement a dynamic flow analysis for JavaScript. Our formalization and implementation observe a program's execution in a training run and generate flow constraints from the observations. We show that a solution of the constraints yields a safe approximation to the program's dataflow if each path in every function is executed at least once in the training run. As a by-product, we can reconstruct types for JavaScript functions from the results of the flow analysis.

Our implementation shows that dynamic flow analysis is feasible for JavaScript. While our formalization concentrates on a core language, the implementation covers full JavaScript. We evaluated the implementation using the SunSpider benchmark.

Keywords: Type inference · JavaScript · Flow analysis · Dynamic languages

1 Introduction

Flow analysis is an important tool that supports program understanding and maintenance. It tells us which values may appear during evaluation at a certain point in a program. Most flow analyses are static analyses, which means they are computed without executing the program. This approach has the advantage that information can be extracted directly from the program text. But it has the disadvantage that significant effort is required to hone the precision of the analysis and then to implement it, for example, in the form of an abstract interpreter.

Constructing the abstract interpreter is particularly troublesome if the language's semantics is complicated or when there are many nontrivial primitive operations. First, the implementer has to come up with suitable abstract domains to represent the analysis results. Then, a sound abstraction has to be constructed for each possible transition and primitive operation of the language. Finally, all these domains and abstract transition functions must be implemented. To obtain good precision, an abstract domain often includes a singleton abstraction, in

© Springer Nature Switzerland AG 2019
D. Van Horn and J. Hughes (Eds.): TFP 2016, LNCS 10447, pp. 75–93, 2019.
https://doi.org/10.1007/978-3-030-14805-8_5

which case the abstract interpreter necessarily contains a concrete interpreter for the language augmented with transitions for the more abstract points in the domain. Clearly, constructing such an abstraction presents a significant effort.

We follow the ideas of An and others [1] who propose dynamic type inference for Ruby, a class-based scripting language where classes have dedicated fields and methods. The benefit of their approach is that existing instrumentation tools can be used, which minimizes the implementation effort, and that high precision (i.e., context-sensitive flow information) is obtained for free.

This paper adapts their approach to dynamic type inference to JavaScript. As JavaScript is not class-based, the adaptation turns out to be nontrivial, although the principal approach—generating typing constraints during execution—is the same. Regarding the differences, in the Ruby work, class names are used as types. In (pre-ES6) JavaScript, there are no named classes, so we have to identify a different notion of type. Our solution is drawn from the literature on flow analysis: we use creation points [13], the program points of **new** expressions, as a substitute for class and function types. We argue that this notion is fairly close to using a class name: The typical JavaScript pattern to define a group of similarly behaving objects is to designate a constructor function, which may be identified by the program point of its definition, and then use this constructor in the **new** expression to create objects of that "class". Hence, the prototype of the constructor could substitute for a class, but it is hard to track. The program point of the **new** is much easier to track and it also approximates the class at a finer degree as the constructor. For simplicity, we use the latter. Choosing program points to approximate run-time entities means that we switch our point of view from type system to flow analysis.

Another difference between JavaScript and Ruby is the definition of what constitutes a type error. The Ruby work considers message-not-understood errors, the typical type error in a class-based object-oriented language. In JavaScript, no such concept exists. In fact, there are only two places in the standard semantics that trigger a run-time type error:

- trying to access a property of **undefined** or **null** and
- trying to invoke a non-function as a function.

We concentrate on the second error and set up our formal system to only avoid failing function calls. The first error may be tracked with similar means and is omitted in favor of a simpler system.

After looking at an example of our approach in Sect. 2, to build intuition, we construct a formal system for a JavaScript core language in Sect. 3. This core language simplifies some aspects of JavaScript to make proofs easier. We describe the analysis in detail, which consists of a training semantics and a monitoring semantics, and prove its soundness. Section 4 presents a practical implementation, which is evaluated in Sect. 5. Section 6 compares our work with previous work, and finally Sect. 7 concludes this paper.

```
1  function test(x){,
2    return{
3      if(x.val)                        e  <= [val : g]
4        then x.val = inc(x.val)
5        else x.val = 1                 e  <= [val : g], Num <= g
6    }
7  }
8  function inc(x){,
9    return x+1
10 }
11 function main(x){var foo bar result,
12   return {
13     foo = new null;                  13 <= [val : c], Num <= c
14     foo.val = 0;                     13 <= [val : c], Num <= c
15     bar = new foo;                   15 <= 13
16     bar.foo = new foo;               15 <= [foo : d], 16 <= d, 16 <= 13
17     result = test(foo);             1  <= e -> f, 13 <= e, Num <= f
18     inc(result);}}                   8  <= h -> i, f <= h, Num <= i
-----------------------------------------------------------------------
e = main();                            11 <= a -> b, () <= a, i <= b
```

Fig. 1. Example program written in core JavaScript, with generated constraints

2 Example

Figure 1 shows an example program, written in the core JavaScript language that will be defined in the next section. On the right are the constraints generated by the flow analysis. Objects and functions are identified in the constraints by the line number they were created on. The symbols *a, b, c...* appearing in the constraints are type variables. Functions are defined as **function** f(x){var y*,**return** e}, where f is the name of the function, x the name of the argument, y* a list of local variables, and e the function body.

Function calls, like the one on line 18, result in three constraints. First, we constrain the object we call to be a function (8 <= *h* -> *i*), second, we constrain the argument (*f* <= *h*) and third, we constrain the type of the return value (Num <= *i*). When a new object is created, as in line 15, we generate the constraint 15 <= 13, since we want the type of the new object to be a subtype of the type of the old object.

Line 14 assigns a value to a property of an object. The assignment results in two constraints, 13 <= [val : *c*] to constrain the type of the object to have the property val and Num <= *c* to constrain the type of the object's property to a supertype of Num.

The function inc does not generate any constraints, because it only accesses local variables. The function test only generates constraints for the else-branch, because we do not visit the then-branch.

After execution, the type of every object can be inferred using these constraints.

3 Formal System

The formal system employs a JavaScript core language with the syntax defined in Fig. 2. It features the usual JavaScript constructs like constants, variables,

Expressions

$$e ::= c \mid x \mid fundec^\ell \mid e(e) \mid e; e \mid prim(e) \mid x = e$$
$$\mid \mathtt{if}^\ell \ e \ \mathtt{then} \ e \ \mathtt{else} \ e \mid \mathtt{new}^\ell \ e \mid e.n \mid \ e.n = e$$

Constants $\quad c ::= num \mid str \mid bool \mid \mathtt{null} \mid \mathtt{udf}$

Function $\quad fundec^\ell ::= \mathtt{fun}^\ell \ f(x)\{\mathtt{var} \ y^*, \mathtt{return} \ e\}$

Variables $\quad x, f, n \in$ set of names

Primitives $\quad prim \in$ set of primative operation

Labels $\quad \ell \in$ set of Labels

Program $\quad prog ::= fundec^* \triangleright e$

Fig. 2. Syntax of the JavaScript core language

heaps $H ::= (l \mapsto obj)^*$

activation record $S ::= (x \mapsto v)^*$

values $v ::= l \mid c$

object $obj ::= (v, (n \mapsto v)^*)$

wrapped values $\omega ::= v : \bar{\tau}$

abstract types $\bar{\tau} ::= \tau \mid \alpha$

paths $\Phi ::= \phi^*$

path $\phi ::= p^*$

literal $p ::= \ell \mid \neg\ell$

constraints $C ::= (\tau \leq \tau')^*$

$Falsey ::= \mathtt{udf} \mid \mathtt{null} \mid 0 \mid \text{""} \mid \mathtt{false}$

$l \in$ Heap addresses

$\alpha \in$ Type variables

$n \in$ Property names

Fig. 3. Semantic objects

functions, function application, primitive operations, conditional, assignment to local variables, new object creation (where the argument is the prototype), property get and property set. Function definition, **new**, and conditional are marked with program labels ℓ to address them in the inference phase. The most notable difference to full JavaScript is the omission of all reflective features: there is no **eval** and no bracket notation to access properties. Thus, there is an a-priori fixed set of properties and all property manipulation happens via the dot notation. This restriction simplifies our semantics considerably compared to existing semantics for JavaScript.

Figure 3 declares the semantic objects for the core language. We keep state in heaps H and activation records S. The heap contains a mapping from locations to objects. An activation record, or stack entry, is a mapping from variables to values. A value is either a heap address l or a constant c. Objects obj contain their prototype and a mapping from property names to values. The property names "$fun", "$vars" and "$tyvar" are reserved and cannot be used by the programmer. Their use will become clear in the next section.

There are type variables α and concrete types τ. Concrete types, as defined in Fig. 4, are composed of one or more type summands. To record execution paths, we define path sets Φ and single paths ϕ, which are lists of potentially negated program labels of conditionals. A positive label ℓ indicates a then-branch taken, a negated label $\neg\ell$ indicates an else-branch. Lastly, a constraint set C collects constraints of the abstract form $\bar{\tau} \leq \bar{\tau}'$. Such a constraint indicates that $\bar{\tau}$ is a subtype of $\bar{\tau}'$.

$$\text{types } \tau ::= \sum_{i \in T, T \subseteq \{\bot, u, b, s, n, f, o\}} \varphi_i$$

$$\text{row } \varrho ::= str : \bar{\tau}, \varrho \mid \alpha$$

undefined	$\varphi_\bot$	$::= \text{Udf}$
null	φ_u	$::= \text{Null}$
boolean	φ_b	$::= \text{Bool}$
string	φ_s	$::= \text{String}$
number	φ_n	$::= \text{Number}$
function	φ_f	$::= \text{Function}(\bar{\tau} \to \bar{\tau})$
object	φ_o	$::= \text{Obj}(\varrho)$

Fig. 4. Types

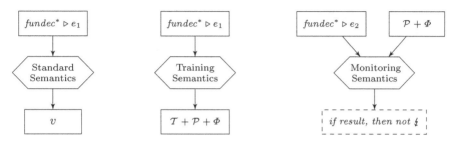

Fig. 5. Overview of formal system

The formal system comprises three parts as shown in Fig. 5. The standard semantics evaluates a top-level expression e_1 in the context of a program $fundec^*$. The training semantics augments the standard semantics by collecting type constraints and execution paths. Flow information in the form of a type equivalence map $\mathcal{P}$ and types $\mathcal{T}$ is inferred from the resulting constraints.

The monitoring semantics is an artifact to prove the soundness of the inferred types. It evaluates the same program for a different top-level expression. It also takes the equivalence map and the set of paths collected by the training semantics. The monitoring semantics is constructed such that no type errors occur during execution if the equivalence information is respected and if all execution paths in every function have been exercised by the training semantics.

3.1 Training Semantics

The training semantics collects type constraints and keeps track of execution paths. The main challenge in the construction of this semantics was to identify the correct abstraction of functions and objects by *program locations*. As any function can serve as a constructor in JavaScript, it is not straightforward to recognize a constructor application and give it a proper type. We omit the standard semantics, which can be obtained by erasing the collection of constraints and paths from the training semantics.

Figure 6 defines a big-step evaluation judgment of the form $H; S; e \longrightarrow H'; S'; \omega \mid C; \phi; \Phi$. Given heap H and activation record S, the expression e evaluates to an augmented value ω with updated heap and activation record

TVarLookup
$$\frac{S(x) = \omega}{H; S; x \longrightarrow H; S; \omega \mid \{\}; \{\}; \{\}}$$

TPCall
$$\frac{H; S; e \longrightarrow H'; S'; v : \_ \mid C; \phi; \Phi \qquad \llbracket prim \rrbracket v = \omega}{H; S; prim(e) \longrightarrow H'; S'; \omega \mid C; \phi; \Phi}$$

TNew
$$\frac{\begin{array}{c} H; S; e \longrightarrow H'; S'; v : \bar{\tau} \mid C; \phi; \Phi \qquad l = \text{fresh location} \\ \alpha' = \ell \quad \text{if } (\bar{\tau} = \alpha) \text{ then } (C' = \alpha' \leq \alpha) \text{ else } (C' = \{\}) \\ obj = (v : \bar{\tau}, \{\}) \qquad H'' = H'\{l \mapsto obj : \alpha'\} \end{array}}{H; S; \mathtt{new}^\ell e \longrightarrow H''; S'; l : \alpha' \mid C, C'; \phi; \Phi}$$

TVarAss
$$\frac{H; S; e \longrightarrow H'; S'; \omega \mid C; \phi; \Phi \qquad S'' = S'\{x \mapsto \omega\}}{H; S; x = e \longrightarrow H'; S''; \omega \mid C; \phi; \Phi}$$

TFun
$$\frac{l = \text{fresh location} \qquad \alpha = \ell \qquad H' = H\{l \mapsto (\mathtt{null}, \$\mathrm{fun} \mapsto fundec, \$\mathrm{vars} \mapsto S \downarrow_{fv(fundec)}) : \alpha\}}{H; S; fundec \longrightarrow H'; S; l : \alpha \mid \{\}; \{\}; \{\}}$$

TProp
$$\frac{H; S; e \longrightarrow H'; S'; l : \alpha \mid C; \phi; \Phi \qquad C' = \alpha \leq [n : \alpha.n] \qquad H'; l.n \longrightarrow \omega}{H; S; e.n \longrightarrow H'; S'; \omega \mid C, C'; \phi; \Phi}$$

TPropSet
$$\frac{\begin{array}{c} H; S; e \longrightarrow H'; S'; l : \alpha \mid C; \phi; \Phi \qquad H'; S'; e' \longrightarrow H''; S''; v : \bar{\tau} \mid C'; \phi'; \Phi' \\ C'' = \alpha \leq [n : \alpha.n], \bar{\tau} \leq \alpha_n \qquad H''' = H''\{l \mapsto H''(l)\{n \mapsto v : \alpha.n\}\} \end{array}}{H; S; e.n = e' \longrightarrow H'''; S''; v : \alpha.n \mid C, C', C''; \phi, \phi'; \Phi, \Phi'}$$

TSeq
$$\frac{H; S; e \longrightarrow H'; S'; \_ \mid C; \phi; \Phi \qquad H'; S'; e' \longrightarrow H''; S''; \omega \mid C'; \phi'; \Phi'}{H; S; (e; e') \longrightarrow H''; S''; \omega \mid C, C'; \phi, \phi'; \Phi, \Phi'}$$

TConditional
$$\frac{H; S; e \longrightarrow H'; S'; c : \tau \mid C; \phi; \Phi}{\text{if } (c \notin Falsey) \text{ then } (p = \ell, e_p = e') \text{ else } (p = \neg\ell, e_p = e'') \qquad H'; S'; e_p \longrightarrow H''; S''; \omega \mid C'; \phi'; \Phi'}{H; S; \mathtt{if}^\ell\ e \text{ then } e' \text{ else } e'' \longrightarrow H''; S''; \omega \mid C, C'; \phi, p, \phi'; \Phi, \Phi'}$$

TCall
$$\frac{\begin{array}{c} H; S; e \longrightarrow H'; S'; l : \alpha \mid C; \phi; \Phi \qquad H'; S'; e' \longrightarrow H''; S''; v : \bar{\tau} \mid C'; \phi'; \Phi' \\ H''(l) = (\_, \$\mathrm{fun} \mapsto \mathtt{fun}\ f(x^f)\{(\mathtt{var}\ y)^*, \mathtt{return}\ e^f\}, \$\mathrm{vars} \mapsto S^f, ...) : \alpha \\ S^{f'} = S^f\{f \mapsto l : \alpha, x^f \mapsto v : \alpha_{\mathrm{arg}}, (y \mapsto \mathtt{udf}\ :\ Udf)^*\} \qquad C^{\mathrm{call}} = \alpha \leq \alpha_{\mathrm{arg}} \longrightarrow \alpha_{\mathrm{ret}}, \bar{\tau} \leq \alpha_{\mathrm{arg}} \\ H''; S^{f'}; e^f \longrightarrow H'''; \_; v' : \bar{\tau}' \mid C''; \phi''; \Phi'' \qquad C^{\mathrm{ret}} = \bar{\tau}' \leq \alpha_{\mathrm{ret}} \end{array}}{H; S; e(e') \longrightarrow H'''; S''; v' : \alpha_{\mathrm{ret}} \mid C, C^{\mathrm{call}}, C', C^{\mathrm{ret}}; \phi, \phi'; \Phi, \Phi', \phi'', \Phi''}$$

Prototype lookup

TPropLookup
$$\frac{H(l)[n] = \omega}{H; l.n \longrightarrow \omega}$$

TProtoLookup
$$\frac{n \notin H(l) \qquad H; H(l)_{\mathrm{proto}}.n \longrightarrow \omega}{H; l.n \longrightarrow \omega}$$

Top-level initialization rule

TRun
$$\frac{(H, S) = \text{initialize}(fundec^*) \qquad H; S; e \longrightarrow \_; \_; \_ \mid C; \_; \Phi}{fundec^* \rhd e \uparrow (\mathcal{T}, \mathcal{P}) = \text{Solve}(C); \Phi}$$

Fig. 6. Training semantics

H' and S'. The C-component contains the constraints collected during evaluation, ϕ contains the evaluation path inside the currently executed function, and Φ contains paths collected during evaluation. An evaluation path records the outcomes of the conditionals that were executed.

Most rules are standard, apart from the constraint collection, path recording, and passing of observed paths and constraints. Variables are looked up directly in the activation record. TPCALL performs primitive operations and is assumed to only return non-object values. Variable assignment is performed by updating the activation record. Rule TSEQ evaluates the first expression, then the second, and returns the value of the second. TCONDITIONAL checks if the condition evaluates to true or false and acts accordingly. Function literals are converted to objects by the TFUN rule. Function objects do not have a prototype, the actual function is stored in the "$fun" property, and the free variables of e are stored in "$vars". This treatment of functions is analogous to the actual semantics of JavaScript. Prototypes are set when a new object is created using the TNEW rule. We explicitly allow creating a new object from either an object or just a regular value. If a regular value like **null** is used, then the object has no prototype. Prototype lookup is performed by TPROPLOOKUP and TPROTOLOOKUP, when a property of an object is requested in the TPROP rule. Lookup relies on a different judgment $H; l.n \longrightarrow \omega$, with heap H, heap location l, and property name n that returns a wrapped value ω.

The rule TCALL also deserves some extra explanation. From the heap, we retrieve the desired function, which must be an object as mentioned above. We construct a new activation record by taking the bound variables in "$vars" and adding references to the function (for recursive calls), to the argument, and to local variables. We execute the actual function with this new activation record.

Four of the evaluation rules collect constraints.

TNew. When a new object is created, it should have at least the same type as its prototype, but it may have additional properties. Therefore, we constrain the type of the new object to be a subtype of the type of its prototype.

TProp. A property lookup requires the property to be present in the type of the object.

TPropSet. Setting a property requires existence of the property and the type of the new value is a subtype of the property's type.

TCall. The type of the object that is called as a function is constrained to be a function. The type of the argument must be a subtype of the function argument. The return type of the function should be a subtype of the outcome of the function call.

Two rules record the paths taken by the execution

TConditional. Either a positive or negative label is added to the current path, depending on the value of the condition.

TCall. The path taken by the dispatch is added to the set of observed paths Φ.

The TCALL rule furthermore wraps a new type variable around the argument value passed to the function, it assigns types to the freshly initialized local variables, and wraps a new type variable around the value returned from the function. The type variables are connected to the prior type wrappings through the above-mentioned constraints.

At top level, we have a different judgment, $fundec^* \triangleright e \uparrow \mathcal{T}; \mathcal{P}; \Phi$, that is evaluated by the TRUN rule. This rule initializes the heap and the top-level bindings from the list of function declarations. It then evaluates the top-level expression e. Afterwards, it solves the constraints and returns a mapping from type variables to inferred types $\mathcal{T}$, an equivalence set mapping $\mathcal{P}$, and the observed paths Φ. Whenever the constraint solver determines that two type variables must be equal, it records this fact in mapping $\mathcal{P}$, which is implemented using a union-find algorithm, as in Henglein's binding-time analysis [9].

3.2   Monitoring Semantics

The rule set in Fig. 7 defines the monitoring semantics. This big-step semantics is defined in terms of the outcome $\mathcal{P}, \Phi$ of a preceding training run and it is restricted to execute only paths that have been trained according to Φ. Hence, the evaluation judgment has the form $H; S; e \mid \phi \longrightarrow H'; S'; v \mid \phi'$, where ϕ is the path that the evaluation has to follow, and ϕ' contains the remainder of the path after evaluation. To avoid clutter, we leave the parameter Φ implicit. It is only used in the MCALL rule.

Some rules deviate from the standard semantics to take paths into account:

MConditional. This rule only applies if the outcome of the condition coincides with the head of the path the execution has to take.

MCall. To execute the method dispatch, the rule nondeterministically selects a path for the function body from the set of trained paths Φ.

MNew. The type variable of the newly created object is also stored in the reserved property "$tyvar".

MFun. The type variable for the function is stored in the function object.

MRun. Besides the usual initialization, this rule executes the monitor rule on the top-level expression.

There are three new rules compared to the standard semantics.

Monitor. This rule applies a meta-function mon to the top-level expression which replaces all property assignments and function calls with their underlined version to enforce their evaluation with MTLPROPSET and MTLCALL.

Error. This rule defines what we consider a type error: when a non-function object is used as a function. The rules for error propagation are standard and omitted for space reasons.

MTLPropSet. This rule verifies if the property assignments from the top-level expression e meet the precondition required in the soundness proof.

MTLCall. This rule verifies that the object in function position is indeed a function. If so, it proceeds with the standard function call rule MCALL.

MVarLookup
$$\frac{S(x) = v}{H; S; x \mid \phi \longrightarrow H; S; v \mid \phi}$$

MPCall
$$\frac{H; S; e \mid \phi \longrightarrow H'; S'; v \mid \phi' \qquad [\![prim]\!]v = v'}{H; S; prim(e) \mid \phi \longrightarrow H'; S'; v' \mid \phi'}$$

MNew
$$\frac{H; S; e \mid \phi \longrightarrow H'; S'; l \mid \phi' \qquad l' = \text{fresh label}}{\alpha = \ell \qquad obj = (v, \$tyvar \mapsto \alpha) \qquad H' = H\{l' \mapsto obj\}}{H; S; \text{new}^\ell e \mid \phi \longrightarrow H'; S; l \mid \phi'}$$

MVarAss
$$\frac{H; S; e \mid \phi \longrightarrow H'; S'; v \mid \phi'}{S'' = S'\{x \mapsto v\}}{H; S; x = e \mid \phi \longrightarrow H'; S''; v \mid \phi'}$$

MFun
$$\frac{l = \text{fresh location}}{\alpha = \ell \qquad H' = H\{l \mapsto (\text{null}, \$fun \mapsto fundec,}{\$vars \mapsto S \downarrow_{fv(fundec)}, \$tyvar \mapsto \alpha)\}}{H; S; fundec^\ell \mid \phi \longrightarrow H; S; o \mid \phi}$$

MProp
$$\frac{H; S; e \mid \phi \longrightarrow H'; S'; l \mid \phi' \qquad H'; l.n \longrightarrow v}{H; S; e.n \mid \phi \longrightarrow H'; S'; v \mid \phi'}$$

MPropSet
$$\frac{H; S; e \mid \phi \longrightarrow H'; S'; l \mid \phi'}{H'; S'; e' \mid \phi' \longrightarrow H''; S''; v \mid \phi''}{H''' = H''\{l \mapsto H''(l)\{n \mapsto v\}\}}{H; S; e.n = e' \mid \phi \longrightarrow H'''; S''; v \mid \phi''}$$

MSeq
$$\frac{H; S; e \mid \phi \longrightarrow H'; S'; \_ \mid \phi'}{H'; S'; e' \mid \phi' \longrightarrow H''; S''; v \mid \phi''}{H; S; (e; e') \mid \phi \longrightarrow H''; S''; v \mid \phi''}$$

MConditional
$$\frac{H; S; e \mid \phi \longrightarrow H'; S'; c \mid p, \phi'}{\text{if } (c \notin Falsey) \text{ then } (p = \ell, e_p = e') \text{ else } (p = \neg \ell, e_p = e'') \qquad H'; S'; e_p \mid \phi' \longrightarrow H''; S''; v \mid \phi''}{H; S; \text{if}^\ell e \text{ then } e' \text{ else } e'' \mid \phi \longrightarrow H''; S''; v \mid \phi''}$$

MCall
$$\frac{H; S; e \mid \phi \longrightarrow H'; S'; l \mid \phi' \qquad H'; S'; e' \mid \phi \longrightarrow H''; S''; v \mid \phi''}{H''(l) = (\_, \$fun \mapsto \text{fun } f(x^f)\{(\text{var } y)^*, \text{return } e^f\}, \$vars \mapsto S^f, \$tyvar \mapsto \alpha, ...)}{S^{f} = S^f\{f \mapsto l, x^f \mapsto v, (y \mapsto udf)^*\} \qquad \bar{\phi} \in \Phi \qquad H'; S^{f}; e^f \mid \bar{\phi} \longrightarrow H''; v' \mid \_}{H; S; e(e') \mid \phi \longrightarrow H''; S'; v' \mid \phi'}$$

MTLPropSet
$$\frac{H; S; e \mid \phi \longrightarrow H'; S'; l \mid \phi' \qquad H'; S'; e' \mid \phi' \longrightarrow H''; S''; v \mid \phi''}{runtype_{H''}(v) \in \mathcal{P}(runtype_{H''}(l).n) \qquad H''' = H''\{l \mapsto H''(l)\{n \mapsto v\}\}}{H; S; \underline{e.n = e'} \mid \phi \longrightarrow H'''; S''; v \mid \phi''}$$

MTLCall
$$\frac{H; S; e \mid \phi \longrightarrow H'; S'; l \mid \phi' \qquad H''(l) = obj}{\$fun \in obj \qquad H; S; e(e') \mid \phi \longrightarrow H''; S'; v' \mid \phi'}{H; S; \underline{e(e')} \mid \phi \longrightarrow H''; S'; v' \mid \phi'}$$

Error
$$\frac{H; S; e \mid \phi \longrightarrow H'; S'; l \mid \phi'}{H'; S'; e' \mid \phi' \longrightarrow H''; S''; v \mid \phi''}{H''(l) = obj \qquad \$fun \notin obj}{H; S; e(e') \mid \phi \longrightarrow \lightning}$$

Top-level initalization rules

MRun
$$\frac{(H, S) = \text{initialize}(fundec^*)}{H; S; mon(e) \mid \{\} \longrightarrow \_; \_; v \mid \{\}}{\mathcal{T}; \mathcal{P}; \Phi \vdash fundec^* \triangleright e \uparrow v}$$

Monitor
$$\frac{\{\}; \{\}; mon(e) \mid \{\} \lightning}{\mathcal{T}; \mathcal{P}; \Phi \vdash fundec^* \triangleright e \lightning}$$

Rules for prototype lookup

MPropLookup
$$\frac{H(l)[n] = v}{H; l.n \longrightarrow v}$$

MProtoLookup
$$\frac{n \notin H(l) \qquad H; H(l)_{\text{proto}}.n \longrightarrow v}{H; l.n \longrightarrow v}$$

Fig. 7. Monitoring semantics rules

The function $runtype_H$ converts values to types. For location values l, a type variable is retrieved from the heap. A constant value results in a concrete type.

$$runtype_H = \{l \mapsto H(l)[\$\text{tyvar}], num \mapsto \text{Number}, str \mapsto \text{String},$$
$$bool \mapsto \text{Bool}, null \mapsto \text{Null}, udf \mapsto \text{Udf}\}$$

3.3   Soundness

In this section, we show that the types and flows inferred by this system are sound. Formally, we prove the following soundness theorem.

Theorem 1 (Soundness). *Suppose there is a training run $fundec^* \triangleright e_1 \uparrow T; \mathcal{P}; \Phi$, with T the types and $\mathcal{P}$ the equivalence mapping resulting from constraint solving and Φ the set of traversed paths.*

Then there cannot be an expression e_2 that evaluates to $\frac{1}{2}$ with the monitoring semantics using the previously inferred types and traversed paths, notated as $T; \mathcal{P}; \Phi \vdash fundec^* \triangleright e_2 \frac{1}{2}$.

That is, if the training run has inferred a set of types for a certain program, then there can be no expression that triggers a not-a-function error inside of the program *fundec*, given the types, equivalence information, and coverage of the training run. Note that applications inside the top-level expression e_2 **are** checked at run time because of the application of *mon* in the MRun rule.

Before we begin with the proof sketch, we introduce a simulation to relate a training run to a monitoring run and we define stability.

Definition 1 (Simulation). *The simulation relation on $H_t; S_t$ and $H_m; S_m$ under equivalence mapping $\mathcal{P}$, denoted by $H_t; S_t \sim_{\mathcal{P}} H_m; S_m$, holds iff the following holds.*

- $\forall x \in dom(S_t)$, $S_t(x) = l_t : \alpha_t$ *iff* $S_m(x) = l_m$ *and* $runtype_{H_m}(l_m) \in \mathcal{P}(\alpha_t)$.
- $\forall l_t \in dom(H_t)$, *whenever* $H_t(l_t) = obj_t : \alpha$ *such that* $obj_t.p = v_t : \alpha'$, *we have* $\mathcal{P}(\alpha') = \mathcal{P}(\alpha.p)$.
- $\forall l_m \in dom(H_m)$, *whenever* $H_m(l_m) = obj_m$ *such that* $obj_m.p = v_m$, *we have* $runtype_{H_m}(v_m) \in \mathcal{P}(runtype_{H_m}(l_m).p)$.

Definition 2 (Training heap stability). *H_t is training-stable under equivalence mapping $\mathcal{P}$ iff, for all $l_t \in dom(H_t)$, whenever $H_t(l_t) = obj : \alpha$ such that $obj.p = v_t : \alpha'$, we have $\mathcal{P}(\alpha') = \mathcal{P}(\alpha.p)$.*

Definition 3 (Monitoring heap stability). *H_m is monitoring-stable under equivalence mapping $\mathcal{P}$ iff, for all $l_m \in dom(H_m)$, whenever $H_m(l_m) = obj$ such that $obj.p = v_m$, we have $runtype_{H_m}(v_m) \in \mathcal{P}(runtype_{H_m}(obj).p)$.*

Lemma 1 (Simulation Splitting). *Suppose that $H_t; S_t \sim_{\mathcal{P}} H_m; S_m$. Then H_t is training stable and H_m is monitoring stable.* $\qquad\square$

Lemma 2 (Every training heap is stable). *For all heaps in the training run it holds that the heap is training-stable.* $\qquad\square$

Lemma 3 (Simulation from stability). *Suppose that H_t is training stable, H_m is monitoring stable, and $S_t \sim_{\mathcal{P}} S_m$ under H_m (i.e., Item 1 in Definition 1 is the mean). Then $H_t; S_t \sim_{\mathcal{P}} H_m; S_m$.* □

Lemma 4 (Preservation). *Suppose there is a training derivation fundec$^* \triangleright e_0 \uparrow \mathcal{T}, \mathcal{P}, \Phi$ with a subderivation for the judgment $H_t; S_t; e_1 \longrightarrow H'_t; S''_t; \_ : \bar{\tau}_t \mid \_ ; \phi_t$. Let H_m, S_m, and ϕ_m be such that $H_t; S_t \sim_{\mathcal{P}} H_m; S_m$ and $\phi_m = \phi_t$.*

If $H_m; S_m; e_1|\phi_m \longrightarrow R$, then $R = H'_m; S'_m; v_m|\phi'_m$, runtype$_{H_m}(v_m) \in \mathcal{P}(\bar{\tau}_t)$ and $H'_t; S'_t \sim_{\mathcal{P}} H'_m; S'_m$. □

With the definitions and lemmas listed above we can prove Theorem 1.

Proof. (Sketch) The proof is by induction on the derivation of $H_m; S_m; e_1|\phi_m \longrightarrow R$ in the monitoring semantics. The only difficult case is dealing with MCALL.

On the callee and argument e and e' we can just apply the induction hypothesis. At this point, we also obtain that the simulation relation must hold.

To proceed, we need to find a subderivation in the training semantics that is suitable for executing the function body, that is, its entry state must simulate the current monitoring state. As we have simulation after executing e and e', we know that the (type variable of the) function e_m^f from the monitoring run is in the equivalence set of the (type variable of the) function e_t^f. This situation can only arise if the function was called at some point in the training run.

Now, our preconditions hold and we can apply the induction hypothesis once more to e_m^f. The only thing left to show is that we end up with simulation again. From Lemma 1 we have that H'''_m is monitoring stable, from Lemma 2 we have that H'''_t is training stable. With Lemma 3 we obtain $H'''_t; S'''_t \sim_{\mathcal{T}} H'''_m; S'''_m$. □

The full proof is available elsewhere [15]. Lemma 4 only holds within the execution. We need to do some extra work at top level, which is explicated in the following lemma.

Lemma 5 (Top-Level Preservation). *Let fundec$^* \triangleright e_0 \uparrow \mathcal{T}, \mathcal{P}, \Phi$ be a training execution. Let H_m be such that monitoring heap simulation holds.*

If $H_m; S_m; mon(e_2)|\phi \longrightarrow R$, then $R = H'_m; S'_m; v_m|\phi'$ and H'_m is monitoring stable.

Proof. We perform induction on the monitoring semantics. In all cases except $mon(e_2) \equiv \underline{e.n = e'}$ and $mon(e_2) \equiv \underline{e(e')}$ can we directly apply the induction hypothesis.

In the case where $mon(e_2) \equiv \underline{e.n = e'}$, we apply the induction hypothesis to both e and e'. We now need to show that H'''_m is monitoring stable. This heap has one updated field. For this field, it must hold that runtype$_{H''_m}(v_m) \in \mathcal{P}(runtype_{H''_m}(l_m).n)$. But this precondition is enforced by rule MTLPROPSET.

If $mon(e_2) \equiv \underline{e(e')}$, then the derivation rule enforces that e must result in a function. □

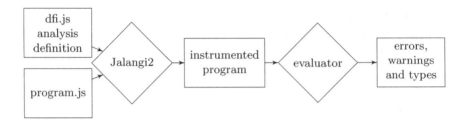

Fig. 8. Analysis pipeline diagram

4   Implementation

Our implementation is based on the formal system. During execution, the analysis observes what types occur by instrumenting the program to collect constraints. Based on these observations, it infers the types of the program.

4.1   Overview

The instrumentation is performed with Jalangi2 [11], a dynamic analysis framework for JavaScript. Figure 8 gives an overview of the instrumentation. The framework takes the original JavaScript program and instruments it according to the analysis definition. Running the instrumented program yields errors, warnings, and inferred types.

The constraints that are collected have the form (*base*, *property*, *type*), where *base* is the item which has the *property*, and *type* is the type of that property. There are three kinds of base items: objects, functions, and frames. For an object, a property represents a field, for a function, a property is either an argument or **return**, and for a frame, a property is a variable.

Types are defined as (*type*, *value*, [*location*]), where *type* is a primitive JavaScript type (number, boolean, string, undefined, null, object, function), *value* a primitive value, and [*location*] a list of source locations where the type has been observed. Values are included in the type if only one value is observed for a particular property. Otherwise, top ($\top$) is reported.

Programmers may annotate their programs with trusted type signatures for both functions and frames. These signatures are extracted during evaluation and verified against the observed types.

Programs are instrumented with constraint collection in the following places.

Function invocation. For each argument passed to the function, a constraint of the form (*fname*, *arg_n*, *type*) is generated, where *fname* is the name of the function invoked, n the index of the argument, and *type* the type of the argument. We also generate a constraint for the return value. Additionally, we check if the function is used as a constructor. If so, we also constrain the new object.

Field read. On a field read, we traverse the prototype chain to find the object providing the field. Then we constrain the provider to contain that property with the type of the value that was read.

Field write. When a field is written, we constrain the object to have that field with the type of the value we assign to it.

Variable read. When a local variable is read, we constrain the current frame that the variable belongs to.

Variable write. Same as with variable read, we constrain the current frame.

Literal string. Type annotations are provided as literal strings in the source code. From these annotations, we generate trusted constraints.

After the program has been executed, the constraints are processed. First, the constraints are solved. Then, the analysis check for type errors. Type errors are defined as conflicts between the annotated type and the inferred type. For each annotation, we check if it matches the inferred types. If not, an error is issued.

Besides errors, which are clashes between type annotations and inferred types, the algorithm also reports warnings. Warnings are issued when type inconsistencies are found. Roughly, an inconsistency is defined as one property having more than one type. In practice, it turns out that there are several cases where it is fine to have more than one type for a property. Pradel et al. [16], who have implemented a dynamic type inconsistency analysis for JavaScript, suggest methods for pruning inconsistencies that are probably not problematic. We implemented some of their methods.

Null-related warning. The value null, unlike undefined, does not occur in JavaScipt, unless the programmer explicitly assigns it. Hence, the type Null only occurs intentionally, so that null-related warnings can be pruned.

Degree of inconsistency. Polymorphic code generates many inconsistency warnings, which are most likely false positives. We therefore define a maximum number of types (i.e., 2) that we consider to be inconsistent.

Max difference. Besides pruning on base types, we also measure the difference between object types. The programmer can set the maximum difference between object types that should cause a warning.

These pruning metrics are only applied to warnings, and can be configured or turned off by the programmer.

4.2 Complete Example

This subsection explores a complete example to demonstrate how a programmer can use the implementation. Listing 1 shows the source code for the program "access-nsieve" from the SunSpider benchmark [22]. The program calculates three large prime numbers.

The program has been augmented with three type annotations, on lines 4, 13 and 29. These annotations are straightforward and result from inspecting the source code.

```
1   // The Great Computer Language Shootout
2   // http://shootout.alioth.debian.org/
3   //
4   // modified by Isaac Gouy
5   "function pad:{number->number->string}"
6   function pad(number,width){
7       var s = number.toString();
8       var prefixWidth = width - s.length;
9       if (prefixWidth>0){
10          for (var i=1; i<=prefixWidth; i++) s = " " + s;
11      }
12      return s;
13  }
14  "function nsieve:{number->Array->number}"
15  function nsieve(m, isPrime){
16      var i, k, count;
17
18      for (i=2; i<=m; i++) { isPrime[i] = true; }
19      count = 0;
20
21      for (i=2; i<=m; i++){
22          if (isPrime[i]) {
23              for (k=i+i; k<=m; k+=i) isPrime[k] = false;
24              count++;
25          }
26      }
27      console.log(count);
28      return count;
29  }
30  "function sieve:{undefined}"
31  function sieve() {
32      for (var i = 1; i <= 3; i++ ) {
33          var m = (1<<i)*10000;
34          var flags = Array(m+1);
35          nsieve(m, flags);
36      }
37  }
38
39  sieve();
```

Listing 1. access-nsieve.js from SunSpider benchmark

The type annotations are not required for the implementation to work. Alternatively, the programmer can inspect the inferred types by hand. The benefit of supplying type annotations is that the algorithm will verify them for the programmer and issue errors where a clash occurs.

The annotations will be extracted during the execution of the instrumented version of the program. Figure 9 shows the type constraints collected during execution of this program. The constraints are first condensed and then checked against the trusted type annotations.

The output of this process is shown in Fig. 10. The program returns two type errors for this program, namely "pad not observed in frame global" and "function pad not observed". These errors arise because the function "pad" is never called and therefore the function was never observed and no constraints were generated. We observed no warnings for this program.

5   Evaluation

To evaluate our implementation, we applied it to the SunSpider benchmark [22] where we hand-annotated every program with types. The results of our

```
'frame global':                          'frame nsieve':
    sieve:    'function sieve'               i:        number
    Array:    'function Array'               m:        number
    nsieve:   'function nsieve'              isPrime:  Array
    result:   number                        count:    number
    expected: number                        k:        number

'frame sieve':                            'function nsieve':
    sum:      number                         arg0:     number
    i:        number                         arg1:     Array
    m:        number                         return:   number
    flags:    Array
                                         'function sieve':
                                             return:   number
```

Fig. 9. Constraints generated for Listing 1, omitting values and locations

```
We detected 2 type error(s)                  sum with type: number(T)
                                             i with type: number(T)
pad not observed in frame global             m with type: number(T)
function pad not observed                    flags with type: Array
                                         frame nsieve has the following properties:
We inferred the following types:             i with type: number(T)
                                             m with type: number(T)
frame global has the following properties:   isPrime with type: Array
    sieve with type: function sieve          count with type: number(T)
    Array with type: function Array          k with type: number(T)
    nsieve with type: function nsieve    function nsieve has the following type:
    result with type: number(14302)          arg0 number(T) -> arg1 Array -> return number(T)
    expected with type: number(14302)    function sieve has the following type:
frame sieve has the following properties:    return number(14302)
```

Fig. 10. Output for access-nsieve.js

evaluation are listed in Fig. 11. All three aforementioned pruning methods were turned on. Programs that did not result in an error or warning are not listed.

Most errors (114) are caused by unused code. This code is annotated, but not executed so that no constraints are generated. No constraints means no types can be inferred, so the annotations cannot coincide with the inferred types.

Fifteen errors are artifacts of our type annotation system, that turned out to be too limited for two programs in the benchmark. The annotation language does not allow recursive types.

In three cases, errors were caused by native functions. Here the problem is that we are unable to generate constraints for native code.

Seven of the 139 errors were actual programming errors. The programs "crypto-md5" and "crypto-sha1" both contained problematic code. These problems were also discovered by Pradel et al. [16].

When looking at the inconsistency warnings, we observe 17 true warnings. In "3d-cube", some function returns either undefined or an Array, depending on the arguments. This could lead to problems when accessing the Array. Both "crypto-md5" and "crypto-sha1" resulted in warnings, identifying the same problems. "date-format-xparb" contains the function "leftPad", which has an inconsistent return type. This problem is also found by Pradel et al. [16].

As shown by the results and discussion above, our analysis yields useful errors and warnings that can be used by programmers to increase the quality of their programs.

		Total	3d-cube	3d-raytrace	access-nbody	access-nsieve	bitops-nsieve-bits	crypto-aes	crypto-md5	crypto-sha1	date-format-tofte	date-format-xparb	math-cordic	math-partial-sums	regexp-dna	string-validate-input
Errors	Unused Code	114	3	2	0	2	2	8	18	18	47	0	2	11	1	0
	Type Limits	15	0	9	6	0	0	0	0	0	0	0	0	0	0	0
	Native Fncts	3	0	0	0	0	0	0	0	0	0	0	0	0	0	3
	True Errors	7	0	0	0	0	0	0	6	1	0	0	0	0	0	0
Warnings	False	13	0	6	0	0	0	1	0	0	5	0	0	0	0	1
	True	17	1	0	0	0	0	0	12	2	0	2	0	0	0	0

Fig. 11. Breakdown of errors and warnings

6   Related Work

Quite some work has been done on bringing type checking and type inference to object oriented dynamic languages such as Ruby, Python and JavaScript.

Anderson and Giannini describe a formal static type inference system for a core JavaScript language with limited syntax [2]. This work builds upon previous work by the same authors together with Drossopoulou [3]. They show that this type system is sound.

Thiemann lays the groundwork for a static type system for JavaScript [24]. In this work, he also presents a JavaScript core language. For this language, typing is defined and type soundness is proved. This core language and the type structure are used in later work with Jensen and Møller to construct a static analyzer for JavaScript [12]. Their analyzer is based on the standard monotone framework with significant extensions to improve precision. Flow graphs are constructed and analysis lattices and transfer functions are presented. The downside of their method is that it is quite intricate and therefore hard to implement.

Facebook has also developed a static type inference system for JavaScript called Flow [6]. There are no formal publications about this system, but according to Facebook, it is based on control and data-flow analysis and aims at inferring types and finding type errors.

Instead of trying to implement a static type system for JavaScript directly, many alternative strategies have been explored to tackle this problem and to overcome the shortcomings of static type inference for dynamic languages. Lerner et al. present TeJaS, an extensible type systems for JavaScript [14]. Chugh et al. have developed Dependent JavaScript (DJS), wich is a typed dialect of JavaScript [5]. Ren and Foster have worked on doing just-in-time static type checking [17].

Furr et al. introduce a static type inference algorithm for Ruby [7]. Their implementation, called DRuby, is similar in complexity to the aforementioned systems for JavaScript. The authors reduced the burden for their implementation by compiling Ruby to an intermediate language, which has an explicit flow.

For Python, Michael Salib developed Starkiller, a comprehensive static type inference system [19]. Starkiller aims to remove the burden of constantly checking types at run time before every operation.

All these approaches are static analyses. JavaScript is a dynamic language and many properties of programs including types are only known at run time. As noted by Jakob et al. [10], static analyses either yield many false positives or restricts the expressiveness of the language. Cartwright and Fagan introduced the concept of Soft Typing to overcome these limitations [4]. They argue that both static and dynamic typing have their drawbacks and that soft typing could potentially provide the best of both worlds. The idea is to do some static type inference first and insert dynamic checks in cases where static inference falls short. Cartwright and Wright implemented such a system for Scheme [25]. More recent work on gradual typing further investigates these ideas [21].

Soft typing has been applied to JavaScript by Hackett and Guo in Spider-Monkey [8]. Their hybrid inference algorithm first performs a static "may have type" analysis on the program. This analysis generates constraints and identifies at what points in the program the constraints may be incomplete. Using this information, type barriers are inserted in the program. During execution, a "must have type" analysis is performed, using the previously inserted information. The type information is used to reduce the run time of the program by omitting some run-time type checks. The only information reported back to the programmer is how many times a dynamic check was needed. More recently, Swamy et al. introduce TS*, a sound gradual type system for JavaScript [23]. An obvious downside to hybrid approaches like soft typing is that a complex static type inference system has to be developed.

Pradel et al. [16] present a dynamic type inconsistency analysis for JavaScript, called TypeDevil. Their system is implemented with the Dynamic Analysis Framework Jalangi2 [20]. It checks JavaScript programs for inconsistent properties, which have more than one type. However, they only develop a practical implementation and do not present a complete formal type inference system. An et al. [1] present a complete dynamic inference algorithm for Ruby. They note that doing a dynamic analysis has several benefits. Implementing such an analysis is much easier and less error prone than a static or hybrid one, since one does not have to capture the whole language and every possible flow. Furthermore, the results respect flow sensitivity. Similar results are achieved by Saftoiu, who has developed JSTrace, a dynamic type discovery system for JavaScript, based on program traces [18].

7   Conclusion

We show that dynamic flow analysis for JavaScript is feasible. To demonstrate that the general idea is useful, we develop a formal system for a JavaScript core language and prove its soundness.

To demonstrate that the concept of dynamic flow analysis for JavaScript is also useful in practice, we develop an implementation based on the same principles as the formal system. We implemented a prototype dynamic flow analysis system for JavaScript. We evaluated our system on benchmark programs. From this evaluation we obtained useful errors and warnings that allow developers to improve the quality of their JavaScript code.

References

1. An, J.D., Chaudhuri, A., Foster, J.S., Hicks, M.: Dynamic inference of static types for Ruby. In: Ball, T., Sagiv, M. (eds.) Proceedings of the 38th ACM SIGPLAN-SIGACT Symposium on Principles of Programming Languages, POPL 2011, Austin, TX, USA, 26–28 January 2011, pp. 459–472. ACM (2011)
2. Anderson, C., Giannini, P.: Type checking for JavaScript. Electr. Notes Theor. Comput. Sci. **138**(2), 37–58 (2005)
3. Anderson, C., Giannini, P., Drossopoulou, S.: Towards type inference for JavaScript. In: Black, A.P. (ed.) ECOOP 2005. LNCS, vol. 3586, pp. 428–452. Springer, Heidelberg (2005). https://doi.org/10.1007/11531142_19
4. Cartwright, R., Fagan, M.: Soft typing. In: Proceedings of the ACM SIGPLAN 1991 Conference on Programming Language Design and Implementation (PLDI), Toronto, Ontario, Canada, 26–28 June 1991, pp. 278–292 (1991)
5. Chugh, R., Herman, D., Jhala, R.: Dependent types for JavaScript. In: Proceedings of the 27th Annual ACM SIGPLAN Conference on Object-Oriented Programming, Systems, Languages, and Applications, OOPSLA 2012, Part of SPLASH 2012, Tucson, AZ, USA, 21–25 October 2012, pp. 587–606 (2012)
6. Facebook Flow (2016). https://flowtype.org/. Accessed 21 June 2016
7. Furr, M., An, J.D., Foster, J.S., Hicks, M.W.: Static type inference for Ruby. In: Shin, S.Y., Ossowski, S. (eds.) Proceedings of the 2009 ACM Symposium on Applied Computing (SAC), Honolulu, Hawaii, USA, 9–12 March 2009, pp. 1859–1866. ACM (2009)
8. Hackett, B., Guo, S.: Fast and precise hybrid type inference for JavaScript. In: Vitek, J., Lin, H., Tip, F. (eds.) ACM SIGPLAN Conference on Programming Language Design and Implementation, PLDI 2012, Beijing, China, 11–16 June 2012, pp. 239–250. ACM (2012)
9. Henglein, F.: Efficient type inference for higher-order binding-time analysis. In: Hughes, J. (ed.) FPCA 1991. LNCS, vol. 523, pp. 448–472. Springer, Heidelberg (1991). https://doi.org/10.1007/3540543961_22
10. Jakob, R., Thiemann, P.: A falsification view of success typing. In: Havelund, K., Holzmann, G., Joshi, R. (eds.) NFM 2015. LNCS, vol. 9058, pp. 234–247. Springer, Cham (2015). https://doi.org/10.1007/978-3-319-17524-9_17
11. Jalangi2 GitHub (2015). https://github.com/Samsung/jalangi2. Accessed 9 July 2015
12. Jensen, S.H., Møller, A., Thiemann, P.: Type analysis for JavaScript. In: Palsberg, J., Su, Z. (eds.) SAS 2009. LNCS, vol. 5673, pp. 238–255. Springer, Heidelberg (2009). https://doi.org/10.1007/978-3-642-03237-0_17
13. Jones, N.D., Muchnick, S.S.: Flow analysis and optimization of Lisp-like structures. In: Aho, A.V., Zilles, S.N., Rosen, B.K. (eds.) Conference Record of the Sixth Annual ACM Symposium on Principles of Programming Languages, San Antonio, Texas, USA, 1979 January, pp. 244–256. ACM Press (1979)

14. Lerner, B.S., Politz, J.G., Guha, A., Krishnamurthi, S.: TeJaS: retrofitting type systems for JavaScript. In: DLS 2013, Proceedings of the 9th Symposium on Dynamic Languages, Part of SPLASH 2013, Indianapolis, IN, USA, 26–31 October 2013, pp. 1–16 (2013)
15. Naus, N.: Dynamic type inference for JavaScript. Master Thesis (2015)
16. Pradel, M., Schuh, P., Sen, K.: TypeDevil: dynamic type inconsistency analysis for JavaScript. In: 37th IEEE/ACM International Conference on Software Engineering, ICSE 2015, Florence, Italy, 16–24 May 2015, vol. 1, pp. 314–324. IEEE (2015)
17. Ren, B.M., Foster, J.S.: Just-in-time static type checking for dynamic languages. In: Proceedings of the 37th ACM SIGPLAN Conference on Programming Language Design and Implementation, PLDI 2016, Santa Barbara, CA, USA, 13–17 June 2016, pp. 462–476 (2016)
18. Saftoiu, C.: JSTrace: run-time type discovery for JavaScript. Technical report, Brown University (2010)
19. Salib, M.: Faster than C: static type inference with Starkiller. In: PyCon Proceedings, Washington DC, vol. 3 (2004)
20. Sen, K., Kalasapur, S., Brutch, T.G., Gibbs, S.: Jalangi: a tool framework for concolic testing, selective record-replay, and dynamic analysis of JavaScript. In: Meyer, B., Baresi, L., Mezini, M. (eds.) Joint Meeting of the European Software Engineering Conference and the ACM SIGSOFT Symposium on the Foundations of Software Engineering, ESEC/FSE 2013, Saint Petersburg, Russian Federation, 18–26 August 2013, pp. 615–618. ACM (2013)
21. Siek, J., Taha, W.: Gradual typing for objects. In: Ernst, E. (ed.) ECOOP 2007. LNCS, vol. 4609, pp. 2–27. Springer, Heidelberg (2007). https://doi.org/10.1007/978-3-540-73589-2_2
22. SunSpider 1.0.2 JavaScript Benchmark (2016). https://webkit.org/perf/sunspider/sunspider.html. Accessed 5 July 2016
23. Swamy, N., et al.: Gradual typing embedded securely in JavaScript. In: The 41st Annual ACM SIGPLAN-SIGACT Symposium on Principles of Programming Languages, POPL 2014, San Diego, CA, USA, 20–21 January 2014, pp. 425–438 (2014)
24. Thiemann, P.: Towards a Type system for analyzing JavaScript programs. In: Sagiv, M. (ed.) ESOP 2005. LNCS, vol. 3444, pp. 408–422. Springer, Heidelberg (2005). https://doi.org/10.1007/978-3-540-31987-0_28
25. Wright, A.K., Cartwright, R.: A practical soft type system for Scheme. ACM Trans. Program. Lang. Syst. **19**(1), 87–152 (1997)

A Type Inference System Based on Saturation of Subtyping Constraints

Benoît Vaugon[1(✉)] and Michel Mauny[1,2]

[1] U2IS, ENSTA ParisTech, Université Paris-Saclay,
828 bd des Maréchaux, 91762 Palaiseau Cedex, France
`benoit.vaugon@gmail.com`
[2] Inria Paris, 2 Rue Simone Iff, CS 42112, 75589 Paris Cedex 12, France

Abstract. This paper (This work is part of the first author's Ph.D. thesis [15].) presents a powerful and flexible technique for defining type inference algorithms, on an ML-like language, that involve subtyping and whose soundness can be proved. We define a typing algorithm as a set of inference rules of three distinct forms: *typing* rules collect subtyping constraints to be satisfied, *instantiation* rules instantiate type schemes, and *saturation* rules specify how to check the validity and consistency of collected constraints. Essentially, type inference then proceeds in two intertwined phases: one that extracts constraints and the other that saturates the sets of constraints. Our technique extends easily to the treatment of high-level features such as polymorphism, overloading, variants and pattern-matching, or generalized algebraic data types (GADTs).

1 Introduction

The presentation of type synthesis of a program as the collection of constraints to be satisfied by its sub-expressions, followed by their resolution, is now classical. To cite only a few of them, [7,9,12] consider and solve equality constraints, and [4,14] consider subtyping constraints.

In this work, we follow a "collect-and-saturate" approach in the spirit of [1] and [14], rather than "collect-and-solve". The main differences between our approach and [1,14] is that we have a much simpler type language and a richer constraint language, providing in particular disjunctions[1] and negations of constraints. Moreover, we use a uniform formalism that allows us to both represent typing proofs and effectively implement a type inference algorithm. Finally, we do not try to generate *solutions* to our sets of constraints: we saturate them in order to check their consistency, an idea already present in [1]. In contrast with constraint resolution, saturation allows us to continue to check compatibility of constraints for which finding a solution would become undecidable.

---

[1] Disjunctions should not be confused with union types.

© Springer Nature Switzerland AG 2019
D. Van Horn and J. Hughes (Eds.): TFP 2016, LNCS 10447, pp. 94–112, 2019.
https://doi.org/10.1007/978-3-030-14805-8_6

Our formalism is not really original: it is well known that syntax-directed inference rules can be used to define functions. Still, using them to define complete inference algorithms and to prove their soundness is original, as far as we know. The main contribution of this paper is therefore to develop a "collect-and-saturate" approach of subtyping constraints in a uniform framework, and show that it extends rather easily to high-level features of functional programming language.

This paper is organized as follows: Sect. 2 presents the programming language that we consider, Sect. 3 presents the type algebra and the constraint language, and Sect. 4 introduces our base type inference system. Section 5 states the properties of this system and Sect. 6 briefly describes its implementation. Finally, Sect. 7 gives some hints about possible extensions of the type system and the appendix lists the full set of inference rules.

2 The Language

The language that we consider here is given in Fig. 1: it is a functional language in the spirit of ML, with constants, primitive operations, data constructors (K_i) and pattern-matching with an optional default case.

```
e ::= x | λ x .  e | e₁ e₂                                              λ-calculus
    | c                                                                  constants
    | (e₁, e₂)                                                               pairs
    | p¹ e | p² e₁ e₂              primitive operations, including projections
    | K e                                                        data constructors
    | let x = e₁ in e₂                                          local declarations
    | if e₁ then e₂ else e₃                                            conditional
    | match e with K₁ x₁ → e₁ || ...|| Kₙ xₙ → eₙ                 pattern-matching
    | match e with K₁ x₁ → e₁ || ...|| Kₙ xₙ → eₙ || x_d → e_d
```

Fig. 1. The expression language

The language has a classical call-by-value semantics[2].

3 Types and Constraints

Types are distinguished according to whether they come from building values (we call them "left-types", that will occur at the left of subtyping constraints)

---

[2] Note that the evaluation order does not interfere with typing, and laziness would not complicate the treatment that is given here.

or from value deconstruction ("right-types") such as pattern-matching or function application. Right-types include types of the form $\{K_1\ \alpha_1\ \|\ \dots\}$ which correspond to deconstruction of variants by pattern-matching.

$$\tau^l ::= \alpha \mid (\alpha_1,\ \dots,\ \alpha_n)\ t \mid K\ \alpha$$
$$\tau^r ::= \alpha \mid (\alpha_1,\ \dots,\ \alpha_n)\ t$$
$$\mid \{\ K_1\ \alpha_1\ \|\ \dots\ \|\ K_n\ \alpha_n\ \}$$
$$\mid \{\ K_1\ \alpha_1\ \|\ \dots\ \|\ K_n\ \alpha_n\ \|\ \alpha_d\ \}$$

Types

$$C ::= \tau^l \leqslant \tau^r \mid \tau^r \not\leqslant \tau^l$$
$$\Psi ::= C_1\ \vee\ \dots\ \vee\ C_n$$
$$\Phi ::= \Psi_1\ \wedge\ \dots\ \wedge\ \Psi_n$$

Constraints

$$\sigma ::= [\ \forall \alpha_1\ \dots\ \alpha_n\ .\quad \alpha \mid \Phi\ ]$$

Type schemes

$$\Gamma ::= (x_1,\ \sigma_1),\ \dots,\ (x_n,\ \sigma_n)$$

Typing environments

Fig. 2. Types and constraints

We use a single type construction $((\alpha_1, \dots, \alpha_n)\ t)$, with a postfix notation, to encode all native type constructors like int, string, etc. (for which $n = 0$), as well as product types $((\alpha_1, \alpha_2)\ \times)$ and arrow types $((\alpha_1, \alpha_2)\ \rightarrow)$. For the sake of readability, we use in the following the standard infix notations $(\alpha_1 \times \alpha_2)$ and $(\alpha_1 \rightarrow \alpha_2)$.

Using the same notation for all type constructors is possible since our saturation mechanism does not need any information about the variance of type parameters. Indeed, at saturation time, the type constructors $(\times)$ and $(\rightarrow)$ are always treated in the same way. Thanks to our typing rules, the initial orientation of constraints associated to a given type constructor is always sufficient to encode variance.

Note that our grammar of types is non-recursive. This property simplifies termination proofs, inference rules, and the encoding of type schemes. However, it remains possible to encode what we commonly call *recursive types* using cyclic dependencies in sets of constraints, like for example: $(\alpha \leqslant \beta \wedge \beta \leqslant \alpha \rightarrow \alpha)$. Enabling recursive subtyping constraints is not a problem for the inference mechanisms presented here, but could be confusing for the programmer since they would allow to write down code elements (functions, for instance) that will be typable but whose usage will be rejected in all contexts. As usual, it is possible to forbid the production of recursive typing constraints by adding a verification on generated sets of constraints that detects cyclic dependencies between type variables.

Typing environments are equipped with two classical operations: one for adding a new binding $(x,\ \sigma)$ in a type environment Γ, written $\Gamma \oplus (x,\ \sigma)$, and the other to extract the type scheme associated to a variable x in Γ, written $\Gamma[x]$.

Constraints can be direct $(\leqslant)$ or negated $(\not\leqslant)$, the latter occurring for instance when dealing with precise typing of pattern matching (not presented in this paper, see [15]). A conjunction Φ, which we sometimes call a *constraint set*, is made of disjunctions Ψ. When we write a disjunction as $\Psi \vee C$, we call Ψ the *alternative* to C.

Alternative constraints should not be confused with more common *disjunctive types* or *union types* that may be encoded with simple conjunctions between subtyping constraints. Disjunctions will only be useful for extensions to the language, introduced further. In particular, used with a negation, they allow to express *implications*. They also naturally appear when we negate a conjunction, as we need to implement GADTs with complete inference. The grammars of types and constraints are given in Fig. 2.

4   Inference systems

4.1   Inference Rules

In our formalism, an inference system has three different kinds of rules, namely *typing* rules, that we sometimes call "T-rules", *instantiation* rules (I-rules), and *saturation* rules (S-rules).

Typing Rules. The typing rules (whose names start with a "T") collect constraints. There is usually exactly one such rule per syntax construct. T-rules have the following shape:

$$\text{Txxx} \ \frac{\cdots \qquad \cdots \qquad \cdots}{\Phi, \Gamma \vdash \Psi \vee e : \alpha \rhd \Phi'}$$

Their conclusion should be read as "*under the set of constraints Φ, in the environment Γ: either e can be of type α, producing constraints which, when saturated with Φ, generate Φ'; or the disjunction Ψ is valid and compatible with Φ, and the saturation of $\Phi \wedge \Psi$ generates Φ'*". The set Φ' is the enrichment of Φ that is produced when the type synthesis of e has been performed. Of course, when $e : \alpha$, Φ' constraints α, and the "type" of e can be expressed as "α such that Φ'".

Saturation Rules. Their names start with a "S" and they have the following shapes:

$$\text{Sxxx} \ \frac{\cdots \qquad \cdots \qquad \cdots}{\Phi \vdash \Psi \vee \tau^l \leqslant \tau^r \rhd \Phi'}$$

They should be read as: "*either $\tau^l \leqslant \tau^r$ is valid and compatible with Φ, or the disjunction Ψ is non-empty and compatible with Φ, Φ' being the resulting set of constraints*".

Instantiation Rules. Similar to S-rules, I-rules have the shape:

$$\text{Ixxx} \ \frac{\cdots \qquad \cdots \qquad \cdots}{\Phi \vdash \Psi \vee \sigma \leqslant \tau^r \,\rhd\, \Phi'}$$

and compare a type scheme σ with a type.

In the following, we call "T-node" (resp. I-node, S-node) a node that is an instance of a T-rule (resp. I-rule, S-rule). We give, in Appendix A, the complete set of rules for the language given in Fig. 1.

Structure of Inference Trees. A successful type inference produces an inference tree composed of three successive layers. The lower layer (in green on Fig. 3) is built from typing rules, and is therefore isomorphic to the program. The middle layer, in red, is made of instantiation rules used when type schemes are generated for polymorphic constants (such as the empty list), polymorphic primitives (for instance, pair projections), and polymorphic constructs of the language (*e.g.* the let construct). Finally, the topmost layer is made of saturation rules (in blue).

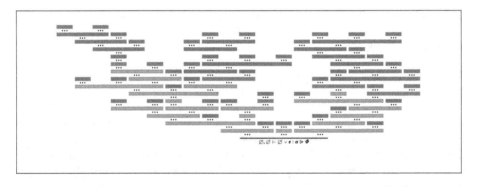

Fig. 3. The different layers of an inference tree (Color figure online)

It is important to notice that the constraint set Φ *flows* through the tree. It is enriched with new constraints in the saturation subtrees, and used by saturation rules that check compatibility of constraints, and by typing rules that generate type schemes at generalization time. We *only add* new constraints in Φ and there is no rule for "cleaning" it. In practice, optimizations are needed to remove subsets of *dead* or *redundant* constraints from Φ. They are not presented here, and can be found in Chap. 6 of [15].

4.2   Typability of an Expression

Before giving examples of inference rules, and expressing the properties of our system, we need a few definitions and notations about type schemes.

Definition 1 (Order relation on type schemes). *Two type schemes* $[\,\forall\alpha_1\ldots\alpha_n\,.\,\alpha_0\mid\Phi\,]$ *and* $[\,\forall\alpha_1'\ldots\alpha_{n'}'\,.\,\alpha_0'\mid\Phi'\,]$ *satisfy* $[\,\forall\alpha_1\ldots\alpha_n\,.\,\alpha_0\mid\Phi\,]\leqslant$ $[\,\forall\alpha_1'\ldots\alpha_{n'}'\,.\,\alpha_0'\mid\Phi'\,]$ *if there exists a substitution* R *of variables to variables (like a renaming, but not necessarily injective) such that:*

- $R(\alpha_0)=\alpha_0'$
- $R(\{\alpha_1,\ldots,\alpha_n\})\subset\{\alpha_1',\ldots,\alpha_{n'}'\}$
- $\forall\alpha\,.\,\alpha\notin\{\alpha_1,\ldots,\alpha_n\}\Rightarrow R(\alpha)=\alpha$
- $R(\Phi)\subset\Phi'$

Intuitively, when we have $\sigma_1\leqslant\sigma_2$, a value of type σ_1 can be used where a value of type σ_2 is expected. In other words, σ_1 is a subtype of σ_2.

We also need a generalization function, which, when given a typing environment, generalizes a type variable together with its constraints. Here is its definition:

$$\mathrm{GEN}(\alpha,\Phi,\Gamma)\quad\triangleq\quad[\forall(\mathrm{FTV}(\Phi)\setminus\mathrm{FTV}(\Gamma))\,.\,\alpha\mid\Phi]$$

Given a particular inference system, we finally define a relation $(\_:\_)$ that relates an expression e and a type scheme σ:

Definition 2 ($e:\sigma$). *We write* $e:\sigma$ *if, when given a type variable* α, *the two following properties hold:*

- *there exists* Φ *such that we have a proof tree of* $\varnothing,\varnothing\vdash\varnothing\vee e:\alpha\rhd\Phi$
- $\mathrm{GEN}(\alpha,\Phi,\varnothing)\leqslant\sigma$

We say that e is *typable* if there exists σ such that $e:\sigma$. Note that if $e:\sigma$, then $e:\sigma'$ for any σ' supertype of σ.

4.3 Examples of Inference Rules

The T-rule for a conditional expression (if e_1 then e_2 else e_3) generates a right-type bool (in deconstruction position) for the test e_1, and propagates the constraints from the two branches e_2 and e_3 to the result type α:

$$\mathrm{TIF}\ \frac{\begin{array}{cc}\mathtt{let}\ \alpha'\ \mathit{fresh}\\[2pt]\Phi_1\vdash\Psi\vee\alpha'\leqslant\mathtt{bool}\rhd\Phi_2\qquad\Phi_2,\Gamma\vdash\Psi\vee e_1:\alpha'\rhd\Phi_3\\[2pt]\Phi_3,\Gamma\vdash\Psi\vee e_2:\alpha\rhd\Phi_4\qquad\Phi_4,\Gamma\vdash\Psi\vee e_3:\alpha\rhd\Phi_5\end{array}}{\Phi_1,\Gamma\vdash\Psi\vee\mathtt{if}\ e_1\ \mathtt{then}\ e_2\ \mathtt{else}\ e_3:\alpha\rhd\Phi_5}$$

For most rules and in particular for TIF, the chaining of Φ's is arbitrarily chosen. In such cases, swapping children of rules does not change the set of typable programs. The order in which sub-expressions are analyzed and in which constraints are added in Φ is then chosen to follow the program source order, improving by the way the quality of error messages. The construction order of Φ is however constrained when a Φ is used by typing rules themselves, for example by the generalization mechanism applied on the let construction.

Abstractions build functional values, this is the reason why the T-rule for abstractions constraints the resulting type α to the left with an arrow type:

$$\text{TLAMBDA} \quad \frac{\textbf{let } \alpha_1, \alpha_2 \textit{ fresh} \qquad \Phi_1, \Gamma \oplus x : \alpha_1 \vdash \Psi \vee e : \alpha_2 \vartriangleright \Phi_2 \qquad \Phi_2 \vdash \Psi \vee \alpha_1 \to \alpha_2 \leqslant \alpha \vartriangleright \Phi_3}{\Phi_1, \Gamma \vdash \Psi \vee \lambda\, x\,.\, e : \alpha \vartriangleright \Phi_3}$$

S-rules decompose constraints and saturate them by transitivity of subtyping. For this, we define auxiliary functions that extract components of constraint sets. As an example, the RIGHTS function extracts from Φ all right-types and alternatives Ψ associated to a given α:

$$\text{RIGHTS}(\alpha,\ \Phi) \quad \triangleq \quad \{(\Psi, \tau^r) \mid (\Psi \vee \alpha \leqslant \tau^r) \in \Phi\}$$

When adding a new disjunction $\Psi \vee \tau^l \leqslant \alpha$, we extract from Φ all right-types τ^r bigger than α, and their alternatives Ψ', and we generate disjunctions $\tau^l \leqslant \tau^r$, with $\Psi \vee \Psi'$ as alternative:

$$\text{STRANSRIGHT} \quad \frac{\textbf{let } (\Psi_1, \tau_1^r), \ldots, (\Psi_n, \tau_n^r) = \text{RIGHTS}(\alpha,\ \Phi_1) \qquad \Phi_1 \vdash \Psi \vee \Psi_1 \vee \tau^l \leqslant \tau_1^r \vartriangleright \Phi_2 \quad \cdots \quad \Phi_n \vdash \Psi \vee \Psi_n \vee \tau^l \leqslant \tau_n^r \vartriangleright \Phi_{n+1}}{\Phi_1 \vdash \Psi \vee \tau^l \leqslant \alpha \vartriangleright \Phi_{n+1}}$$

When a τ^l of the form $K\ \alpha$, corresponding to the type inference of the application of a data constructor K, has to be compared to a $\{\ldots, K\ \alpha', \ldots\}$ coming from typing a pattern-matching that accepts values built with K, we propagate the subtype relation to type variables associated to the arguments of the data constructor:

$$\text{SVARIANTMATCH} \quad \frac{\Phi_1 \vdash \Psi \vee \alpha \leqslant \alpha' \vartriangleright \Phi_2}{\Phi_1 \vdash \Psi \vee K\ \alpha \leqslant \{\ldots, K\ \alpha', \ldots\} \vartriangleright \Phi_2}$$

The saturation of constraints checks the validity and the compatibility of constraints (see the definitions below). When the validity of a constraint set cannot be checked by a saturation rule, the type inference fails and a type error is reported.

Definition 3 (Validity of a subtyping constraint C). *A subtyping constraint C is said to be* valid *if there exists a saturation rule whose conclusion has the form $\Phi \vdash \Psi \vee C \vartriangleright \Phi'$, that is, if it is possible to perform at least one saturation step from $\Phi \vdash \Psi \vee C \vartriangleright \Phi'$.*

In other words, a subtyping constraint is valid if it has one of the following forms:

- $\alpha \leqslant (\alpha_1', \ldots, \alpha_n')\ t$
- $\alpha \leqslant \alpha'$
- $(\alpha_1, \ldots, \alpha_n)\ t \leqslant \alpha'$
- $(\alpha_1, \ldots, \alpha_n)\ t \leqslant (\alpha_1', \ldots, \alpha_n')\ t$
- $\alpha \leqslant \{\ldots, K\ \alpha', \ldots\}$
- $K\ \alpha \leqslant \{\ldots, K\ \alpha', \ldots\}$
- $K\ \alpha \leqslant \alpha'$

Obviously, a disjunction of subtyping constraints Ψ is said to be valid if at least one of its members (a subtyping constraint) is valid. Similarly, a conjunction of subtyping relations Φ is valid if all its members are valid.

Definition 4 (Saturation of a constraint set Φ). *A set of constraints Φ is said to be* saturated *if it satisfies all the following properties:*
▶ *Comparison of parameterized types with the same name:*

- $\forall\,\Psi, \alpha_1, \ldots, \alpha_n, t, \alpha'_1, \ldots, \alpha'_n.$
  $(\Psi \vee (\alpha_1, \ldots, \alpha_n)\ t \leqslant (\alpha'_1, \ldots, \alpha'_n)\ t) \in \Phi \Rightarrow$
  $(\Psi \vee \alpha_1 \leqslant \alpha'_1) \in \Phi \wedge\ \ldots\ \wedge (\Psi \vee \alpha_n \leqslant \alpha'_n) \in \Phi\ \wedge$
  $(\Psi \vee \alpha'_1 \leqslant \alpha_1) \in \Phi \wedge\ \ldots\ \wedge (\Psi \vee \alpha'_n \leqslant \alpha_n) \in \Phi$

- $\forall\,\Psi, \alpha_1, \ldots, \alpha_n, t, \alpha'_1, \ldots, \alpha'_n.$
  $(\Psi \vee (\alpha_1, \ldots, \alpha_n)\ t \nleqslant (\alpha'_1, \ldots, \alpha'_n)\ t) \in \Phi \Rightarrow$
  $(\Psi\ \vee\ \alpha_1 \nleqslant \alpha'_1\ \vee\ \ldots\ \vee\ \alpha_n \nleqslant \alpha'_n\ \vee\ \alpha'_1 \nleqslant \alpha_1\ \vee\ \ldots\ \vee\ \alpha'_n \nleqslant \alpha_n) \in \Phi$

▶ *When a disjunction member is invalid, the rest must be present in Φ:*

- $\forall\,\Psi, \alpha.\ (\Psi \vee \alpha \nleqslant \alpha) \in \Phi \Rightarrow \Psi \in \Phi$

- $\forall\,\Psi, \alpha_1, \ldots, \alpha_n, t, \alpha'_1, \ldots, \alpha'_p, u.$
  $(\Psi \vee (\alpha_1, \ldots, \alpha_n)\ t \leqslant (\alpha'_1, \ldots, \alpha'_p)\ u) \in \Phi \Rightarrow \Psi \in \Phi$

▶ *Transitivity through an α:*

- $\forall\,\Psi_1, \tau^l, \alpha, \Psi_2, \tau^r.$
  $(\Psi_1 \vee \tau^l \leqslant \alpha) \in \Phi \wedge (\Psi_2 \vee \alpha \leqslant \tau^r) \in \Phi \Rightarrow (\Psi_1 \vee \Psi_2 \vee \tau^l \leqslant \tau^r) \in \Phi$

- $\forall\,\Psi_1, \alpha, \tau^l, \Psi_2, \tau^r.$
  $(\Psi_1 \vee \alpha \leqslant \tau^r) \in \Phi \wedge (\Psi_2 \vee \alpha \nleqslant \tau^l) \in \Phi \Rightarrow (\Psi_1 \vee \Psi_2 \vee \tau^r \nleqslant \tau^l) \in \Phi$

- $\forall\,\Psi_1, \tau^l, \alpha, \Psi_2, \tau^r.$
  $(\Psi_1 \vee \tau^l \leqslant \alpha) \in \Phi \wedge (\Psi_2 \vee \tau^r \nleqslant \alpha) \in \Phi \Rightarrow (\Psi_1 \vee \Psi_2 \vee \tau^r \nleqslant \tau^l) \in \Phi$

The saturation of a set of constraints computes its smallest saturated superset.

4.4   Example

A complete example of the usage of these rules may be found in pages 46–47 of [15]. It details the inference tree obtained by type checking the expression (**not true**):

$$\frac{\qquad\qquad\bigtriangledown\qquad\qquad}{\varnothing, \varnothing \vdash \varnothing \vee \textbf{not true} : \alpha \triangleright \Phi}$$

As expected, the constructed Φ is, after cleaning, equivalent to:

$$\{\forall \alpha\,.\,\alpha \mid \textbf{bool} \leqslant \alpha\}$$

5   Properties

Theorem 1 (Termination). *For a given finite expression e, the type inference of e (obtained by building the inference tree for $\varnothing, \varnothing \vdash \varnothing \vee e : \alpha \vartriangleright \varPhi$ following the given inference rules), always terminates.*

Since each inference rule builds exactly one node of the inference tree, proving that inference trees are always finite suffices to prove termination of the type inference.

Sketch of the Proof. In order to prove that all inference trees have a finite size, we start by showing that the "typing part" of such a tree is finite since it is isomorphic to the syntax tree of the program, then that it contains only a finite number of I-nodes since they only appear at the frontier of the "typing part", and then that all S-subtrees have a finite size thanks to the structure of our types and constraints.

Theorem 2 (Soundness). *For any expression e and any type scheme σ such that $e : \sigma$, one of the following properties holds:*

- *evaluating e does not terminate,*
- *e evaluates to a value v and $v : \sigma$.*

The detailed proof of this theorem can be found in [15]. As in [5], we use a small-step semantics and a proof technique *à la Felleisen* (see [16]). The soundness theorem is a direct consequence of the two following lemmas:

- [Progress]: expressions that are not values and whose evaluation is blocked are untypable.
- [Subject Reduction]: if an expression e_1 is typable and evaluates to e_2 then e_2 is typable.

6   Implementation

The formalism that we have used for defining our inference systems can receive a direct implementation. Performing the type inference for an expression e only needs to build the inference tree by using the rules of the inference system under consideration.

At each step of building the tree, either no rule can be applied, and the type inference stops, raising an error, or there is exactly one rule that applies, and type inference goes on, deterministically. This property is true for the "typing part", as well as for "instantiation part" and the "saturation part". Furthermore, each rule precisely mentions the type variables to be generated, and there is no (implicit) global operation to perform, such as, for instance, renaming of type variables.

It is therefore extremely easy to extract a working implementation of an inference algorithm from such a type inference system. Given an expression e

```
let rec type_expr phi_1 env psi expr a =
  [...]
  | EIf (e1, e2, e3) ->
    let a' = Var.fresh() in
    let phi_2 = leq phi_1 psi (Var a') TBool  in
    let phi_3 = type_expr phi_2 env psi e1 a' in
    let phi_4 = type_expr phi_3 env psi e2 a  in
    let phi_5 = type_expr phi_4 env psi e3 a  in
    phi_5
  | ELambda (x, e) ->
    let a_1 = Var.fresh() and a_2 = Var.fresh() in
    let sub_env = (x, schema_of_var var1) :: env in
    let phi_2 = type_expr phi_1 sub_env psi e a_2 in
    let phi_3 = leq phi_2 psi (Arr a_1 a_2) (Var a) in
    phi_3
  [...]
```

Fig. 4. Systematic implementation of typing rules TIF and TLAMBDA

as input, one only has to generate a fresh type variable α and try to derive the inference tree from the root: $\overline{\varnothing, \varnothing \vdash \varnothing \vee e : \alpha \triangleright \Phi}$. If the construction of this tree succeeds, it generates a set of constraints Φ and the inferred type for e is GEN$(\alpha, \Phi, \varnothing)$.

Of course, it is not necessary to keep the whole inference tree in memory and a simple recursive algorithm is sufficient to extract constraints, check their compatibility and compute Φ. Such an implementation consists in three recursive functions, one for each kind of inference rule (typing, instantiation and saturation) in which each rule is implemented as a case. Figure 4 shows how the *typing* function may be systematically be derived from *typing* rules.

Of course, proceeding this way results in an implementation much less efficient than unification-based systems that use mutable data structures to represent type variables, and the famous union-find algorithm (*cf.* [3,6]). Our systems simply cannot use unification, and we cannot use those tools directly to deal with our subtyping constraints.

The fact is that such a direct implementation of our systems produces an extremely inefficient resulting type inference program. The reason is threefold:

1. disjunctions are problematic: they are the source of combinatorial explosions in the saturation mechanisms;
2. the generalization mechanism naively encapsulates the whole set of constraints and provokes an explosion of the number of type variables generated at each instantiation, as well as an explosion of the number of α-renamed constraints;
3. the saturation mechanism keeps in Φ constraints that are consequences of others and generates an explosion of the number of items returned by LEFTS and RIGHTS, resulting in useless constraints and computations.

Another difficulty with this naive implementation technique lies in the readability of the type schemes provided to the user: their size becomes quickly huge (for the reasons above), and a simple clean up using dependency analysis is practically insufficient for having readable results.

However, we found two effective ways to improve the performance of our type inference prototype:

- clean up the sets of constraints contained in type schemes. In particular, we implemented a dependency analysis in the spirit of [10]. However, since the main performance issues in our systems come from disjunctions, we need to go further and develop other orthogonal techniques:
  - an improved dependency analysis using weak dependencies between several disjunctions of constraints;
  - a reinforcement of saturation, considering all disjunctions "modulo rotation". Furthermore, Pottier in [10] removes constraints using a detection of "equivalent subsets of constraints". We use the same idea but with a more aggressive definition of "equivalence". Rather than simply detecting isomorphic sub-graphs of constraints, we use the definition of *a set of constraints is less general than another one*, originally designed to typecheck polymorphic recursion.
- use a dedicated representation of constraint sets containing disjunctions: this representation allows for optimizing the primitives that are used by cleaning algorithms, and limits some redundant computations during saturation.

These techniques have been tested and seem to work well in practice. They bring gains of several orders of magnitude in computing time as well as in the size of constraint sets. The cleaning mechanisms provide us with a further advantage: they also improve the readability of type schemes.

7   Extensions

The main advantages of the inference mechanism presented in this paper are its flexibility and its extensibility. Indeed, the first author's Ph.D. thesis [15] extends the basic type system presented here in three orthogonal directions. We simply show here some hints about how these extensions work.

7.1   A Finer Typing of Pattern Matching on Variants

The goal of this extension is to accept codes like the one given at Fig. 5, where the types of parameters x and y depend on the actual value of **kind**. This problem has been already studied elsewhere: some authors define a dedicated form of *implication*, *e.g.* by extending the grammar of types, defining *conditional types* [2,8] and others extend the grammar of constraints, defining *conditional constraints* [11].

```
let sum x y kind = match kind with
  | INTEGERS -> x + y
  | STRINGS  -> concat x y in
let n = 2 * (sum 3 4 INTEGERS) in
let s = concat ">␣" (sum "Hello␣" "world" STRINGS) in
[...]
```

Fig. 5. An example of matching with different return types

Despite the fact that it is more intuitive to extend the grammar of types with expressions saying "if the argument is of type X then the result is of type Y", this technique fails to link the type of an argument with arbitrary other types, *i.e.* types that are not directly related to this argument like, for example, the type of a previous argument or the type of a variable from an outer function.

The work of Pottier [11], using conditions at the level of constraints, avoids this problem and is the closest to ours. The main difference is that we do not design here a dedicated implication mechanism but instead use negations and disjunctions provided by our general framework.

The idea here consists in simply modifying the typing mechanism of pattern matching by associating in Φ, for each case, the variant being matched to the subtyping constraints extracted from the body of the case. This way, if a typing error occurs later because of a constraint coming from a case, instead of raising a type error immediately, we just mark that case as impossible.

It appears that our language of constraints is sufficient to express this kind of relation between variants and other arbitrary constraints. For each case, we simply use a negation to encode the fact that the set of values denoted by the type variable associated to the matched expression does not contain the variant from the current pattern, and disjunctions to link this constraint with those obtained when typing the body of the case. The saturation mechanism presented in this paper finishes the job.

7.2 A New Generalization Mechanism

The extension of pattern matching presented above is nearly sufficient to encode objects by message passing and without any extension of the language. In this setting, an *object* is simply a function taking a method name (encoded as a variant) as its first argument and performing pattern matching to jump to the code associated to that method.

Unfortunately, the underlying type system is not powerful enough to accept codes like the following one, rather classical in object oriented languages like OCaml:

```
let f obj =
  println (obj ToString);
  obj GetWidth + 10 in
let mkobj width meth =
  match meth with
  | ToString -> concat "width:" (string_of_int width)
  | GetWidth -> width in
let obj = mkobj 42 in
f obj
```

Indeed, the `obj` parameter of `f` is used multiple times in different typing contexts, and the saturation leads to a clash on multiple occurrences of the unique type variable associated to `obj`.

The first motivation for our extension of polymorphism is to accept this kind of code. Many papers have been dedicated to extend the ML polymorphism, defining in particular different extensions and restrictions of the k-CFA, as described in [13].

The basic idea of our extension consists in delaying instantiation by extending the language of left-types (τ^l) with schemes (σ) and changing the instantiation rule into a saturation one performing instantiation as late as possible.

The recurrent problem with this kind of extension is that it breaks the termination of type inference. The originality of our approach concerns the technique that we use to ensure the termination by limiting the generalization power of our system, technique that can be understood by the programmer. Indeed, our technique simply limits the depth of nested polymorphic instantiation through function parameters in a context-free way. As we can see in [15], this technique is, once more, based on an extension of language of constraints.

7.3 GADTs with Complete Inference

In our context, we encode GADTs by:

- Adding a construction to the language to declare GADTs with local typing constraints.
- Adapting pattern matching on variants to GADTs by inserting in Ψ the negation of constraints specified by the user, like in our first extension (Sect. 7.1).
- Extending the type language with a new construction for existential types.

The problem that usually breaks inference in the presence of GADTs is the management of existential types. In our system, this problem appears in saturation rules that take constraints containing existential types in their conclusion. Thanks to the presence of disjunctions and negations in the language of constraints, our saturation mechanism is able to automatically propagate constraints on existential types to other types occurring in the definition of the GADTs.

Each of these extensions makes intensive usage of the saturation mechanism, and the first and third ones perform heavy use of negations and disjunctions. This highlights the interest of a general framework like ours that factorizes formalization, implementation and optimization of a saturation mechanism on constraints using all operators from first order logic.

8   Conclusion

We have presented in this paper a type inference system based of saturation of subtyping constraints, providing terminating and sound inference algorithms. This system has been successfully extended to perform type inference of the following language features:

- overloading (with dynamic dispatch),
- more precise typing of pattern matching (that keeps the relationship between input patterns and output results),
- a generalization of ML polymorphism that enables polymorphic usages of function arguments,
- type inference for GADTs with subtyping.

We gave hints on how these extensions work. All but overloading are fully described in the first author's Ph.D. thesis [15].

A   Appendix

We give here the complete set of rules for the language given in Fig. 1.

Meta-functions

$$\text{LEFTS}(\alpha, \ \varPhi) \triangleq \{(\varPsi, \tau^l) \mid (\varPsi \vee \tau^l \leqslant \alpha) \in \varPhi\}$$
$$\text{RIGHTS}(\alpha, \ \varPhi) \triangleq \{(\varPsi, \tau^r) \mid (\varPsi \vee \alpha \leqslant \tau^r) \in \varPhi\}$$
$$\overline{\text{LEFTS}}(\alpha, \ \varPhi) \triangleq \{(\varPsi, \tau^r) \mid (\varPsi \vee \tau^r \not\leqslant \alpha) \in \varPhi\}$$
$$\overline{\text{RIGHTS}}(\alpha, \ \varPhi) \triangleq \{(\varPsi, \tau^l) \mid (\varPsi \vee \alpha \not\leqslant \tau^l) \in \varPhi\}$$

The T meta-function associates a type scheme to constants and primitives. For instance:

- $T(3) \quad \triangleq \ [\ \forall \alpha \ . \ \alpha \mid \texttt{int} \leqslant \alpha \ ]$
- $T(\texttt{not}) \triangleq \ [\ \forall \alpha \alpha_1 \alpha_2 \ . \ \alpha \mid \alpha_1 \to \alpha_2 \leqslant \alpha \ \wedge \ \alpha_1 \leqslant \texttt{bool} \ \wedge \ \texttt{bool} \leqslant \alpha_2 \ ]$

Typing

TCONST
$$\frac{\varPhi \vdash \varPsi \vee T(\texttt{c}) \leqslant \alpha \rhd \varPhi'}{\varPhi, \varGamma \vdash \varPsi \vee \texttt{c} : \alpha \rhd \varPhi'}$$

TVAR
$$\frac{\textbf{when } \varGamma[\texttt{x}] \textit{ defined} \qquad \varPhi \vdash \varPsi \vee \varGamma[\texttt{x}] \leqslant \alpha \rhd \varPhi'}{\varPhi, \varGamma \vdash \varPsi \vee \texttt{x} : \alpha \rhd \varPhi'}$$

TAPPLYPRIM1

$$\frac{\begin{array}{c}\texttt{let}\ \alpha_1, \alpha_2\ \textit{fresh}\qquad \Phi \vdash \Psi \vee T(\mathrm{p}^1) \leqslant \alpha_1 \to \alpha_2 \rhd \Phi'\\ \Phi' \vdash \Psi \vee \alpha_2 \leqslant \alpha \rhd \Phi''\qquad \Phi'', \Gamma \vdash \Psi \vee \mathsf{e}_1 : \alpha_1 \rhd \Phi'''\end{array}}{\Phi, \Gamma \vdash \Psi \vee \mathrm{p}^1\ \mathsf{e}_1 : \alpha \rhd \Phi'''}$$

TAPPLYPRIM2

$$\frac{\begin{array}{c}\texttt{let}\ \alpha_0, \alpha_1, \alpha_2, \alpha_3\ \textit{fresh}\qquad \Phi \vdash \Psi \vee \alpha_0 \leqslant \alpha_2 \to \alpha_3 \rhd \Phi'\\ \Phi' \vdash \Psi \vee \alpha_3 \leqslant \alpha \rhd \Phi''\qquad \Phi'' \vdash \Psi \vee T(\mathrm{p}^2) \leqslant \alpha_1 \to \alpha_0 \rhd \Phi'''\\ \Phi''', \Gamma \vdash \Psi \vee \mathsf{e}_1 : \alpha_1 \rhd \Phi''''\qquad \Phi'''', \Gamma \vdash \Psi \vee \mathsf{e}_2 : \alpha_2 \rhd \Phi'''''\end{array}}{\Phi, \Gamma \vdash \Psi \vee \mathrm{p}^2\ \mathsf{e}_1\ \mathsf{e}_2 : \alpha \rhd \Phi'''''}$$

TLAMBDA

$$\frac{\texttt{let}\ \alpha_1, \alpha_2\ \textit{fresh}\qquad \Phi, \Gamma \oplus (\mathsf{x}, \alpha_1) \vdash \Psi \vee \mathsf{e} : \alpha_2 \rhd \Phi'\qquad \Phi' \vdash \Psi \vee \alpha_1 \to \alpha_2 \leqslant \alpha \rhd \Phi''}{\Phi, \Gamma \vdash \Psi \vee \lambda\, \mathsf{x}\,.\,\mathsf{e} : \alpha \rhd \Phi''}$$

TAPP

$$\frac{\begin{array}{c}\texttt{let}\ \alpha_1, \alpha_2, \alpha_3\ \textit{fresh}\qquad \Phi \vdash \Psi \vee \alpha_1 \leqslant \alpha_2 \to \alpha_3 \rhd \Phi'\\ \Phi' \vdash \Psi \vee \alpha_3 \leqslant \alpha \rhd \Phi''\qquad \Phi'', \Gamma \vdash \Psi \vee \mathsf{e}_1 : \alpha_1 \rhd \Phi'''\qquad \Phi''', \Gamma \vdash \Psi \vee \mathsf{e}_2 : \alpha_2 \rhd \Phi''''\end{array}}{\Phi, \Gamma \vdash \Psi \vee \mathsf{e}_1\ \mathsf{e}_2 : \alpha \rhd \Phi''''}$$

TPAIR

$$\frac{\begin{array}{c}\texttt{let}\ \alpha_1, \alpha_2\ \textit{fresh}\\ \Phi, \Gamma \vdash \Psi \vee \mathsf{e}_1 : \alpha_1 \rhd \Phi'\qquad \Phi', \Gamma \vdash \Psi \vee \mathsf{e}_2 : \alpha_2 \rhd \Phi''\qquad \Phi'' \vdash \Psi \vee \alpha_1 \times \alpha_2 \leqslant \alpha \rhd \Phi'''\end{array}}{\Phi, \Gamma \vdash \Psi \vee (\mathsf{e}_1,\ \mathsf{e}_2) : \alpha \rhd \Phi'''}$$

TCONSTR

$$\frac{\texttt{let}\ \alpha'\ \textit{fresh}\qquad \Phi, \Gamma \vdash \Psi \vee \mathsf{e} : \alpha' \rhd \Phi'\qquad \Phi' \vdash \Psi \vee \mathsf{K}\,\alpha' \leqslant \alpha \rhd \Phi''}{\Phi, \Gamma \vdash \Psi \vee \mathsf{K}\ \mathsf{e} : \alpha \rhd \Phi''}$$

TIF

$$\frac{\begin{array}{c}\texttt{let}\ \alpha'\ \textit{fresh}\qquad \Phi \vdash \Psi \vee \alpha' \leqslant \mathtt{bool} \rhd \Phi'\\ \Phi', \Gamma \vdash \Psi \vee \mathsf{e}_1 : \alpha' \rhd \Phi''\qquad \Phi'', \Gamma \vdash \Psi \vee \mathsf{e}_2 : \alpha \rhd \Phi'''\qquad \Phi''', \Gamma \vdash \Psi \vee \mathsf{e}_3 : \alpha \rhd \Phi''''\end{array}}{\Phi, \Gamma \vdash \Psi \vee \texttt{if}\ \mathsf{e}_1\ \texttt{then}\ \mathsf{e}_2\ \texttt{else}\ \mathsf{e}_3 : \alpha \rhd \Phi''''}$$

TLET

$$\frac{\begin{array}{c}\texttt{let}\ \alpha'\ \textit{fresh}\\ \Phi, \Gamma \vdash \Psi \vee \mathsf{e}_1 : \alpha' \rhd \Phi'\qquad \Phi', \Gamma \oplus (\mathsf{x}, \mathrm{GEN}(\alpha', \Phi', \Gamma)) \vdash \Psi \vee \mathsf{e}_2 : \alpha \rhd \Phi''\end{array}}{\Phi, \Gamma \vdash \Psi \vee \texttt{let}\ \mathsf{x} = \mathsf{e}_1\ \texttt{in}\ \mathsf{e}_2 : \alpha \rhd \Phi''}$$

TMATCH

$$\mathtt{let} \ \alpha_e, \alpha_1, \ldots, \alpha_n \ \mathit{fresh}$$
$$\Phi \vdash \Psi \vee \alpha_e \leqslant \{\mathsf{K}_1 \ \alpha_1 \ \| \ \ldots \ \| \ \mathsf{K}_n \ \alpha_n\} \rhd \Phi_0 \qquad \Phi_0, \Gamma \vdash \Psi \vee \mathsf{e} : \alpha_e \rhd \Phi_1$$
$$\Phi_1, \Gamma \oplus (\mathsf{x}_1, \ \alpha_1) \vdash \Psi \vee \mathsf{e}_1 : \alpha \rhd \Phi_2$$
$$\ldots$$
$$\Phi_n, \Gamma \oplus (\mathsf{x}_n, \ \alpha_n) \vdash \Psi \vee \mathsf{e}_n : \alpha \rhd \Phi_{n+1}$$

$$\Phi, \Gamma \vdash \Psi \vee \mathtt{match} \ \mathsf{e} \ \mathtt{with} \ \mathsf{K}_1 \ \mathsf{x}_1 \to \mathsf{e}_1 \ \| \ \ldots \ \| \ \mathsf{K}_n \ \mathsf{x}_n \to \mathsf{e}_n : \alpha \rhd \Phi_{n+1}$$

TMATCHDEFAULT

$$\mathtt{let} \ \alpha_e, \alpha_1, \ldots, \alpha_n, \alpha_d \ \mathit{fresh}$$
$$\Phi \vdash \Psi \vee \alpha_e \leqslant \{\mathsf{K}_1 \ \alpha_1 \ \| \ \ldots \ \| \ \mathsf{K}_n \ \alpha_n \ \| \ \alpha_d\} \rhd \Phi_0 \qquad \Phi_0, \Gamma \vdash \Psi \vee \mathsf{e} : \alpha_e \rhd \Phi_1$$
$$\Phi_1, \Gamma \oplus (\mathsf{x}_1, \ \alpha_1) \vdash \Psi \vee \mathsf{e}_1 : \alpha \rhd \Phi_2$$
$$\ldots$$
$$\Phi_n, \Gamma \oplus (\mathsf{x}_n, \ \alpha_n) \vdash \Psi \vee \mathsf{e}_n : \alpha \rhd \Phi_{n+1}$$
$$\Phi_{n+1}, \Gamma \oplus (\mathsf{x}_d, \ \alpha_d) \vdash \Psi \vee \alpha_e \leqslant \{\mathsf{K}_1 \ \alpha_1 \ \| \ \ldots \ \| \ \mathsf{K}_n \ \alpha_n\} \vee \mathsf{e}_d : \alpha \rhd \Phi_{n+2}$$

$$\Phi, \Gamma \vdash \Psi \vee \mathtt{match} \ \mathsf{e} \ \mathtt{with} \ \mathsf{K}_1 \ \mathsf{x}_1 \to \mathsf{e}_1 \ \| \ \ldots \ \| \ \mathsf{K}_n \ \mathsf{x}_n \to \mathsf{e}_n \ \| \ \mathsf{x}_d \to \mathsf{e}_d : \alpha \rhd \Phi_{n+2}$$

Instantiation

INST

$$\mathtt{let} \ \alpha'_1, \ldots, \alpha'_n \ \mathit{fresh} \qquad \Phi \vdash \Psi \vee \alpha_0[\alpha_i \mapsto \alpha'_i]_{i=1}^n \leqslant \tau^r \rhd \Phi_1$$
$$\Phi_1 \vdash \Psi \vee \Psi_1[\alpha_i \mapsto \alpha'_i]_{i=1}^n \rhd \Phi_2 \qquad \cdots \qquad \Phi_p \vdash \Psi \vee \Psi_p[\alpha_i \mapsto \alpha'_i]_{i=1}^n \rhd \Phi_{p+1}$$

$$\Phi \vdash \Psi \vee [\, \forall \alpha_1 \ \ldots \ \alpha_n \, . \, \alpha_0 \mid \Psi_1 \wedge \cdots \wedge \Psi_p \,] \leqslant \tau^r \rhd \Phi_{p+1}$$

Saturation

To prevent our algorithm from entering an infinite loop in the presence of cyclic relations between type variables, before checking the compatibility of a constraint with Φ, we check whether this constraint is already present in Φ. If not, one of SNEWCONSTRAINT($\leqslant$) or SNEWCONSTRAINT($\nleqslant$) is used, and we add the new constraint in Φ and generate a property annotated with a question mark ($\overset{?}{\vdash}$) consumed by rules defined further. If so, one of the axioms SALREADYPROVED($\leqslant$) or SALREADYPROVED($\nleqslant$) is used and no more constraint is generated.

SNEWCONSTRAINT($\leqslant$)

$$\frac{\mathtt{when} \ (\Psi \vee \tau^l \leqslant \tau^r) \notin \Phi \qquad \Phi \wedge (\Psi \vee \tau^l \leqslant \tau^r) \overset{?}{\vdash} \Psi \vee \tau^l \leqslant \tau^r \rhd \Phi'}{\Phi \vdash \Psi \vee \tau^l \leqslant \tau^r \rhd \Phi'}$$

SNEWCONSTRAINT($\nleqslant$)

$$\frac{\mathtt{when} \ (\Psi \vee \tau^l \nleqslant \tau^r) \notin \Phi \qquad \Phi \wedge (\Psi \vee \tau^l \nleqslant \tau^r) \overset{?}{\vdash} \Psi \vee \tau^l \nleqslant \tau^r \rhd \Phi'}{\Phi \vdash \Psi \vee \tau^l \nleqslant \tau^r \rhd \Phi'}$$

$$\mathrm{SAlreadyProved}(\leqslant)$$
$$\underline{\textbf{when } (\Psi \vee \tau^l \leqslant \tau^r) \in \Phi}$$
$$\Phi \vdash \Psi \vee \tau^l \leqslant \tau^r \rhd \Phi$$

$$\mathrm{SAlreadyProved}(\not\leqslant)$$
$$\underline{\textbf{when } (\Psi \vee \tau^l \not\leqslant \tau^r) \in \Phi}$$
$$\Phi \vdash \Psi \vee \tau^l \not\leqslant \tau^r \rhd \Phi$$

$$\mathrm{SLeqSameVar}$$
$$\overline{\Phi \overset{?}{\vdash} \Psi \vee \alpha \leqslant \alpha \rhd \Phi}$$

$$\mathrm{SNotLeqSameVar}$$
$$\Phi \vdash \Psi \vee \phi \rhd \Phi'$$
$$\overline{\Phi \overset{?}{\vdash} \Psi \vee \phi \vee \alpha \not\leqslant \alpha \rhd \Phi'}$$

$$\mathrm{SLeqSameParamed}$$
$$\underline{\Phi \vdash \{\Psi \vee \alpha_i \leqslant \alpha_i'\}_{i=1}^n \rhd \Phi' \qquad \Phi' \vdash \{\Psi \vee \alpha_i' \leqslant \alpha_i\}_{i=1}^n \rhd \Phi''}$$
$$\Phi \overset{?}{\vdash} \Psi \vee (\alpha_1, \ldots, \alpha_n) \, \mathrm{t} \leq (\alpha_1', \ldots, \alpha_n') \, \mathrm{t} \rhd \Phi''$$

$$\mathrm{SNotLeqSameParamed}$$
$$\underline{\Phi \vdash \Psi \vee \alpha_1 \not\leqslant \alpha_1' \vee \cdots \vee \alpha_n \not\leqslant \alpha_n' \vee \alpha_1' \not\leqslant \alpha_1 \vee \cdots \vee \alpha_n' \not\leqslant \alpha_n \rhd \Phi'}$$
$$\Phi \overset{?}{\vdash} \Psi \vee (\alpha_1, \ldots, \alpha_n) \, \mathrm{t} \not\leqslant (\alpha_1', \ldots, \alpha_n') \, \mathrm{t} \rhd \Phi'$$

$$\mathrm{SLeqDiffParamed}$$
$$\underline{\Phi \vdash \Psi \vee \phi \rhd \Phi'}$$
$$\Phi \overset{?}{\vdash} \Psi \vee \phi \vee (\alpha_1, \ldots, \alpha_n) \, \mathrm{t} \leq (\alpha_1', \ldots, \alpha_p') \, \mathrm{u} \rhd \Phi'$$

$$\mathrm{SNotLeqDiffParamed}$$
$$\underline{\textbf{when } \mathrm{t} \neq \mathrm{u}}$$
$$\Phi \overset{?}{\vdash} \Psi \vee (\alpha_1, \ldots, \alpha_n) \, \mathrm{t} \not\leqslant (\alpha_1', \ldots, \alpha_p') \, \mathrm{u} \rhd \Phi$$

$$\mathrm{SVarLeqParamed}$$
$$\texttt{let } (\Psi_1, \tau_1^l), \ldots, (\Psi_p, \tau_p^l) = \mathrm{LEFTS}(\alpha, \Phi) \qquad \texttt{let } (\Psi_1', \tau_1'^l), \ldots, (\Psi_q', \tau_q'^l) = \overline{\mathrm{RIGHTS}}(\alpha, \Phi)$$
$$\underline{\Phi \vdash \{\Psi \vee \Psi_i \vee \tau_i^l \leqslant (\alpha_1, \ldots, \alpha_n) \, \mathrm{t}\}_{i=1}^p \rhd \Phi'}$$
$$\underline{\Phi' \vdash \{\Psi \vee \Psi_i' \vee (\alpha_1, \ldots, \alpha_n) \, \mathrm{t} \not\leqslant \tau_i'^l\}_{i=1}^q \rhd \Phi''}$$
$$\Phi \overset{?}{\vdash} \Psi \vee \alpha \leq (\alpha_1, \ldots, \alpha_n) \, \mathrm{t} \rhd \Phi''$$

$$\mathrm{SParamedLeqVar}$$
$$\texttt{let } (\Psi_1, \tau_1^r), \ldots, (\Psi_p, \tau_p^r) = \mathrm{RIGHTS}(\alpha, \Phi) \qquad \texttt{let } (\Psi_1', \tau_1'^r), \ldots, (\Psi_q', \tau_q'^r) = \overline{\mathrm{LEFTS}}(\alpha, \Phi)$$
$$\underline{\Phi \vdash \{\Psi \vee \Psi_i \vee (\alpha_1, \ldots, \alpha_n) \, \mathrm{t} \leqslant \tau_i^r\}_{i=1}^p \rhd \Phi'}$$
$$\underline{\Phi' \vdash \{\Psi \vee \Psi_i' \vee \tau_i'^r \not\leqslant (\alpha_1, \ldots, \alpha_n) \, \mathrm{t}\}_{i=1}^q \rhd \Phi''}$$
$$\Phi \overset{?}{\vdash} \Psi \vee (\alpha_1, \ldots, \alpha_n) \, \mathrm{t} \leq \alpha \rhd \Phi''$$

SVARLEQVAR

$$\text{when } \alpha_1 \neq \alpha_2$$

$$\text{let } (\Psi_1^l, \tau_1^l), \ldots, (\Psi_p^l, \tau_p^l) = \text{LEFTS}(\alpha_1, \, \Phi), \, (\varnothing, \alpha_1) \qquad \text{let } (\Psi_1'^l, \tau_1'^l), \ldots, (\Psi_q'^l, \tau_q'^l) = \overline{\text{RIGHTS}}(\alpha_1, \, \Phi)$$

$$\text{let } (\Psi_1^r, \tau_1^r), \ldots, (\Psi_r^r, \tau_r^r) = \text{RIGHTS}(\alpha_2, \, \Phi), \, (\varnothing, \alpha_2) \qquad \text{let } (\Psi_1'^r, \tau_1'^r), \ldots, (\Psi_s'^r, \tau_s'^r) = \overline{\text{LEFTS}}(\alpha_2, \, \Phi)$$

$$\Phi \vdash \{\{\Psi \vee \Psi_i^l \vee \Psi_j^r \vee \tau_i^l \leqslant \tau_j^r\}_{i=1}^r\}_{j=1}^p \triangleright \Phi'$$

$$\cfrac{\Phi' \vdash \{\{\Psi \vee \Psi_i'^l \vee \Psi_j^r \vee \tau_j^r \not\leqslant \tau_i'^l\}_{i=1}^q\}_{j=1}^r \triangleright \Phi'' \qquad \Phi'' \vdash \{\{\Psi \vee \Psi_i^l \vee \Psi_j'^r \vee \tau_j'^r \not\leqslant \tau_i^l\}_{i=1}^p\}_{j=1}^s \triangleright \Phi'''}{\Phi \overset{2}{\vdash} \Psi \vee \alpha_1 \leq \alpha_2 \triangleright \Phi'''}$$

SVARNOTLEQVAR

$$\text{when } \alpha_1 \neq \alpha_2$$

SVARNOTLEQPARAMED

$$\text{let } (\Psi_1, \tau_1^r), \ldots, (\Psi_p, \tau_p^r) = \text{RIGHTS}(\alpha, \, \Phi)$$

$$\cfrac{\Phi \vdash \{\Psi \vee \Psi_i \vee \tau_i^r \not\leqslant (\alpha_1, \ldots, \alpha_n) \, \mathrm{t}\}_{i=1}^p \triangleright \Phi'}{\Phi \overset{2}{\vdash} \Psi \vee \alpha \not\leqslant (\alpha_1, \ldots, \alpha_n) \, \mathrm{t} \triangleright \Phi'}$$

$$\text{let } (\Psi_1^r, \tau_1^r), \ldots, (\Psi_p^r, \tau_p^r) = \text{RIGHTS}(\alpha_1, \, \Phi), \, (\varnothing, \alpha_1)$$

$$\text{let } (\Psi_1^l, \tau_1^l), \ldots, (\Psi_q^l, \tau_q^l) = \text{LEFTS}(\alpha_2, \, \Phi), \, (\varnothing, \alpha_2)$$

$$\cfrac{\Phi \vdash \{\{\Psi \vee \Psi_i^r \vee \Psi_j^l \vee \tau_i^r \not\leqslant \tau_j^l\}_{j=1}^q\}_{i=1}^p \triangleright \Phi'}{\Phi \overset{2}{\vdash} \Psi \vee \alpha_1 \not\leqslant \alpha_2 \triangleright \Phi'}$$

SPARAMEDNOTLEQVAR

$$\text{let } (\Psi_1, \tau_1^l), \ldots, (\Psi_p, \tau_p^l) = \text{LEFTS}(\alpha, \, \Phi) \qquad \Phi \vdash \{\Psi \vee \Psi_i \vee (\alpha_1, \ldots, \alpha_n) \, \mathrm{t} \not\leqslant \tau_i^l\}_{i=1}^p \triangleright \Phi'$$

$$\cfrac{}{\Phi \overset{2}{\vdash} \Psi \vee (\alpha_1, \ldots, \alpha_n) \, \mathrm{t} \not\leqslant \alpha \triangleright \Phi'}$$

References

1. Aiken, A., Wimmers, E.L.: Type inclusion constraints and type inference. In: Functional Programming and Computer Architecture, pp. 31–41. ACM, Copenhagen (1993)
2. Aiken, A., Wimmers, E.L., Lakshman, T.K.: Soft typing with conditional types. In: Principles of Programming Languages, pp. 163–173. ACM, Portland (1994)
3. Charguéraud, A., Pottier, F.: Machine-checked verification of the correctness and amortized complexity of an efficient union-find implementation. In: Urban, C., Zhang, X. (eds.) ITP 2015. LNCS, vol. 9236, pp. 137–153. Springer, Cham (2015). https://doi.org/10.1007/978-3-319-22102-1_9
4. Dolan, S., Mycroft, A.: Polymorphism, subtyping and type inference in MLsub. In: Principles of Programming Languages (2017)
5. Eifrig, J., Smith, S., Trifonov, V.: Type inference for recursively constrained types and its application to OOP. Electron. Notes Theor. Comput. Sci. **1**, 132–153 (1995)
6. Henglein, F.: Efficient type inference for higher-order binding-time analysis. In: Hughes, J. (ed.) FPCA 1991. LNCS, vol. 523, pp. 448–472. Springer, Heidelberg (1991). https://doi.org/10.1007/3540543961_22
7. Martelli, A., Montanari, U.: An efficient unification algorithm. Trans. Program. Lang. Syst. **4**(2), 258–282 (1982)
8. Palmer, Z., Menon, P.H., Rozenshteyn, A., Smith, S.: Types for flexible objects. In: Asian Symposium on Programming Languages and Systems, pp. 99–119 (2014)
9. Jones, S.P., Vytiniotis, D., Weirich, S., Washburn, G.: Simple unification-based type inference for GADTs. SIGPLAN Not. **41**(9), 50–61 (2006)
10. Pottier, F.: A framework for type inference with subtyping. In: International Conference on Functional Programming, pp. 228–238, September 1998

11. Pottier, F.: A versatile constraint-based type inference system. Nordic J. Comput. **7**(4), 312–347 (2000)
12. Simonet, V., Pottier, F.: Constraint-based type inference for guarded algebraic data types. Research Report 5462. INRIA, January 2005
13. Smith, S.F., Wang, T.: Polyvariant flow analysis with constrained types. In: Smolka, G. (ed.) ESOP 2000. LNCS, vol. 1782, pp. 382–396. Springer, Heidelberg (2000). https://doi.org/10.1007/3-540-46425-5_25
14. Trifonov, V., Smith, S.: Subtyping constrained types. In: Cousot, R., Schmidt, D.A. (eds.) SAS 1996. LNCS, vol. 1145, pp. 349–365. Springer, Heidelberg (1996). https://doi.org/10.1007/3-540-61739-6_52
15. Vaugon, B., Sous-typage par saturation de contraintes: théorie et implémentation. Ph.D. thesis. Université Paris-Saclay (2016). https://pastel.archives-ouvertes.fr/tel-01356695/document
16. Wright, A.K., Felleisen, M.: A syntactic approach to type soundness. Inf. Comput. **115**, 38–94 (1992)

Programming

Project Report: Dependently Typed Programming with Lambda Encodings in Cedille

Ananda Guneratne, Chad Reynolds, and Aaron Stump[(✉)]

Computer Science, The University of Iowa, Iowa City, IA, USA
{ananda-guneratne,chad-reynolds,aaron-stump}@uiowa.edu

Abstract. This project report presents Cedille, a dependent type theory based on lambda encodings. Cedille is an extension of the Calculus of Constructions with new type features enabling induction and large eliminations (computing a type by recursion on a term) for lambda encodings, which are not available for lambda-encoded data in related type theories. Cedille is presented through a number of examples, including both programs and proofs.

1 Introducing Cedille

In this report, we describe a new project aimed at developing a dependently typed programming language called Cedille, based on lambda encodings. In dependent type theory, lambda encodings were abandoned in the 1980s, due to several serious problems: induction is provably not derivable [9], and one cannot use lambda encodings across multiple levels of the type theory making it impossible to compute both terms and types by recursion on lambda-encoded data. For these reasons, languages like Coq and Agda are based on a datatype subsystem, including case expressions or pattern matching, and special additional typing and reduction rules. With lambda encodings, one can avoid all this, and work with a pure lambda calculus. This simplifies the design and meta-theory of the language. Furthermore, one can use higher-order encodings, which correspond to datatype definitions with negative occurrence of the datatype being defined. These are disallowed in systems like Coq and Agda, but are allowed in languages like System F. Such datatypes have been proposed for representing expressions with binders, a long-standing challenge in functional programming and type theory (see, e.g., [26]).

The third author has developed new solutions to the problems of induction and large eliminations, in a type theory called the Calculus of Dependent Lambda Eliminations (CDLE), which has been proven consistent as a logic [23]. The main ideas are (1) to add a special form of recursive types where constructors are first declared, for purposes of stating a dependent elimination principle (which must mention the constructors), and then defined using a lambda encoding;

A. Guneratne and C. Reynolds are doctoral students.

© Springer Nature Switzerland AG 2019
D. Van Horn and J. Hughes (Eds.): TFP 2016, LNCS 10447, pp. 115–134, 2019.
https://doi.org/10.1007/978-3-030-14805-8_7

and (2) to use a lifting operation to lift simply typed terms to the type level, for large eliminations. In this report, we describe our initial experience with an implementation of CDLE called Cedille. We begin with an informal look at type checking (Sect. 2), and the user interface for Cedille (Sect. 3). Next, we recall the Parigot encoding, which is recommended for Cedille programming (Sect. 4). We then discuss equational reasoning in Cedille in general (Sect. 5), and through some examples with Parigot-encoded natural numbers (Sects. 6 and 7). Next we give some examples with lists (Sect. 8), and a somewhat longer proof example, for transitivity of `compare` on natural numbers (Sect. 9). Finally, we consider a beginning example of a higher-order lambda encoding (Sect. 10), and conclude (Sect. 11).

1.1   Related Work

Probably the best-known lambda encoding is the Church encoding [4], typable in System F [3,8]. The inherent inefficiency of predecessor, proved by Parigot [20], was addressed later by the same author, who proposed a new lambda encoding with constant-time predecessor [19]. The size of the normal form of Parigot-encoded natural number n is $O(2^n)$, but this does not result in inefficient computation using modern functional programming implementations [11]. Stump and Fu survey various lambda encodings and compare their runtime performance [24].

Coq and Agda are two prominent interactive theorem provers based on constructive type theory [7,15]. Coq is based on the Calculus of Inductive Constructions (CIC) [27]. This formalism adds inductive datatypes to the Extended Calculus of Constructions [14], which is itself based on the original Calculus of Constructions [5]. The problems noted above – underivability of induction, lack of large eliminations (needed for deriving propositions like $0 \neq 1$), and (inessentially) inefficiency of accessor functions like predecessor – motivated the addition of inductive types as primitive [6]. Agda has a somewhat different basis than Coq: it uses predicative polymorphism only, where Coq has both predicative and impredicative quantification;, and it is based on pattern-matching equations including axiom K, which is not derivable in CIC [10]. Still, for purposes of comparison with Cedille, it is very similar to Coq, as it is also based on a primitive notion of inductive datatype. In contrast, in Cedille, all data are lambda-encoded and there are no primitive inductive types.

It is worth noting that while Coq and Agda remain active testbeds for new research in theorem proving and verification based on constructive type theory, ours is not the only project seeking new foundations. Geuvers and Basold propose a new type theory based solely on inductive and co-inductive types, without even function space as a primitive type form [1]. Work continues to create new systems for homotopy type theory (e.g., [2,25]). One motivation for that work is to allow interchange of isomorphic structures, a central concern also for Morphoid Type Theory [16]. These efforts focus on different aspects of type theory than that targeted by Cedille, which seeks to provide a more fundamental account of data via lambda encodings.

2   Type Checking in Cedille

The starting point for the CDLE type theory on which Cedille is based is the Calculus of Constructions (CC), extended with support for implicit arguments, taken from the Implicit Calculus of Constructions [18]. Implicit inputs to functions are ones which exist just for purposes of specification: they can be mentioned in the types of later arguments. A basic example for dependently typed programming is taking in the length of a vector as an implicit argument. Vector operations like reverse, for example, do not need to inspect this length computationally; it is just there to allow the statement of the type of the input (and output) vector. In Cedille, an **erasure function** is applied to terms to erase these implicit arguments, and other typing annotations, from terms, before equational reasoning.

To this basic type theory (CC plus implicit arguments), Cedille adds typing features to support induction and large eliminations with lambda encodings. Let us now consider these features and informally introduce the type-checking algorithm, using the example of the datatype of booleans.

```
rec Bool | tt : Bool , ff : Bool =
  ∀ P : Bool → ⋆ .
    P tt → P ff → P self
  with
    tt = Λ P . λ a . λ b . a ,
    ff = Λ P . λ a . λ b . b .
```

Fig. 1. The Cedille definition of the datatype of booleans

Figure 1 shows the Cedille definition for the inductive type Bool. Cedille supports top-level definition of inductive types using the rec keyword. Such definitions first <u>declare</u> types for the constructors of the datatype (here tt and ff) in terms of the name of the datatype (here Bool). At the end of the rec statement, after the with keyword, the constructors are then <u>defined</u> using a lambda-encoding. In between, a type is given which the named datatype is defined to equal. We call this the **body** of the datatype definition, in this case:

∀ P : Bool → ⋆ . P tt → P ff → P self

This type is allowed to mention the name of the datatype recursively, but only in a *positive* position (to the left of an even number of functional constructs in the type). Note that Coq and Agda require strict positivity (to the left of no functional constructs in the type). Here, we are saying that Bool is the type of those terms t such that for any property P of booleans, if one proves the property for tt and also for ff, then the property is proved also for t. The quantification over predicates on booleans is why the definition must be recursive. The dependence of the type of t on t itself is captured using the special variable self. Technically, this self reference is expressed using dependent intersection types [12], though the Cedille implementation hides all other details for these.

As just noted, the definition in Fig. 1 ends with definitions for the constructors tt and ff, in this case using the Church encoding. These definitions are type-checked in a context where the name of the datatype is definitionally equal to the body, and the constructors are all assumed to have the typings and definitions given in the rec declaration. Importantly, however, the constructors may not occur free in the erasure of the body. This means that they can only be mentioned in erased positions, for purposes of dependent typing. Erased arguments are denoted with a minus sign in Cedille's input syntax. For Bool, they need not be mentioned at all. Cedille implements local type inference [21], allowing us to elide the types for the bound variables in the definitions of tt and ff. The capital lambda symbol is used to bind erased arguments. Erasing the definitions of tt and ff of Fig. 1 indeed gives the standard definitions for Church-encoded boolean true and false (namely λ a . λ b . a and λ a . λ b . b).

$$\text{and} \Leftarrow \text{Bool} \rightarrow \text{Bool} \rightarrow \text{Bool} =$$
$$\lambda \text{ x . } \lambda \text{ y . x } \cdot (\lambda \text{ b : Bool . Bool) y ff .}$$

Fig. 2. Definition of boolean conjunction

Figure 2 shows the Cedille definition of boolean conjunction. Cedille definitions use the symbol $\Leftarrow$ to separate the symbol being defined from the type against which the defining term will be checked. Such definitions are processed in checking mode with local type inference; i.e., the term and the type are both inputs to the typing algorithm. The definition in Fig. 2 erases to the standard one for Church-encoded booleans.

Note that to apply x, we must specify the instantiation of the predicate P from Fig. 1, here (λ b : Bool . Bool). Application of an expression to a type is denoted using ·. This instantiation is rather verbose, and can be avoided using McBride's idea of "elimination with a motive" [17]: we can instruct the type checker to use the type against which we are checking the application of x (namely Bool), to construct this predicate automatically. The Cedille notation for elimination with a motive is θ, and the more concise definition is then just:

and $\Leftarrow$ Bool $\rightarrow$ Bool $\rightarrow$ Bool =
  λ x . λ y . θ x y ff .

In this case, the motive (λ b : Bool . Bool) ignores the input b. When we come below to proving theorems, however, the motives will make use of such inputs, to state non-trivial predicates to be proved.

As an example of Cedille's second novel typing construct, Fig. 3 shows the standard impredicative definitions of types True and False, and a function mapping booleans to these types. In consistent pure type theories like the Calculus of Constructions, one cannot apply an expression at multiple levels of the language: Church-encoded booleans can be defined at the term level or at the type level, but they cannot be used across levels. Cedille features a lifting operator ↑ for lifting predicatively typed terms (no type quantifiers) to the type level. The expression ↑ X . b · (λ b : Bool . X) : (☆ → ☆ → ☆) says that we are lifting the term b · (λ b : Bool . X) to the type level. The bound type variable X is a name that can be used to stand, at the type level, for the kind ⋆. The lifting expression specifies the resulting kind using a *lifting type* ☆ → ☆ → ☆. This lifting type is needed for type-level conversions involving these lifting types; otherwise the conversion relation would need to depend on the typing relation. We avoid this by including the lifting type in the syntax. We intend in future work to infer the lifting type during typing so it does not have to appear in the input syntax (while remaining part of the abstract syntax during conversion). A basic example of a conversion for lifting types is seen if we apply Bool-to-type to tt. Lifting tt to the type level yields, with the help of the lifting type, the following:

λ A : ⋆ . λ B : ⋆ . A

This is applied to True and False, reducing via type-level β-reduction to True. (Note that True and False are types, while tt and ff are terms.)

Note that lifting enables us to perform type-level computation with instantiations of impredicatively typed data, while competing approaches like level-polymorphism are restricted to predicative quantification (and hence not usable in practice for lambda encodings, though see Leivant's work on finitely stratified polymorphism [13]).

Typing is done modulo a relation of definitional equality, which automatically equates certain terms and types. Terms are equated if $\beta\eta$-equal, and types if they are β-equal or related by certain conversions for lifting types as just mentioned. As usual in type theory, it is customary to consider some notion(s) of provable equality, in addition to definitonal. We consider this topic shortly (Sect. 5).

```
True  ⇐ ⋆ = ∀ X : ⋆ . X → X .
False ⇐ ⋆ = ∀ X : ⋆ . X .
Bool-to-type ⇐ Bool → ⋆ =
    λ b : Bool . ↑ X . b · (λ b : Bool . X) : (☆ → ☆ → ☆) · True · False .
```

Fig. 3. Function mapping booleans to True and False

3   User Interface for Cedille

Before we look at further aspects of the Cedille language and examples of using it, let us consider briefly the user interface. Users interact with Cedille via an emacs interface, whose version at the time of writing is in around 1800 lines of elisp. This interface communicates with the backend Cedille tool, whose current version is around 4300 lines of Agda, not including parsers automatically generated from just under 300 lines of grammars. The basic interaction between the frontend (the emacs interface) and the backend is for the frontend to request that the backend parse a `.ced` file, namely the one the user is viewing in emacs. If the buffer is parsable, the backend sends back an annotated parse tree in a certain standard format. The format for the parse tree is as a list of **spans**, where a span is a starting and ending character position in the file, together with a name for the kind of parse-tree node this span represents, and a list of extra annotations. The frontend uses a generic elisp library called **se** (for "structured editing") to reassemble a parse tree from the list of spans. It is then possible to navigate through the text in the emacs buffer following the syntactic structure of the code. One highlights a span, and then can navigate up, down, left, or right in the parse tree with single keystrokes (e.g., "p" for up in the parse tree), shifting the highlighted span as one goes.

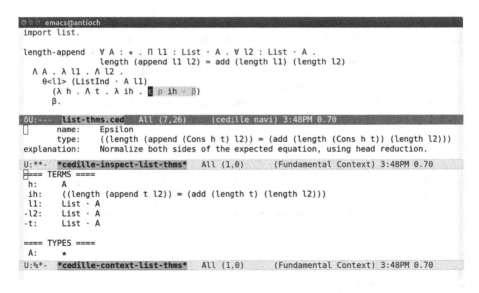

Fig. 4. Screenshot showing Cedille navigation mode within emacs. The top buffer displays a Cedille source file with a proof of a simple theorem (the length of appending two lists is equal to the sum of the lengths of the lists). The middle buffer is the inspect buffer, showing information about the span which is highlighted in the top (source) buffer. The bottom buffer shows the context for the highlighted span; the context is the set of local variables with their types or kinds.

This basic architecture has so far proven extremely flexible. The backend exports essentially all available typing information as extra annotations on the spans it is sending to the frontend. So for each node in the parse tree, the user of the emacs mode can view the type of that node, and any further annotations the backend has supplied. This information is brought up in a buffer called the **inspect** buffer. Once the input file has been parsed by the backend, the emacs mode enters a special minor mode for navigation. During navigation, the buffer is read-only. Single keystrokes are then used for navigation commands and to toggle display of the inspect buffer, which is updated automatically during navigation. This makes it very quick to comb through the substantial amount of type information one gets with dependent typing. There are also keystrokes to navigate through type errors reported by the backend. The frontend recognizes which spans have errors through the inclusion of an additional attribute `error`. A screenshot showing the inspect buffer for a simple example is shown in Fig. 4.

As the interface has been developed, further functionality has almost always been easily supported by simply adding more attributes to the spans. Attributes that are just used for such functionality are filtered out of the inspect buffer by default. An example is functionality to jump to the position in a (possibly different) source file where a symbol is defined. This is implemented in the frontend with the help of a `location` attribute, which the backend adds to the spans for every occurrence of a symbol. With similar additional help from the backend, to recognize which nodes are binders and which children of those nodes are the bound variables, the frontend computes the typing context at any given point in the code, and displays it in a **context** buffer. This buffer has its own minor mode allowing sorting and filtering of the context based on various parameters. A final additional buffer is a **summary** buffer, which lists all the top-level typings in a file. This is useful to see a summary of the lemmas proved in a long source file, for example. From the summary buffer, one can jump to the position in the source file for a summarized typing, with a single keystroke.

So Cedille's interface is based on the goal of providing easy navigation of all available typing information. The architecture commits to this goal by having the backend provide all this information at once as annotations to the parse tree it sends to the frontend. This is fundamentally different from the interfaces for tools like Coq and Agda, which are based on a more traditional querying style of interaction with the backend. In these tools, it is not possible to navigate through source files and see all the typing information for the subexpressions in the file. The Cedille implementation provides this additional power in a very small number of lines of code (the total line count is just over 5000 lines), thanks to this basic architectural decision to have the backend send all typing information to the frontend. The frontend then helps the user navigate and sort through the information. This architecture should be relevant for other implementations seeking to aid a user in understanding complex information computed locally for some sources. Note that similar functionality is provided by the Merlin tool for OCaml.

4   Parigot-Encoded Natural Numbers

Having considered the user interface, let us return to the details of lambda encodings in Cedille. The Parigot encoding combines the best qualities of the

Church and Scott encodings, allowing for both recursion and pattern matching. Where the Church encoding defines numbers as their own iterators, the Parigot encoding defines them as their own primitive recursors: the predecessor number is made available to the function which is applied in the successor case. We illustrate this encoding for the standard example of natural numbers. In Cedille, this is defined as follows:

```
rec Nat | S : Nat → Nat , Z : Nat =
  ∀ P : Nat → ⋆ .
    (Π n : Nat . P n → P (S n)) → P Z → P self
  with
    S = λ n . Λ P . λ s . λ z . s n (n · P s z) ,
    Z = Λ P . λ s . λ z . z.
```

The first line declares the constructors S and Z for Nat. The second and third lines define Nat as the type for lambda expressions that can verify any property P about nats, given a proof that P n implies P (S n) and a proof that P Z. In other words, it provides a way to prove statements about Nats using mathematical induction. Note that, as is often done in other languages like Coq or Agda, one could use this form of induction to derive other induction principles, like strong induction, as theorems. The fourth through sixth lines define the constructors for Nat. S is the successor, a lambda term that takes a Nat and gives back the next higher Nat; and Z is zero.

Under this definition, the first four Nats are:

```
0 = Λ P . λ s . λ z . z.
1 = Λ P . λ s . λ z . s 0 z
2 = Λ P . λ s . λ z . s 1 (s 0 z)
3 = Λ P . λ s . λ z . s 2 (s 1 (s 0 z))
```

Thus, each Nat contains within it every nat that came before it, allowing for easy retrieval of the predecessor. To accomplish this, any function f that is input for s must be of type ∀ X . Nat → (X → X), which is to say that it must begin by taking in the predecessor. Note that this means that the Church encoding can easily be recovered by simply choosing an s that discards the predecessor argument. For example, we can convert Parigot-encoded 3 to Church-encoded 3 as follows:

```
λ s' . 3 · (λ x : Nat . Nat) (λ pn . s')
  = λ s' . λ z . (λ pn . s') 2 ((λ pn . s') 1 ((λ pn . s') Z z))
  = λ s' . λ z . s' (s' (s' z))
```

To define add, we write:

```
add ⇐ Nat → Nat → Nat = λ n . λ m . θ n (λ pn . S) m .
```

where pn binds the predecessor of n (and is not used at all in the computation). As for the predecessor itself, retrieving it is simple:

```
P ⇐ Nat → Nat = λ n . θ n ( λ pn . λ _ . pn ) n .
```

5 Equational Reasoning in Cedille

While it is well-known that various forms of equality can be defined in type theory, our experience so far has suggested that there are some desirable forms of reasoning which require a built-in equality type, denoted t $\simeq$ t' in Cedille. The intended semantics is that the term t is β-equivalent to t'. For pure closed terms, this coincides with being $\beta\eta$-equivalent, providing a semantic justification for the use of $\beta\eta$-equivalence in Cedille.

syntax	description
β	prove T if it is an equation whose sides are, after erasure, β-equivalent
ε t	if T is an equation, β-reduce both sides to head-normal form, and check t against this. With εl instead of ε, just reduce the lhs of T (and similarly, just the rhs with εr)
ρ t - t'	if t proves an equation, replace the lhs with the rhs in T, and check t' against this
δ t	if t proves an equality between head-normal forms with distinct head variable, then prove (any) T, as such an equality contradicts the theory of β-equality
π n t	if t proves an equality between head-normal forms with the binders $\lambda\bar{x}$ and same head variable, then prove that the n'th argument of the head of the lhs is equal to the corresponding argument of the rhs; where those arguments must be prefixed by the same binders $\lambda\bar{x}$.
χ T' - t	confirm that T and T' are convertible, and then check t against T'.
χ - t	synthesize a type T' for t and then confirm that T and T' are convertible.

Fig. 5. Term constructs for equational reasoning in Cedille, when checking against a type T

Figure 5 summarizes some of Cedille's built-in equational reasoning principles. These are term constructs, used to prove equations or deduce facts from equations. Greek symbols are used to separate the namespace for these constructs from that for user-defined symbols. An important concept here is that of head-normal form. Recall that a head-normal form is a term of the form $\lambda\bar{x}.x_i\ \bar{t}$, where $\bar{x}$ is a nonempty sequence of variables bound at the top of the term, x_i is one of these variables, called the **head variable**, and $\bar{t}$ is a possibly empty sequence of terms given as arguments to that head variable. We found that reduction to head-normal form keeps terms more readable than reduction to normal form. Note that as mentioned above, equational reasoning is performed on erased terms, which are pure untyped lambda terms where all typing annotations have been erased.

As explained in Fig. 5, β is used to prove an equation T where both sides are $\beta\eta$-equivalent. For example, the simple lemma

and-tt-0 $\Leftarrow$ Π x : Bool . and tt x $\simeq$ x = λ x. β .

uses this construct to prove our **and** operation applied to boolean true, tt, and any boolean, x, is equivalent to the value of that boolean x.

The ε construct is used to β-reduce portions of an equation to head-normal form. In our Cedille programming, the typical use case we have for ε is reduction of an equation in preparation for use of ρ. Our ρ construct is applied to rewrite the left-hand side of the current equation, T, being reasoned about using its argument equation, for the purpose of stepping towards a proof of T. Examples of ε and ρ in Cedille code can be seen later in Sects. 6 and 8.

Another equational principle is π, which is a kind of injectivity for head-normal forms. For a simple example, suppose we have a proof p that $\lambda c.c\ a$ equals $\lambda c.c\ b$. Then $\pi 0\ p$ would prove that $\lambda c.a$ equals $\lambda c.b$. A more realistic example of a proof using this construct is given in Sect. 7.

The δ construct is for the case where a proof that both sides are equal according to the built-in equality is impossible. As explained in Fig. 5, this means that each side of the equation has distinct head variables while in head-normal form. As an example:

```
Bool-contra ⇐ (tt ≃ ff) → False = λ u . δ u .
```

shows δ in use. Looking back at the definitions of tt and ff, we can see the difference in head variable, as the terms are already in head-normal form. This is similar to the "absurd pattern" in Agda.

In theorem provers like Coq, there are tactics (**change**) for changing the current goal type T which the user is seeking to inhabit (i.e., prove) to some other goal type which is definitionally equal to the T. There are many reasons to want to do this, but the most critical is that while the core type theory is defined modulo definitional equality, one often has additional operations, defined via tactics or some other construct outside the core type theory, which do <u>not</u> work modulo definitional equality. These operations may be sensitive to the exact syntactic form of the goal type. In the case of Cedille, our ρ construct for rewriting is such an operation. To check a ρ-term, Cedille looks for a subexpression of the goal type T which is definitionally equal to the left-hand side of a proven equation. It may happen that a certain goal type T does not contain any such subexpression, but is convertible to a type which does. For example, consider trying to prove

```
(λ x . f (g x)) a ≃ f a
```

assuming g a ≃ a. The left-hand side of the goal equation is convertible to f (g a), to which a rewrite with the assumed equation could be applied. But the original left-hand side (of the goal) does not contain any subterm convertible to g a. It is necessary first to β-reduce the left-hand side of the goal, and then such a subexpression appears. In a case like this, one can use a χ-term to change the form of the goal equation to f (g a) ≃ f a. The rewrite can then be applied.

6   Proving the Injectivity of Addition

In Sect. 4, we defined natural numbers (Nats) using the Parigot encoding. Now, we want to make use of this definition to prove statements about the Nats. For example, consider the following proof that the function add x is injective for all x of type Nat:

```
Add-inj ⇐ Π x : Nat . Π y : Nat . Π z : Nat .
          add x y ≃ add x z → y ≃ z =
  λ x . λ y . λ z . θ x

  % Inductive Step
    ( λ px . λ h . λ pf .
       h ( Succ-Inj ( add px y ) ( add px z ) (
       ρ ( Add-Succ-Comm-0 px y ) -
       ρ ( Add-Succ-Comm-0 px z ) -
       pf )))

  % Base Case
    ( λ pf . ρ ( Add-Ident-0 y ) -
             ρ ( Add-Ident-0 z ) - pf ).
```

We divide this theorem into a proof for the base case and a proof for the inductive step. To verify its correctness, we must ensure that the β terms in both steps are recognized as valid by Cedille. This involves making substitutions until we have an equality of the form t ≃ t.

The θ x term at the head of the λ expression tells Cedille that we are going to do a proof by induction on x (a "split" on x). Given this splitting, we are then expected to provide a proof for the inductive step followed by a proof for the base case.

Consider first the base case. The λ pf means that we are giving as input a proof that

add Z y ≃ add Z z

where the substitution of Z for x is inferred from the context. The type of λ pf is determined using Cedille's local type inference algorithm. Cedille's user interface can display this type to the user. Given this proof, we then do a rewrite (using the ρ construct) with an instance of the Add-Ident-0 theorem, which states that for all n,

add Z n ≃ n

i.e. that zero is the identity for addition. Recall from Fig. 5 that the syntax of ρ expressions is ρ t - t', where t is a proof an equation which is used to rewrite the type for checking t'. By applying Add-Ident-0 to y, we get a proof of add Z y ≃ y; similarly we apply Add-Ident-0 to z. The two ρ expressions rewrite the type of pf using these equations, obtaining a proof that y ≃ z.

Now we consider the more complex inductive step proof. First, we have as inputs the following: px, the predecessor to x; h, our inductive hypothesis which states that (add px y $\simeq$ add px z) $\rightarrow$ y $\simeq$ z ; and pf, a proof that add (S px) y $\simeq$ add (S px) z. The obvious route to take here is to eliminate the S terms on both sides of pf and then give pf as an input to h to obtain y $\simeq$ z. The first step is to get S to the outside of the add terms, where it will be easier to eliminate. We achieve this with the help of the Add-Succ-Comm-0, which proves for any Nats n,m that

add (S n) m $\simeq$ S (add n m)

By applying this theorem to both px,y and px,z, we transform pf to

S (add px y) $\simeq$ S (add px z)

Now that S is on the outside of the term, we can make use of Succ-Inj, a proof of the injectivity of the successor function, which states that

(S x $\simeq$ S y) $\rightarrow$ x $\simeq$ y

for all Nats x,y. By using (add px y),(add px z) as our x,y, we obtain a proof of

add px y $\simeq$ add px z

We can plug this into our hypothesis h to get y $\simeq$ z, completing our proof.

7   Using the pi Construct

The example proof of the injectivity of add x worked by making use the ρ construct to rewrite the input proof. In this section, we showcase a different proof tool: the π construct. We want to prove that

Π x : Nat . Π y : Nat . (S x $\simeq$ S y) $\rightarrow$ x $\simeq$ y

in order to support our proof of Add-inj. The proof may be written as follows:

S-inj $\Leftarrow$ Π x : Nat . Π y : Nat . (S x $\simeq$ S y) $\rightarrow$ x $\simeq$ y =
  λ x . λ y . λ pf . π1 pf .

Here, the purpose of π1 is to prove that the terms at argument position 1 (where these positions start from 0) of the head-normal form of S x $\simeq$ S y are equal. The terms in the resulting equality are prefixed by the same λ-abstractions as the starting head-normal form. The head-normal form of S x $\simeq$ S y is

λ s . λ z . s x (x s z) $\simeq$ λ s . λ z . s y (y s z)

So applying π1 to h produces a proof of

λ s . λ z . x s z $\simeq$ λ s . λ z . y s z

The sides of this equation are then η-equivalent to x and y, respectively. So the type of the proof π1 h is definitionally equal to x $\simeq$ y, as desired.

8   Examples with Lists

Here is the Cedille definition for lists:

```
rec List (A : ⋆) :  | Cons : A → List → List , Nil : List =
  ∀ P : List → ⋆ .
     (Π h : A . Π t : List . P t → P (Cons h t)) →
     P Nil →
     P self
  with
     Cons = λ e . λ l .  Λ P . λ c . λ n . c e l (l · P c n),
     Nil = Λ P . λ c . λ n . n .
```

Looking at this definition, we can see that operations on the list datatype will follow a specific pattern. Each function will accept arguments for the Cons and Nil cases, and then pass these functions to the list. This encoding inherently captures the foldr form familiar to many functional programmers. If we give a Cedille foldr definition:

```
foldr ⇐ ∀ A : ⋆ . ∀ B : ⋆ .
          (A → (List · A) → B → B) → B → List · A → B =
Λ A . Λ B . λ f . λ b . λ l . θ l f b .
```

We can see that the list encoding does the work of foldr here. Below is an example of how similar the foldr and non-foldr definitions are, using the example of reversing the elements of a list:

```
singleton ⇐ ∀ A : ⋆ . A → List · A =
  Λ A . λ a . (Cons · A) a (Nil · A) .

reverseCons ⇐ ∀ A : ⋆ .
                A → (List · A) → (List · A) → (List · A) =
  Λ A . λ h . λ t . λ r . (append · A) r (singleton · A h) .

reverse ⇐ ∀ A : ⋆ . (List · A) → (List · A) =
  Λ A . λ l . θ l (reverseCons · A) (Nil · A) .

reverse2 ⇐ ∀ A : ⋆ . (List · A) → (List · A) =
  Λ A . (foldr · A · (List · A)) (reverseCons · A) (Nil · A) .
```

Typically in functional programming fold allows for smaller definitions, but the need to pass types to our polymorphic definition gives the non-foldr version a slight edge in conciseness.

For an example theorem, let us prove that the inverse of the reverse function is itself. This requires a lemma, reverse-last, but the proof of these two properties is only marginally longer than the statement of the properties themselves.

```
reverse-last ⇐
  ∀ A : ⋆ . Π l : List · A . Π a : A .
    reverse (append l (Cons a Nil)) ≃ Cons a (reverse l) =
  Λ A . λ l . λ a . θ l
    (λ h . λ t . λ ih . εl ρ ih - β)
    β .


reverse-involution ⇐
  ∀ A : ⋆ . Π l : List · A . reverse (reverse l) ≃ l =
  Λ A . λ l . θ l
    (λ h . λ t . λ ih .
       εl ρ (reverse-last · A (reverse · A t) h) - ρ ih - β)
    β .
```

The reverse-involution definition is our focus here, and we can break down this definition into two main pieces: our statement to prove and then the proof of these statements. Looking at the first and second lines of the definition, we see that it is stating that for any type, A, and for any list, l, the reverse of the reverse of a list is beta-equivalent to that list. On the third line we need parameters for the type and the list, and finally the θ l computes the predicate with which to instantiate the parameter l (as explained in Sect. 2 above).

Next, we have the proofs for both the Cons and Nil instances of a list. The equational steps in these two proofs are as follows:

Cons case:
$$\text{Cons h t} = \text{reverse (reverse (Cons h t))}$$
$$=_{\beta} \text{reverse (append (reverse t) (Cons h Nil))}$$
$$=_{\rho \text{ reverse-last}} \text{Cons h (reverse (reverse t))}$$
$$=_{\rho \text{ IH}} \text{Cons h t}$$

Nil case:
$$\text{Nil} = \text{reverse (reverse Nil)}$$
$$=_{\beta} \text{Nil}$$

This reasoning is mirrored in the Cedille code. The εl is used to beta-reduce the reverse side of the equation. Then we use our ρ construct to rewrite our equation using the reverse-last lemma, and again to rewrite the equation using our induction hypothesis. Our β construct then finalizes the Cons case and is the entire proof for the Nil case, stating that both sides of the equation are beta-equivalent.

9 Proving the Transitivity of the Comparison Operator

In this section we will define a comparison operator on Nats and prove that it is transitive. This operator returns an element of the following type:

```
rec compare-t | LT : compare-t , EQ : compare-t , GT : compare-t =
  ∀ P : compare-t → ⋆ .
    P LT → P EQ → P GT → P self
  with
    LT = Λ P . λ a . λ b . λ c . a ,
    EQ = Λ P . λ a . λ b . λ c . b ,
    GT = Λ P . λ a . λ b . λ c . c .
```

Note the similarity to Church-encoded booleans; compare-t is a type which may have one of three values, and one of three distinct expressions will be evaluated depending on which of the three values is found. The definition of the compare function is then:

```
compare ⇐ Nat → Nat → compare-t =
  λ n . θ n
    (λ pn . λ hn . λ m . θ m (λ pm . λ _ . hn pm) GT)
    (λ m . θ m (λ _ . λ _ . LT) EQ) .
```

This function splits on the first input (n). If it is a successor, then compare checks the second input, and returns either compare pn pm (if that is a successor too) or GT (if it is zero). Otherwise, if n ≃ Z, compare checks the second input and returns either LT (if it is a successor) or EQ (if it is zero).

Suppose we want to prove a statement about compare. For instance, we might want to prove that compare is transitive. This proof can also be written through case splitting:

```
compare-trans ⇐
    Π x : Nat . Π y : Nat . Π z : Nat . Π o : compare-t .
    ( compare x y ≃ o ) → ( compare y z ≃ o ) →
    ( compare x z ≃ o ) =
  λ x . θ x
    ( λ px . λ hx . λ y . θ y
      ( λ py . λ _ . λ z . θ z
        ( λ pz . λ _ . λ o . λ pf-xy . λ pf-yz .
          ρ ( hx py pz o pf-xy pf-yz ) - β )
        ( λ _ . λ _ . λ pf-yz . ρ ( ς pf-yz ) - β ) )
      ( λ z . θ z
        ( λ _ . λ _ . λ _ . λ pf-xy . λ pf-yz .
          δ ( ρ ( ς pf-xy ) - pf-yz ) )
        ( λ _ . λ pf-xy . λ pf-yz .
          δ ( ρ ( ς pf-xy ) - pf-yz ) ) ) )
    ( λ y . θ y
      ( λ _ . λ _ . λ z . θ z
        ( λ _ . λ _ . λ _ . λ pf-xy . λ _ .
          ρ ( ς pf-xy ) - β )
        ( λ _ . λ pf-xy . λ pf-yz .
          δ ( ρ ( ς pf-xy ) - pf-yz ) ) ) )
```

```
( λ z . θ z
  ( λ _ . λ _ . λ _ . λ pf-xy . λ pf-yz .
      δ ( ρ ( ς pf-xy ) - pf-yz ) )
  ( λ _ . λ pf-xy . λ _ . pf-xy ) ) ) .
```

In this proof, there are four inputs: x, y, z, and a comparison type o. The type of the proof also provides the assumptions that compare x y ≃ o (labeled pf-xy), and compare y z ≃ o (labeled pf-yz). The body of the proof simply splits on each of the x, y, z variables in order for a total of 8 cases. Some of these cases follow trivially from the input proofs. For example, in the case where x, y, and z are all zero (the last line of the proof), we have the proof pf-xy = compare Z Z ≃ o (where the two zeros are x and y) and we are required to prove that pf-xy = compare Z Z ≃ o (where the two zeros are x and z). So we can simply regurgitate the input proof to solve the case.

Other cases may be proven by contradiction using δ. For example, suppose x and y are zero, but z is a successor (the penultimate line of the proof). In this case, we are given proofs that

```
compare Z Z ≃ o
compare Z (S pz) ≃ o
```

and are asked to prove that compare Z (S pz) ≃ o. If we substitute the former into the latter, we end up with a proof of compare Z (S pz) ≃ compare Z Z. However, we also know by the definition of compare that compare Z Z ≃ EQ and compare Z (S pz) ≃ LT. Thus, we use δ along with this contradiction to prove anything we want (in this case, that compare Z (S pz) ≃ o).

The most complicated case is when all three Nats are successors. In this case, we call the inductive hypothesis

```
hx py pz o ⇐
   compare px py ≃ o → compare py pz ≃ o → compare px pz ≃ o
```

with the proofs

```
compare (S px) (S py) ≃ o
compare (S py) (S pz) ≃ o
```

Of course, as we know from the definition of compare, when both inputs are successors compare (S a) (S b) will return compare a b, so these input proofs satisfy the type requirements and thus our inductive hypothesis duly produces a proof of compare px pz ≃ o.

10   Reasoning About Higher-Order Datatypes

Lambda terms can themselves be encoded as lambda terms. One of the simplest ways to accomplish this is using the Church-term (or ctrm) encoding scheme. A ctrm is a lambda term of type

```
ctrm ⇐ ⋆ = ∀ X : ⋆ .
  (X → X → X) → ((X → X) → X) → X .
```

where the first argument determines what happens when one ctrm is applied
to another (App) and the second argument determines what happens when a
symbol is bound to a lambda (Lam). Together, they allow for operations that
depend on the structure of the term itself. To encode a term as a ctrm, we
simply replace each occurrence of an application or lambda binding with the
appropriate function. For example, to encode

$$\lambda \ x \ . \ \lambda \ y \ . \ x \ y$$

we would write

```
example ⇐ ctrm =
  Λ X . λ A . λ L . L ( λ x . L ( λ y . A x y ) ) .
```

Now suppose we want to measure the size of a term, defined by the number of
nodes in its abstract syntax tree. Then we must encode two pieces of information:

1. The size of an application node is 1 plus the sum of the sizes of its child
   nodes.
2. The size of a lambda node is 2 (one for the lambda binder itself, and one for
   the binding occurrence of the variable) plus the size of the bound term, where
   each occurence of the bound symbol has a size of 1.

We can write a size function using this idea:

```
size-app = λ s1 : Nat . λ s2 : Nat . S (add s1 s2) .
size-lam = λ f : Nat → Nat . S ( S ( f (S Z) ) ) .
size = λ t : ctrm . t · Nat size-app size-lam .
```

Applying size to the above example term and β-reducing, we indeed get the
expected value (7).

   Unlike previous examples, ctrm is not declared using a rec-statement, so
there is no way to prove statements inductively about ctrms. However, some
equational reasoning about ctrms is still possible. For example, suppose we want
to prove that the ctrm representations of boolean true and false (tt and ff) are
not equal. We can write:

```
% tt = λ x . λ y . x
ctt ⇐ ctrm = Λ X . λ A . λ L . L (λ x . L (λ y . x)) .

% ff = λ x . λ y . y
cff ⇐ ctrm = Λ X . λ A . λ L . L (λ x . L (λ y . y)) .

ctt-cff-neq ⇐ (ctt ≃ cff) → False = λ pf . δ (π0 (π0 pf)) .
```

Here, we use π0 twice to strip away the lambdas inside the term, leaving us with

$$\lambda \ a \ . \ \lambda \ 1 \ . \ \lambda \ x \ . \ \lambda \ y \ . \ x \simeq \lambda \ a \ . \ \lambda \ 1 \ . \ \lambda \ x \ . \ \lambda \ y \ . \ y$$

At this point, Cedille is able to recognize a contradiction, allowing us to derive False using a δ.

11   Conclusion and Future Work

This report has introduced the Cedille project, which is seeking to develop a new proof assistant and dependently typed programming language, based on lambda encodings. We have seen proofs of standard theorems, carried out here with lambda encodings instead of primitive datatypes. For future work, we intend to explore much further the power of higher-order lambda encodings for datatypes that cannot be defined in traditional type theories with primitive inductive types. Examples are datatypes for representing expressions with locally scoped names, such as object-language syntax, typing derivations, and similar structures. We have preliminary results on devising extended versions of the ctrm datatype above, using rec-defined types, to support inductive reasoning with higher-order encodings. We intend to develop this preliminary work, to take advantage of the latent higher-order power of lambda encodings. We are also working on extending these methods to other classes of datatypes including coinductive and inductive-recursive. Further future work includes continuing development of the frontend and backend tools, based on the architectural decision to export all typing information from the backend to the frontend. There are some operations, like indexing into a library, that need more back-and-forth interaction because the amount of possible information to send is too great. We intend to extend the communication protocol between frontend and backend to account for these. An important development since the work described in this paper is the derivation of induction without using rec, but just dependent intersections, implicit products, and equality types alone [22]. A public release of Cedille remains a little ways off, as we make what will hopefully be the final improvements to the core type theory. Furthermore, developing the tools and library to compete with well-established theorem provers like Coq and Agda will take time.

Acknowledgments. Thanks to the anonymous TFP 2016 pre-proceedings reviewer for helpful comments which helped improve the paper. This work has been supported by NSF on a grant titled "Lambda Encodings Reborn" (award 1524519), and through the DoD MURI project "Semantics, Formal Reasoning, and Tools for Quantum Programming" (award FA9550-16-1-0082). Thanks also to Matthew Heimerdinger and Richard Blair who made contributions to the tool summer 2016.

References

1. Basold, H., Geuvers, H.: Type theory based on dependent inductive and coinductive types. In: Shankar, N. (ed.) IEEE Symposium on Logic in Computer Science (LICS) (2016)
2. Bezem, M., Coquand, T., Huber, S.: A model of type theory in cubical sets. In: Matthes, R., Schubert, A. (eds.) 19th International Conference on Types for Proofs and Programs, TYPES 2013 of LIPIcs, vol. 26, pp. 107–128. Schloss Dagstuhl - Leibniz-Zentrum fuer Informatik (2014)
3. Böhm, C., Berarducci, A.: Automatic synthesis of typed lambda-programs on term algebras. Theor. Comput. Sci. **39**, 135–154 (1985)
4. Church, A.: The Calculi of Lambda Conversion. Princeton University Press, Princeton (1941). Ann. Math. Stud. (6)
5. Coquand, T., Huet, G.: The calculus of constructions. Inf. Comput. **76**(2–3), 95–120 (1988)
6. Coquand, T., Paulin, C.: Inductively defined types. In: Martin-Löf, P., Mints, G. (eds.) COLOG 1988. LNCS, vol. 417, pp. 50–66. Springer, Heidelberg (1990). https://doi.org/10.1007/3-540-52335-9_47
7. The Agda Development Team: Agda, Version 2.5.1 (2016)
8. Fortune, S., Leivant, D., O'Donnell, M.: The expressiveness of simple and second-order type structures. J. ACM **30**(1), 151–185 (1983)
9. Geuvers, H.: Induction is not derivable in second order dependent type theory. In: Abramsky, S. (ed.) TLCA 2001. LNCS, vol. 2044, pp. 166–181. Springer, Heidelberg (2001). https://doi.org/10.1007/3-540-45413-6_16
10. Hofmann, M., Streicher, T.: The groupoid interpretation of type theory. In: Twenty-Five Years of Constructive Type Theory of Oxford Logic Guides, vol. 36, pp. 83–111. Oxford University Press, Oxford (1998)
11. Koopman, P., Plasmeijer, R., Jansen, J.M.: Church encoding of data types considered harmful for implementations. In: Plasmeijer, R., Tobin-Hochstadt, S. (eds.) 26th Symposium on Implementation and Application of Functional Languages (IFL) (2014). Presented version
12. Kopylov, A.: Dependent intersection: a new way of defining records in type theory. In: 18th IEEE Symposium on Logic in Computer Science (LICS), pp. 86–95 (2003)
13. Leivant, D.: Finitely stratified polymorphism. Inf. Comput. **93**(1), 93–113 (1991)
14. Luo, Z.: An extended calculus of constructions. Ph.D. thesis (1990)
15. The Coq Development Team: The Coq Proof Assistant Reference Manual. LogiCal Project, Version 8.5 (2016)
16. McAllester, D.A.: Implementation and abstraction in mathematics. CoRR, abs/1407.7274 (2014)
17. McBride, C.: Elimination with a motive. In: Callaghan, P., Luo, Z., McKinna, J., Pollack, R., Pollack, R. (eds.) TYPES 2000. LNCS, vol. 2277, pp. 197–216. Springer, Heidelberg (2002). https://doi.org/10.1007/3-540-45842-5_13
18. Miquel, A.: The implicit calculus of constructions extending pure type systems with an intersection type binder and subtyping. In: Abramsky, S. (ed.) TLCA 2001. LNCS, vol. 2044, pp. 344–359. Springer, Heidelberg (2001). https://doi.org/10.1007/3-540-45413-6_27
19. Parigot, M.: Programming with proofs: a second order type theory. In: Ganzinger, H. (ed.) ESOP 1988. LNCS, vol. 300, pp. 145–159. Springer, Heidelberg (1988). https://doi.org/10.1007/3-540-19027-9_10

20. Parigot, M.: On the representation of data in lambda-calculus. In: Börger, E., Büning, H.K., Richter, M.M. (eds.) CSL 1989. LNCS, vol. 440, pp. 309–321. Springer, Heidelberg (1990). https://doi.org/10.1007/3-540-52753-2_47
21. Pierce, B.C., Turner, D.N.: Local type inference. ACM Trans. Program. Lang. Syst. **22**(1), 1–44 (2000)
22. Stump, A.: From realizability to induction via dependent intersection. Available from the author's web page, under review as of 19 June 2017
23. Stump, A.: The calculus of dependent lambda eliminations. J. Funct. Program. **27**, e14 (2017)
24. Stump, A., Fu, P.: Efficiency of lambda-encodings in total type theory. J. Funct. Program. **26**, e3 (31 p.) (2016)
25. The Univalent Foundations Program: Homotopy Type Theory: Univalent Foundations of Mathematics, Institute for Advanced Study (2013). https://homotopytypetheory.org/book
26. Washburn, G., Weirich, S.: Boxes go bananas: encoding higher-order abstract syntax with parametric polymorphism. J. Funct. Program. **18**(1), 87–140 (2008)
27. Werner, B.: Une Théorie des constructions inductives. Ph.D. thesis, Paris Diderot University, France (1994)

Threading the Arduino with Haskell

Mark Grebe[2](✉) and Andy Gill[1]

[1] Information and Telecommunication Technology Center,
The University of Kansas, Lawrence, KS, USA
andy.gill@ittc.ku.edu
[2] University of Central Missouri, Warrensburg, MO, USA
grebe@ucmo.edu

Abstract. Programming embedded microcontrollers often requires the
scheduling of independent threads of execution, specifying the interaction and sequencing of actions in the multiple threads. Developing
and debugging such multi-threaded systems can be especially challenging in highly resource constrained systems such as the Arduino line of
microcontroller boards. The Haskino library, developed at the University of Kansas, allows programmers to develop code for Arduino-based
microcontrollers using monadic Haskell program fragments. This paper
describes our efforts to extend the Haskino library to translate monadic
Haskell code to multi-threaded code executing on Arduino boards.

Keywords: Haskell · Arduino · Remote monad · Embedded systems ·
Scheduling

1 Introduction

The Haskino library was written to advance the use of Haskell to program systems based on the Arduino line of micocontrollers. Software written for embedded microcontrollers routinely requires multiple threads of execution to efficiently and easily meet its requirements. The previous version of Haskino [1]
supported only single threaded, run to completion style programming. We have
since extended Haskino to support multi-threaded, concurrent operation.

In this paper, we discuss the following.

- We describe enhancements to the Haskino DSL and expression language,
  which allow for control of a wider variety of Arduino interfaces, such as I^2C
  and character output devices.
- We discuss how the Haskino interpreter has been enhanced with the ability to
  write multi-threaded programs which are cooperatively scheduled, and allow
  inter-thread communication.
- We describe the new Haskino code generator, which allows programmers to
  write native Haskell, yet have that Haskell compiled to a Arduino binary for
  execution on the Arduino.
- We explain the additions that have been made to Haskino to support quick
  prototyping and easy debugging of multi-threaded programs.
- We then instantiate these ideas into a number of concrete examples.

© Springer Nature Switzerland AG 2019
D. Van Horn and J. Hughes (Eds.): TFP 2016, LNCS 10447, pp. 135–154, 2019.
https://doi.org/10.1007/978-3-030-14805-8_8

1.1 Background

The Haskino library has its roots in the hArduino package [2], written by Levent Erkök, which allows programmers to control Arduino boards through a serial connection. In hArduino, the serial protocol used between the host computer and the Arduino, and the firmware which runs on the Arduino, are together known as Firmata [3].

The evolution of Arduino and Haskell libraries is presented in Table 1. The previous version of Haskino extended hArduino by applying the concepts of the strong remote monad design pattern [4] to provide a more efficient way of communicating and generalized the controls over the remote execution. In addition, it added a deep embedding, control structures, an expression language, and a redesigned firmware interpreter to enable standalone software for the Arduino to be developed using Haskell. Although neither version of the Haskino byte code language executed by the interpreter on the Arduino yet contains support for lambdas, functions may be written in the Haskell host code.

The remote monad design pattern splits primitives to be executed on the remote Arduino into commands and procedures. Commands are primitives that do not return a result, and do not have a temporal consequence, such as executing a delay. Procedures are remote primitives that do return a result, or do have a temporal consequence. The remote monad design pattern then uses bundling strategies to combine the commands and procedures efficiently, as they are sent to the remote Arduino.

The current version of Haskino expands the capabilities of Haskino even further. It moves beyond single threaded operation, adding cooperatively scheduled multi-threaded operation. In addition, programming the Arduino with Haskino is no longer limited to interpreted operation. The current version of Haskino is able to take the same monadic code that may be run with the interpreter, and compile it into C code. That C code may then be compiled and linked with a small runtime, to allow standalone operation of an executable with a smaller size than the interpreted code.

Table 1. Haskell and Arduino evolution

	hArduino	Previous Haskino	Current Haskino
Remote monad type	Weak	Strong	Strong
DSL embedding	Shallow	Shallow/deep	Shallow/deep
Firmware/protocol	Firmata	Haskino interpreter	Haskino interpreter/runtime
Interpreted/compiled	Interpreted	Interpreted	Interpreted/compiled
Threading	Single threaded	Single threaded	Multi-threaded

1.2   Arduino Remote Monad

The current version of Haskino uses the remote-monad library developed at the University of Kansas [5] to define the Haskino remote monad. The Arduino type is defined as follows:

```
newtype Arduino a =
    Arduino (RemoteMonad ArduinoCommand ArduinoProcedure a)
  deriving (Functor, Applicative, Monad)
```

The data types for commands and procedures in Haskino are defined as GADTs. ArduinoCommand and ArduinoProcedure data types are shown below, with a subset of their actual constructors as examples.

```
data ArduinoCommand =
    SetPinModeE (Expr Word8) (Expr Word8)
    | DigitalWriteE (Expr Word8) (Expr Bool)
    | AnalogWriteE (Expr Word8) (Expr Word16)

data ArduinoProcedure :: * -> * where
    MillisE       :: ArduinoProcedure (Expr Word32)
    DelayMillisE  :: Expr Word32 -> ArduinoProcedure ()
    DelayMicrosE  :: Expr Word32 -> ArduinoProcedure ()
    DigitalReadE  :: Expr Word8 -> ArduinoProcedure (Expr Bool)
    AnalogReadE   :: Expr Word8 -> ArduinoProcedure (Expr Word16)
```

API functions which are exposed to the programmer are defined in terms of these constructors, as shown for the example of digitalWriteE below:

```
digitalWriteE :: Expr Word8 -> Expr Bool -> Arduino ()
digitalWriteE p b = Arduino $ command $ DigitalWriteE p b
```

The function used to run a remote monad is called **send** by convention, and Haskino makes use of the remote-monad libraries functions to implement its send function. The **send** function transforms the Arduino remote monad into a byte stream which will be sent to the remote Arduino board. **send** takes as a parameter an ArduinoConnection data structure, which specifies the Arduino to send the remote monad. The ArduinoConnection data structure is returned by the **openArduino** function, which takes a boolen to indicate if debugging should be enabled, and the path the serial port where the Arduino board is connected.

```
openArduino :: Bool -> FilePath -> IO ArduinoConnection

send :: ArduinoConnection -> Arduino a -> IO a
send c (Arduino m) = (run $ runMonad $ nat (runAP c)) m
```

1.3   Haskino Expression Language

The previous deep embedding of the Haskino DSL and interpreter provided the capability to handle typed expressions of boolean and unsigned integers of length 8, 16 and 32 bits. This covered the types used by the basic digital and analog input and output functions in the Arduino API. The Data.Boolean [6] package was used so that operators used in expressions may be written in same manner that operations on similar data types are written in native Haskell. The exception is for operations on booleans, in which case the operators have an appended asterisk, such as >* for greater than.

However, to extend the DSL for more complex libraries such as the stepper motor, servo motor, and I^2C libraries, the handling of signed types, floating points, and lists of unsigned 8 bit words has been added to the Haskino DSL expression language. In addition to adding float data types and their basic operations, the expression language was also expanded to include most of the standard math library primitives, including trigonometric functions. Primitives to convert between numeric data types, including toInteger, fromInteger, trunc, round, frac, ceil, and floor have also been added.

Handling reads and writes from I^2C devices, as well as displaying text on LCD and other displays, requires the ability to handle a type for a collection of bytes. As Haskino is a Haskell DSL, the intuitive choice for the collection is a list of Word8. In the new version, Haskino's expression language has been enhanced with primitives for cons, append, length, and element operations on expressions of [Word8]. In addition, show primitives have been added to convert other types into lists of Word8.

2   Haskino Threads

The previous version of Haskino inherited it's concept of threads from Firmata tasks. Tasks in Firmata are sequences of commands which can be executed at a future time. However, as they have no way to store results from one procedure for use in another command or procedure, the usefulness of these tasks is severely limited.

The initial version of Haskino extended the ability of tasks, allocating remote binds to store the results of a procedure and use the result in a subsequent command or procedure. It was, however, still limited to running a single task to completion.

We have subsequently extended Haskino to allow it to handle multiple threads of execution, with communication between the threads, and cooperative multitasking.

As an example of multiple threads running in a Haskino program, we present the following program.

```
blinkDelay :: Expr Word32
blinkDelay = 125
```

```
taskDelay :: Expr Word32
taskDelay = 2000

semId :: Expr Word8
semId = 0

myTask1 :: Expr Word8 -> Arduino ()
myTask1 led = do
    setPinModeE led OUTPUT
    i <- newRemoteRef $ lit (0 :: Word8)
    loopE $ do
        takeSemE semId
        writeRemoteRef i 0
        while i (\x -> x <* 3) (\x -> x + 1) $ do
            digitalWriteE led true
            delayMillisE blinkDelay
            digitalWriteE led false
            delayMillisE blinkDelay

myTask2 :: Arduino ()
myTask2 = do
    loopCount <- newRemoteRef $ lit (0 :: Word8)
    loopE $ do
        giveSemE semId
        t <- readRemoteRef loopCount
        writeRemoteRef loopCount $ t+1
        debugE $ showE t
        delayMillisE taskDelay

initExample :: Arduino ()
initExample = do
    let led = 13
    createTaskE 1 $ myTask1 led
    createTaskE 2 myTask2
    scheduleTaskE 1 1000
    scheduleTaskE 2 1050

semExample :: IO ()
semExample = withArduino True "/dev/cu.usbmodem1421" $ do
    initExample
```

This example creates two tasks. The first task, **myTask1**, sets the mode of the LED pin to output, then goes into an infinite loop. Inside the loop, it takes a semaphore, and when the semaphore is available it blinks the LED rapidly three times. The second task, **myTask2**, executes an infinite loop where it gives the semaphore, then delays for two seconds. The main function, **semExample**, creates the two tasks and schedules them to execute, using the Arduino connected to the specified serial port.

3   Scheduling the Interpreter

The Haskino firmware interpreter runs byte code on the Arduino, the byte code having been generated on the host and transmitted to Arduino using the remote monad function send. To enable scheduling in Haskino, the Haskino firmware interpreter required modification to allow another task to run when the currently executing task was suspended due to a delay or a wait on a resource. The scheduler in the Firmata firmware only ran tasks to completion, so no interruption and resumption of tasks was allowed. The scheduler in the initial version of the Haskino interpreter was modeled after that scheduler, and therefore was limited to run to completion tasks as well.

Haskino defines four conditional structures, an If-Then-Else structure, a While structure, an infinite LoopE structure, and a ForIn structure (which allows a computation to be mapped over a list of 8 bit words). Each of these structures contains the concept of execution of basic code blocks within the interpreter.

To allow the scheduler to interrupt execution of a basic block in a task, and then later restore execution when the task resumes, a method for saving and restoring the execution state of the task is required. In an operating system, this is normally done by saving and restoring the processor's registers, as well as giving each thread its own stack. In the Haskino interpreter, each task has it's own context, which provides the storage for the bound variables. This corresponds to the separate stack for each thread in a traditional operating system.

In addition, the interpreter must also store information in the context which indicates where in the basic block execution of the task was interrupted, such that it may be restored when the task resumes. For all of the control structures containing basic blocks, the location (in bytes from the start of the block) of the command or procedure that was executing when the interruption occurred is stored. For the simplest of the control structures, ForE and While, this is all that is required. The other two control structures require an additional piece of information to be stored. The If-Then-Else structure requires storing which branch code block was being executed, either the Then branch or the Else branch. The ForIn structure requires storing an index indicating which element of the list the code block was being executed for.

As the Haskino control structures may be nested, the scheduler is required to keep track of not just the state of execution in one basic block, but instead must track the state of execution in a stack of basic blocks leading up to the point that code execution was suspended. When the task is later resumed, the interpreter must walk that stack in reverse order, restoring the state of the task for each of the other nested basic blocks.

Currently, there are two procedures which cause the Haskino scheduler to interrupt the execution of a task, and potentially start execution of another. The first of these procedures is the delayMillisE command, which will delay a task for specified number of milliseconds. When the procedure is executed, the state of current task is saved, and the time when the task should resume execution is stored in the task's context. The scheduler then checks if another task is ready to run, based on its next execution time having passed, or a resource it was waiting on having become available. If a ready to run task is found, it's state of execution is restored by the method previously discussed, and it's execution is resumed. A second delay procedure, `delayMicrosE`, exists for those cases where the programmer wishes a task to have a short delay without the possibility of being interrupted. The other procedure which can cause a reschedule is taking a semaphore, which is described in the following section.

4   Inter-thread Communication

Running multiple threads of computation is of limited use if the threads do not have a method of communicating with each other. To enable communication and synchronization between tasks, Haskino provides several methods. First, the RemoteReference class provides atomic storage methods that can be used to pass data between Haskino tasks. RemoteReference's provide an API analogous to the Haskell IORef, allowing a remote reference to be read, written, or modified.

Haskino also provides binary semaphores for synchronization between Haskino tasks. A binary semaphore may be given by one task by issuing the `giveSem` procedure, while the task that wants to synchronize with the first task can do so by issuing the `takeSem` procedure. When a task issues a `takeSem` procedure, and the binary semaphore that it refers to is not available, the task will be suspended. When another task later makes the semaphore available through a `giveSem` procedure, the scheduler will then make the task taking the semaphore ready to run. If the binary semaphore is available when `takeSem` is called, the semaphore is made unavailable. However, the task is not suspended in this case, but continues operation. In addition, if a task is already waiting on an unavailable semaphore when another task calls `giveSem`, the semaphore is left unavailable, but the task waiting on it is made ready to run.

The inclusion of binary semaphores also enables Haskino to handle another important aspect of programming embedded systems, the processing of interrupts. In addition to handling multiple tasks, the Arduino monadic structures may also be attached to handle external Arudino interrupts. For example, the following example uses a simple interrupt handler which gives a semaphore to communicate with a task. It is similar to our earlier two task example, but in this case, the interrupt handling task is attached to the interrupt using the `attachIntE` command, which specifies the pin of the interrupt to attach to.

```
blinkDelay :: Expr Word32
blinkDelay = 125

semId :: Expr Word8
semId = 0
```

```
myTask :: Expr Word8 -> Arduino ()
myTask led =
    loopE $ do
        takeSemE semId
        digitalWriteE led true
        delayMillisE blinkDelay
        digitalWriteE led false
        delayMillisE blinkDelay

intTask :: Arduino ()
intTask = giveSemE semId

initIntExample :: Arduino ()
initIntExample = do
    let led = 13
    setPinModeE led OUTPUT
    let button = 2
    setPinModeE button INPUT
    let myTaskId = 1
    let intTaskId = 2
    createTaskE myTaskId (myTask led)
    createTaskE intTaskId intTask
    scheduleTaskE myTaskId 50
    attachIntE button intTaskId FALLING

intExample :: IO ()
intExample = withArduino True "/dev/cu.usbmodem1421" $ do
    initIntExample
```

5   Code Generation

The interpreted version of the Haskino DSL provides a quick turnaround Arduino development environment, including features for easy debugging. However, it has one major disadvantage. The interpreter takes up a large percentage of the flash program storage space on the smaller capability Arduino boards such as the Uno. The only other resource on such boards for storing interpreted programs to be executed when the Arduino is not tethered to a host computer is EEPROM, which is what the current interpreter uses. However, this resource is also relatively small (1K byte) on these boards. These storage limitations directly limit the complexity of programs which can be developed using the interpreted version of Haskino when not connected to a host computer.

To overcome these limitations, we have developed a compiler that translates the same Haskell DSL source code used to drive the interpreter, into C code. The C code may then be compiled and linked with a C based runtime which is much smaller than the interpreter. The compiler takes as input the same Arduino monad that is used as input to the `withArduino` function to run the interpreter, and the file to write the C code to.

```
compileProgram :: Arduino () -> FilePath -> IO ()
```

5.1 Compiler Structure

The compiler processes the monadic code in a similar fashion to the way that the remote monad send function does for the interpreted version. Instead of reifying the GADT structures which represent the user programs into Haskino interpreter byte code, the compiler instead generates C code.

Each task in the program, including the initial task which consists of the code in the top level monadic structure, is compiled to C code using the `compileTask` function. The `compileTask` function makes use of the compiler's core function, `compileCodeBlock`, to recursively compile the program. The top level code block for the task, may contain sub-blocks for While, IfThenElse, LoopE, and ForIn control structures present in the top level block. A State monad is used by the compiler to track generated task code, tasks which are yet to be compiled as they are discovered in compilation of other task blocks, and statistics such as the number of binds per task, which are used for storage allocation as described in Sect. 5.4.

```
data CompileState = CompileState {
                    level :: Int
                  , intTask :: Bool
                  , ix :: Int
                  , ib :: Int
                  , cmds :: String
                  , binds :: String
                  , refs :: String
                  , forwards :: String
                  , cmdList :: [String]
                  , bindList :: [String]
                  , tasksToDo :: [(Arduino (), String, Bool)]
                  , tasksDone :: [String]
                  , errors :: [String] }

compileTask :: Arduino () -> String -> Bool -> State CompileState ()

compileCodeBlock :: Arduino a -> State CompileState a
```

Expressions and control structures are compiled into their C equivalents, with calls to Haskino runtime functions for expression operators that are not present in the standard Arduino runtime library. ArduinoCommand's and ArduinoProcedure's are likewise translated into calls to either the Arduino standard library, or to the Haskino runtime.

In the following sections, we will explain the C code which is generated by executing the `compileProgram` function on the initExample monad from the semaphore example in Sect. 2.

5.2   Initialization Code Generation

Arduino programs consist of two main functions, `setup()`, which performs the required application initialization, and `loop()`, which is called continuously in a loop for the main application. For Haskino applications, any looping is handled inside of the monadic Haskino code, and the compiled code uses only the `setup()` function. The `loop()` function is left empty, and is only provided to satisfy the link requirement of the Arduino library. The code generated for Haskino initialization for this semaphore example follows:

```
void setup() {
    haskinoMemInit();
    createTask(255, haskinoMainTcb, HASKINOMAIN_STACK_SIZE,
            haskinoMain);
    scheduleTask(255, 0);
    startScheduler();
    }

void loop() {
    }

void haskinoMain() {
    createTask(1, task1Tcb, TASK1_STACK_SIZE, task1);
    createTask(2, task2Tcb, TASK2_STACK_SIZE, task2);
    scheduleTask(1,1000);
    scheduleTask(2,1050);
    taskComplete();
    }
```

The `setup()` function serves three purposes. First, it initializes the memory management of the Haskino runtime, which is described in Sect. 5.6. Second, it creates the initial root task of the application. The compiler generates the code associated with the main monadic function passed to compileMonad as the C function `haskinoMain()`. The `steup()` function creates the initial task by calling `createTask()`, passing a pointer `haskinoMain()`, and schedules the task to start immediately by calling `scheduleTask()`. Finally, the runtime scheduler, described in Sect. 5.5, is started by calling the `startScheduler()` function.

5.3   Task Code Generation

The monadic code passed in each `createTaskE` call in the Haskell code is compiled into a C function, named `taskX()`, where X is the task ID number which is also passed to `createTaskE` (not the name of the monadic function). As an example, the code for the first task from the semaphore example is shown below:

```
void task1() {
    pinMode(13,1);
    ref1 = 0;
    while (1) {
        takeSem(0);
        ref1 = 0;
        for (;(ref1 < 3);ref1 = (ref1 + 1)) {
            digitalWrite(13,1);
            delayMilliseconds(125);
            digitalWrite(13,0);
            delayMilliseconds(125);
            }
    }
    taskComplete();
    }
```

5.4   Storage Allocations

Three types of storage are allocated by the compiler. RemoteReference's are compiled into global C variables, named refX, where X is the id of the remote reference. In the example, two Word8 remote references are used, and compilation of their newRemoteRef calls cause the following global allocations in the generated code (prior to any task functions):

```
uint8_t ref0;
uint8_t ref1;
```

Binds in the Haskino DSL are compiled into local variables, and are therefore allocated on the stack. The number of binds for each code block is tracked by the compiler, and the binds are defined local to the code block in which they are used. They are named similar to remote references, with a name of the form bindX, where X is the id number of the bind assigned by the compiler. In the example, there is one Word8 bind in `myTask2`, used inside of the while loop:

```
        t <- readRemoteRef loopCount
```

Its allocation as the local variable bind0 may be seen in the following code:

```
void task2() {
    ref0 = 0;
    while (1) {
        uint8_t bind0;

        giveSem(0);
        bind0 = ref0;
        ref0 = (bind0 + 1);
        debug(showWord8(bind0));
        delayMilliseconds(2000);
        }
    taskComplete();
    }
```

The task2() generated code above also demonstrates the initialization of the RemoteReference ref0 to its initial value, 0, in the first statement of the generated task. The remote reference ref0 is then incremented in each iteration, making use of the bind0 bind variable. This code also demonstrates the use of the debugging features of Haskino (discussed in Sect. 6), by outputting the loop count contained in bind0, with the debug() call.

Like the tasks in the interpreter, each task in the compiled code requires a context to track its state. In the compiled code, this context consists of the C stack, as well as several other state variables, such as the next time the task should run and a flag indicating if the task is blocked. Together, these make up the task control block (TCB) for the task, which is the finally type of storage allocated by the compiler. The compiler allocates space for the task control block statically, sizing the block based on the size of the fixed elements of the block, a default amount of stack space to account for Arduino library usage, and finally stack space for the number of binds used by the task, which the compiler tracks while generating the code. The following shows the generated code used to define the TCB for three tasks from the semaphore example.

```
void haskinoMain();
#define HASKINOMAIN_STACK_SIZE 100
byte haskinoMainTcb[sizeof(TCB) + HASKINOMAIN_STACK_SIZE];
void task2();
#define TASK2_STACK_SIZE 104
byte task2Tcb[sizeof(TCB) + TASK2_STACK_SIZE];
void task1();
#define TASK1_STACK_SIZE 100
byte task1Tcb[sizeof(TCB) + TASK1_STACK_SIZE];
```

The address of the allocated TCB, as well as the size of the allocated stack are passed to the task creation calls, as can be seen from the creation call for task1 shown below:

```
createTask(1, task1Tcb, TASK1_STACK_SIZE, task1);
```

5.5   Scheduling the Generated Code

The small Haskino runtime system used with the generated C code needs to duplicate the scheduling capabilities of the Haskino interpreter, to allow Haskino programs to be move seamlessly between the two environments. These capabilities are provided by a small multitasking kernel that is a core part of the runtime. Like the Haskino interpreter, generated tasks are cooperative, only yielding the processor at delays and semaphore takes.

The scheduling algorithm used is a simple cooperative algorithm. Since the number of tasks expected is relatively small, a separate ready list is not used. Instead, each time the scheduler is run when a task yields the processor, the list of all tasks is scanned starting at the task after the yielding task for a task whose next time to run is less than or equal to the current time, and is not blocked. Starting the list search at the next task after the yielding task ensures that scheduling will occur in a round robin sequence of the ready tasks, even if each tasks yields with a `delayMilliseconds(0)`.

The compiler inserts a `taskComplete()` call at the end of each generated task. If the task ever reaches this call, it will mark the task as blocked so that it will no longer run. As task control blocks are allocated statically, the task control block memory is not freed.

5.6   Dynamic Memory Management

Both the Haskino interpreter, and the compiler require some form of dynamic memory management to handle the Word8 list expressions which are used in the Haskino expression language for strings and byte array data such as I2C input and output (discussed in Sect. 1.3). In both cases the garbage collection scheme is simple, with memory elements being freed when an associated reference count for the element goes to zero. The interpreter uses the standard libc memory routines `malloc()` and `free()`, which allocates space from the heap.

The libc heap allocation scheme was not practical for use with the generated thread code. With the standard Arduino libc memory management, the program's stack grows down from the top of memory, while the heap grows up from the bottom of available memory. The `malloc()` routine includes a test to make sure that the new memory allocation will not cause the heap to grow above the stack pointer. While this will work with the interpreter, the compiler statically allocates the stack for each of the tasks, and the stack pointer for all of the tasks would then be below the heap, causing any memory allocation to fail.

One possible solution to this issue that was considered was to rewrite the Arduino memory management library to remove the heap/stack collision detection, so that it would be usable with multiple stacks. Instead, to improve speed and determinism of the memory allocation and garage collection in the compiled code, a fixed block allocation scheme was instead chosen. Through a library header file, the programmer is able to choose the number of 16, 32, 64, 128 and 256 byte blocks available for allocation. The runtime then keeps a linked list of the free blocks for each block size, and the memory allocator simple returns the head of the free list of the smallest block size larger the the requested size. If no blocks of that size are available, then the next larger free list is tried until a free block is found, or until the allocation fails.

6   Debugging

The previous version of the Haskino DSL provided rudimentary debugging capabilities through a `debug` local which made use of host Haskell show functions:

```
debug :: String -> Arduino ()
```

However, since the debug parameters were evaluated locally on the host, not in the Haskino interpreter, it could not be used for debugging intermediate results within deeply embedded conditionals or loops, or for debugging within tasks. The current version of the Haskino DSL instead includes a `debugE` Procedure whose expression parameters are evaluated on the Arduino:

```
debugE :: Expr [Word8] -> Arduino ()
```

The evaluated expression is returned to the host via the Haskino protocol, and the message displayed on the host console. It can make use of the show primitives added to the expression language to display the values of remote references or remote binds.

An additional procedure was also added to the DSL language, debugListen, which keeps the communication channel open listening for debug messages. This was required as the channel is normally closed after the last command or procedure has been sent. If the last command is a loop or task scheduling, this procedure may be used to ensure that debug messages are received and displayed on the host while the loop or task executes on the Arduino.

One of the key features of Haskino is that the same monadic code may be used for both interpreted and compiled versions. This allows for quick prototyping with the tethered, interpreted version, and then compiling the code for deployment. This duality of environments is supported with the debugging primitives as well. When compiled, the `debugE` procedure will output the evaluated byte list to the serial port, allowing the same debug output displayed by the interpreted version to be used in debugging the compiled version as well.

7   Examples

To better illustrate the utility of the Haskino system with a multithreading program, we present two slightly more complex examples. The first example demonstrates using Haskino to program multiple tasks with asynchronous timing relationships. The second example demonstrates using tasks to simplify a program which would otherwise require hardware status busy waiting.

7.1   Multiple LED Example

In this first example, an Arduino board has multiple LED lights connected to it (in the example code below, three lights), and each of these lights are required to blink at a different, constant rate.

The basic monadic function for blinking a LED is defined as ledTask, which is parameterized over the pin number the LED is connected to, and the amount of time in milliseconds the LED should be on and off for each cycle. This function sets the specified pin to output mode, then enters an infinite loop turning the LED on, delaying the specified time, turning the LED off, and then again delaying the specified time.

```
ledTask :: Expr Word8 -> Expr Word32 -> Arduino ()
ledTask led delay = do
    setPinModeE led OUTPUT
    loopE $ do
        digitalWriteE led true
        delayMillisE delay
        digitalWriteE led false
        delayMillisE delay
```

The main function of the program, initExample, creates three Hakino tasks, each with a different LED pin number, and a different delay rate. The three created tasks are then scheduled to start at a time in the future that is twice their delay time. The task with an ID of 1 will be the first to run, as it is scheduled to start at the nearest time in the future (1000 ms). It will run until it reaches its first call to delayMillisE. At that point, the scheduler will be called. The scheduler will reschedule task 1 to start again in 500ms, and as no other tasks will yet be started at that time, then call the Arduino delay() function with the same time delay. When the delay() function returns, task 1 will be the only task ready to run, so it will run again until it reaches the second delayMillisE call, when the scheduler will be called and will call delay() as before. When delay() returns the second time, both task 1 and task 2 will be ready to run. Since task 1 was the last to run, the scheduler will search the task list starting at the task after task 1, and will find task 2 ready to run, and it will be started. Task 2 will run until it reaches the delay, at which point the scheduler will be called, and it will restart task 1 since it was also ready to run. This process will continue, with each task running (turning it's LED on or off) until it reaches a delay, at which point it will cooperatively give up its control of the processor and allow another task to run.

```
initExample :: Arduino ()
initExample = do
    let led1 = 6
    let led2 = 7
    let led3 = 8
    createTaskE 1 $ ledTask led1  500
```

```
createTaskE 2 $ ledTask led2 1000
createTaskE 3 $ ledTask led3 2000
scheduleTaskE 1 1000
scheduleTaskE 2 2000
scheduleTaskE 3 4000
```

The final two functions in the example, ledExample and compile are used to run the initExample monad with the interpreter and compiler respectively.

```
ledExample :: IO ()
ledExample = withArduino True "/dev/cu.usbmodem1421" $ do
    initExample

compile :: IO ()
compile = compileProgram initExample "multiLED.ino"
```

This example demonstrates the ability to write a program where using multiple threads to implement concurrency greatly simplifies the task. This code could have been written with straight inline code, but would require calculating the interleaving of the delays for the various LED's. However, in that straight line code, it would be more difficult to expand the number of LEDs, or to handle staggered start times. Both of those cases are easily handled by the multithreaded code, and the amount of code is also smaller in the multithreaded case, since the ledTask function is reused.

7.2 LCD Counter Example

In the second example, an Arduino board has an LCD display shield attached, which also has a set of six buttons (up, down, left, right, select, and enter). The buttons are all connected to one pin, and the analog value read from the pin determines which button is pressed. The example will display a signed integer counter value on the LCD display, starting with a counter value of zero. If the user presses the up button, the counter value will be incremented and displayed. Similarly, if the user presses the down button the counter value will be decremented and displayed.

The main function of the program, lcdCounterTaskInit, creates two Haskino tasks, one for reading the button, and another for updating the display. It also creates a remote reference which will be used for communicating the button press value between the tasks.

```
lcdCounterTaskInit :: Arduino ()
lcdCounterTaskInit =  do
    let button = 0
    setPinModeE button INPUT
    taskRef <- newRemoteRef $ lit (0::Word16)
    createTaskE 1 $ mainTask taskRef
    createTaskE 2 $ keyTask taskRef button
```

```
-- Schedule the tasks to start immediately
scheduleTaskE 1 0
scheduleTaskE 2 0
```

The key task waits for a button press, reading the analog value from the button input pin until it is less than 760 (A value greater than 760 indicates that no button is pressed). The value read from the pin, which indicates which button was pressed, is stored in the remote reference used to communicate between tasks. At this point, the semaphore is given by the task. It then waits for the button to be released, and repeats the loop.

```
keyTask :: RemoteRef Word16 -> Expr Word8 -> Arduino ()
keyTask ref button = do
    let readButton :: RemoteRef Word16 -> Arduino ()
        readButton r = do
            val <- analogReadE button
            writeRemoteRef r val
    releaseRef <- newRemoteRef $ lit (0::Word16)
    loopE $ do
        writeRemoteRef ref 760
        -- wait for key press
        while ref (\x -> x >=* 760) id $ do
            readButton ref
            delayMillisE 50
        giveSemE semId
        writeRemoteRef releaseRef 0
        -- wait for key release
        while releaseRef (\x -> x <* 760) id $ do
            readButton releaseRef
            delayMillisE 50
```

The main task sets up the LCD (with the lcdRegiserE call), and creates a remote reference which will track the counter value. It tens turns on the LCD backlight, and writes the initial counter value to the display. It then enters the main loop, waiting for the key task to give the semaphore. When it receives the sempahore, it reads the key value from the remote reference. Based on the value, it either increments the counter, decrements the counter, or does nothing. The counter value is then read from the remote reference and the display is updated with its value.

```
mainTask :: RemoteRef Word16 -> Arduino ()
mainTask ref = do
    lcd <- lcdRegisterE osepp
    let zero :: Expr Int32
        zero = 0
    cref <- newRemoteRef zero
    lcdBacklightOnE lcd
```

```
lcdWriteE lcd $ showE zero
loopE $ do
    takeSemE semId
    key <- readRemoteRef ref
    debugE $ showE key
    ifThenElse (key >=* 30 &&* key <* 150)
        (modifyRemoteRef cref (\x -> x + 1)) (return ())
    ifThenElse (key >=* 150 &&* key <* 360)
        (modifyRemoteRef cref (\x -> x - 1)) (return ())
    count <- readRemoteRef cref
    lcdClearE lcd
    lcdHomeE lcd
    lcdWriteE lcd $ showE count
```

This second example has demonstrated using a remote reference in conjunction with a semaphore to communicate between Haskino tasks.

8   Comparing Interpreted and Compiled Size

We have stated that the Haskino compiler makes more efficient use of the small amount of storage space available on the Arduino Uno boards than does the Haskino intepreter. Table 2 shows the amount of space used by both the Haskino interpreter, and the runtime used by the compiler, without any user program present. Both the raw size, and the percentage of the available resource are shown.

Table 2. Interpreter and runtime storage sizing with no user program

	Haskino interpreter	Haskino runtime
Flash size	31124 bytes	3052 bytes
RAM size	901 bytes	437 bytes
Uno flash usage	95.0%	9.3%
Uno RAM usage	44.0%	21.3%

Table 3 shows the percentage of available Uno Flash and RAM used by the example programs from Sect. 7.1 (Example 1) and Sect. 7.2 (Example 2). The number of buffers available for dynamic memory management in the runtime is user configurable. The unoptimized numbers for the runtime reflect the default allocation, where the optimize reflect values customized for the specific program.

Note that for Example 2, the LCD Counter example, the RAM requirements for the interpreted version of the program exceeds the memory available on a Uno board, due to the size of the generated byte code for the tasks. This program was tested using an Arduino Mega 2560 board which has 8 Kbytes of RAM, as

Table 3. Interpreter and runtime storage sizing for example programs

	Haskino interpreter	Haskino runtime
Example 1 flash usage	95.0%	14.5%
Example 1 unoptimized RAM usage	56.9%	70.8%
Example 1 optimized RAM usage	-	45.0%
Example 2 flash usage	95.0%	30.4%
Example 2 unoptimized RAM usage	151.6%	70.8%
Example 2 optimized RAM usage	-	47.9%

opposed to the Uno's 2 Kbytes. However, the compiled version fits comfortably within the Uno's 32 Kbytes of flash, and 2 Kbytes of RAM.

While the size of the interpreter means that large programs may not be implemented with it in their entirety, it may still be used to prototype and debug smaller portions of more complicated programs. For example, it may be used to prototype code for interfacing to new hardware, where the hardware interface may not be well understood. Once the interface section is prototyped with the interpreter, the entire program may then be developed with the compiler.

9   Related Work

There is other ongoing work on using functional languages to program embedded systems in general, and the Arduino in specific. A shallowly embedded DSL for programming the Arduino in the Clean language, called ArDSL has been developed [7]. Their work does not make use of the remote monad design pattern, and does not provide a tethered, interpreted mode of operation.

The Ivory language [8,9] provides a deeply embedded DSL for use in programming high assurance systems. It also does not make use of the strong remote monad design pattern, and generates C rather than use a remote interpreter. An additional EDSL built on top of Ivory, called Tower [8], provides the ability to define tasking for multithreaded systems. However, it depends on the support of an underlying RTOS, as opposed to the minimal scheduler of Haskino.

The frp-arduino [10] provides a method of programming the Arduino using Haskell, but using a functional reactive programming paradigm, and once again only compiling to C code.

10   Conclusion and Future Work

Many programs for embedded systems are more efficiently implemented with multiple threads of execution. The Haskino interpreter has been updated to allow development of multithreaded software written in Haskell for the Arduino line of embedded development boards. The updated scheduler for the Haskino interpreter provides cooperative scheduling between tasks, as well as intertask communication.

To overcome the limitation on program size due to limited Arduino resources and the size of the Haskino interpreter, a complimentary compiler has been developed that is able to compile the same monadic Haskell code used by the interpreter into C code. The C code only requires a small runtime library, and takes up much less of the limited storage resources, allowing more complicated programs to be developed.

The updated Haskino therefore provides two complimentary ways of developing multithreaded software in Haskell for the Arduino. The scheduling of multiple threads and inter-thread communication is implemented to work the same in both the Haskino interpreter and the Haskino runtime, allowing multi-threaded programs to be tested and debugged using the interpreter, then compiled to an executable binary for stand alone execution and deployment.

In the future, we also plan on investigating using HERMIT [11] to semi-automatically translate from programs written in a more functional style, such as tail recursion instead of loops, to programs written using the deep embedding. This will improve the applicability of the library. We would also like to expand the scheduler in Haskino, adding priorities and preemption to the current cooperative multithreading. Another area of future investigation is the use of asynchronous programming techniques, such as those currently being used by the JavaScript community, with Haskino.

Acknowledgment. This material is based upon work supported by the National Science Foundation under Grant No. 1350901.

References

1. Grebe, M., Gill, A.: Haskino: a remote monad for programming the Arduino. In: Gavanelli, M., Reppy, J. (eds.) PADL 2016. LNCS, vol. 9585, pp. 153–168. Springer, Cham (2016). https://doi.org/10.1007/978-3-319-28228-2_10
2. Erkok, L.: Hackage package hArduino-0.9 (2014)
3. Steiner, H.C.: Firmata: towards making microcontrollers act like extensions of the computer. In: New Interfaces for Musical Expression, pp. 125–130 (2009)
4. Gill, A., et al.: The remote monad design pattern. In: Proceedings of the 8th ACM SIGPLAN Symposium on Haskell, pp. 59–70. ACM (2015)
5. Gill, A., Dawson, J.: Hackage package remote-monad-0.2 (2016)
6. Elliott, C.: Hackage package boolean-0.2.3 (2013)
7. Koopman, P., Plasmeijer, R.: A shallow embedded type safe extendable DSL for the Arduino. In: Serrano, M., Hage, J. (eds.) TFP 2015. LNCS, vol. 9547, pp. 104–123. Springer, Cham (2016). https://doi.org/10.1007/978-3-319-39110-6_6
8. Hickey, P.C., Pike, L., Elliott, T., Bielman, J., Launchbury, J.: Building embedded systems with embedded DSLs. In: Proceedings of the 19th ACM SIGPLAN International Conference on Functional Programming, pp. 3–9. ACM (2014)
9. Elliott, T., et al.: Guilt free ivory. In: Proceedings of the 8th ACM SIGPLAN Symposium on Haskell, pp. 189–200. ACM (2015)
10. Lindberg, R.: Hackage package frp-arduino-0.1.0.3 (2015)
11. Farmer, A., Sculthorpe, N., Gill, A.: Reasoning with the HERMIT: tool support for equational reasoning on GHC core programs. In: Proceedings of the 8th ACM SIGPLAN Symposium on Haskell, pp. 23–34. ACM (2015)

The Random Access Zipper
Simple, Persistent Sequences

Kyle Headley[✉] and Matthew A. Hammer

University of Colorado Boulder, Boulder, USA
{kyle.headley,matthew.hammer}@colorado.edu

Abstract. We introduce the Random Access Zipper (RAZ), a simple, persistent data structure for editable sequences. The RAZ combines the structure of a zipper with that of a tree: like a zipper, edits at the cursor require constant time; by leveraging tree structure, relocating the edit cursor in the sequence requires log time. While existing data structures provide these time bounds, none do so with the same simplicity and brevity of code as the RAZ. The simplicity of the RAZ provides the opportunity for more programmers to extend the structure to their own needs, and we provide some suggestions for how to do so.

1 Introduction

The singly-linked list is the most common representation of sequences for functional programmers. This structure is considered a core primitive in every functional language, and morever, the principles of its simple design recur throughout user-defined structures that are "sequence-like". Though simple and ubiquitous, the functional list has a serious shortcoming: users may only efficiently access and edit the *head* of the list. In particular, random accesses (or edits) generally require linear time.

To overcome this problem, researchers have developed other data structures representing (functional) sequences, most notably, *finger trees* [8]. These structures perform well, allowing edits in (amortized) constant time and moving the edit location in logarithmic time. More recently, researchers have proposed the *RRB-Vector* [14], offering a balanced tree representation for immutable vectors. Unfortunately, these alternatives lack the simplicity and extensibility of the singly-linked list.

In this paper, we introduce the *random access zipper*, or RAZ for short. Like the common linked list, the RAZ is a general-purpose data structure for persistent sequences. The RAZ overcomes the performance shortcomings of linked lists by using probabilistically-balanced trees to make random access efficient (expected or amortized logarithmic time). The key insight for balancing these trees comes from [12], which introduces the notion of probabilistically-chosen *levels*.[1] To edit sequences in a persistent setting, the RAZ also incorporates the

---

[1] In short, these levels represent the heights of uniformly randomly chosen nodes in a full, balanced binary tree. See Sect. 3.

© Springer Nature Switzerland AG 2019
D. Van Horn and J. Hughes (Eds.): TFP 2016, LNCS 10447, pp. 155–171, 2019.
https://doi.org/10.1007/978-3-030-14805-8_9

design of a zipper [9], which provides the notion of a *cursor* in the sequence. A cursor focuses edits on (or near) a distinguished element. The user may move the cursor locally (i.e., forward and backward, one element at a time), or globally (i.e., based on an index into the sequence), which provides random access to sequence elements.

The RAZ exposes two types to the user, `'a tree` and `'a zip`, which respectively represent an unfocused and focused sequence of elements (of type `'a`). The RAZ exposes the following interface to the user based on these types:

Function : Type		Time Complexity
focus	: `'a tree -> int -> 'a zip`	$O(\log n)$ expected
unfocus	: `'a zip -> 'a tree`	$O(\log n + m \cdot \log^2 m)$ expected
insert	: `dir -> 'a -> 'a zedit`	$O(1)$ worst-case
remove	: `dir -> 'a zedit`	$O(1)$ amortized
replace	: `'a -> 'a zedit`	$O(1)$ worst-case
move	: `dir -> 'a zedit`	$O(1)$ amortized
view	: `'a zip -> 'a`	$O(1)$ worst-case

The second and third columns of the table respectively report the type (in OCaml) and time complexity for each operation; we explain each in turn.

Function `focus` transforms a tree into a zipper, given a position in the sequence on which to place the zipper's cursor. It runs in expected logarithmic time, where n is the number of elements in the sequence. We use expected analysis for this function (and the next) since the tree is balanced probabilistically.

Function `unfocus` transforms a (focused) zipper back to an (unfocused) tree; its time complexity $O(\log n + m \cdot \log^2 m)$ depends on the length of the sequence n, as well as m, the number of zipper-based edits since the last refocusing. We summarize those possible edits below. Assuming that the number m is a small constant, the complexity of `unfocus` is merely $O(\log n)$; when m grows to become significant, however, the current design of the RAZ performs more poorly, requiring an additional expected $O(\log^2 m)$ time to process each edit in building the balanced tree. An algorithm linear in m does exist for this purpose, but a more straightforward one was a better match for the simplicity of this codebase.

Functions `insert`, `replace`, `remove`, `move` each transform the zipper structure of the RAZ. We abbreviate their types using type `'a zedit`, which we define as the function type `'a zip →'a zip`. Function `insert` inserts a given element to the left or right of the cursor, specified by a direction of type `dir`. Function `remove` removes the element in the given direction. Its time complexity is amortized, since removal may involve decomposing subtrees of logarithmic depth; overall, these costs are amortized across edits that require them. Function `replace` replaces the element at the cursor with the given element. Function `move` moves the cursor one unit in the specified direction; just as with `remove`, this operation uses amortized analysis. Finally, function `view` retrieves the element currently focused at the cursor (in constant time).

In the next section, we give an in-depth example of using the operations described above. In particular, we illustrate how the RAZ represents the sequence as a tree and as a zipper, showing how the operations construct and transform these two structures.

In Sect. 3, we present our implementation of the RAZ. It requires well under 200 lines of OCaml, which is publicly available:

https://github.com/cuplv/raz.ocaml.

The code described in this paper comes from the `raz_simp.ml` file. This code includes ten main functions that work over a simple set of datatypes for trees, lists of trees, and zippers, as defined in Sect. 3. In contrast, the finger tree [8] requires approximately 800 lines in the OCaml "Batteries Included" repo [10] to provide similar functionality.

We evaluate the RAZ empirically in Sect. 4. In particular, we report the time required to build large sequences by inserting random elements into the sequence at random positions. Our evaluation demonstrates that the RAZ is very competitive with the finger tree implementation mentioned above, despite the simplicity of the RAZ compared with that of the finger tree.

In Sect. 5, we discuss the design decisions we considered for this implementation and exposition of the RAZ. Section 6 discusses related work, and in particular, alternative structures for persistent sequences. We give a deeper comparison to finger trees, and explain why other balanced trees designed for sets (e.g., red-black trees, or splay trees, etc.) are inappropriate for representing sequences.

2 Example

In this section, we give a detailed example of using the RAZ interface introduced above, and illustrate the internal tree and list structures of the RAZ informally, using pictures. In the next section, we make the code for these functions precise.

Consider the sequence of seven elements $\langle z, a, b, c, y, d, e \rangle$. In the example that follows, the programmer uses the RAZ to perform four operations over this sequence, editing it (functionally) in the process:

- She uses `focus` to place the cursor at offset 4 (element y),
- she uses `remove` to remove the element to the left of the cursor (element c),
- she uses `unfocus` in anticipation of refocusing, and
- she uses `focus` to place the cursor at the sequence's start (element z).

Figure 1 (first image, top) shows the sequence of elements represented by a RAZ. As explained further in Sect. 3, the RAZ interposes randomly-chosen *levels* as meta-data in the sequence; we show these levels, $\langle 4, 6, 1, 2, 5, 3 \rangle$, interposed below the sequence elements. The second image shows the tree form of the RAZ, whose structure is determined by the sequence elements and levels above. This tree represents an unfocused RAZ.

Next, the programmer uses `focus` to place the cursor into the tree, in order to edit its elements. The third image in Fig. 1 shows the zipper that results

Elements and levels for our example sequence:

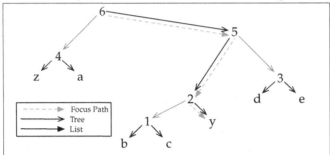

As a tree, levels are internal and determine heights:

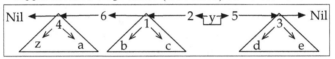

Zipper focused on y. Three (unfocused) sub-trees remain:

Fig. 1. The RAZ represents the sequence of elements $\langle z, a, b, c, y, d, e \rangle$ interposed with levels 1–6 (first image); these levels uniquely determine a balanced tree (second image) that permits log-time focusing on element y (third image).

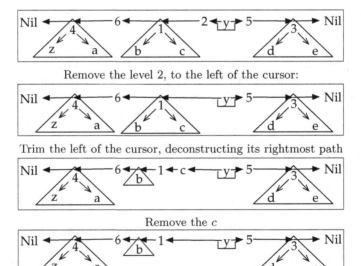

Remove the level 2, to the left of the cursor:

Trim the left of the cursor, deconstructing its rightmost path

Remove the c

Fig. 2. An example of editing a focused RAZ: remove the c to the left of the cursor by removing level 2 (second image), trimming the left tree (third image), and removing the c (last image)

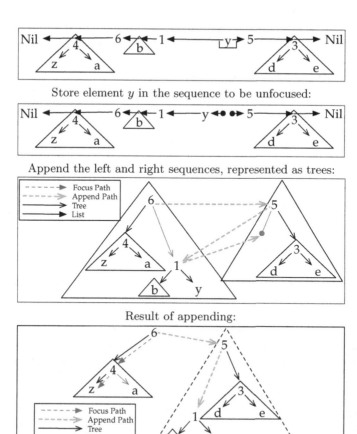

Store element y in the sequence to be unfocused:

Append the left and right sequences, represented as trees:

Result of appending:

Fig. 3. Unfocus the RAZ

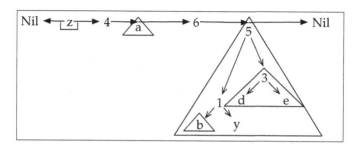

Fig. 4. Focus on the first element, z, creating left and right lists of (unfocused) subtrees.

from focusing the sequence on element y. As can be seen, this structure consists of left and right lists that each contain levels and unfocused subtrees from the original balanced tree. The focusing algorithm produces this zipper by descending the balanced tree along the indicated focus path (second image of Fig. 1), adding levels and subtrees along this path to the left and right lists, according to the branch taken. Notice that the elements nearest to the cursor consist of the subtrees at the end of this path; in expectation, these lists order subtrees in ascending size.

After focusing on element y, the programmer uses the `remove` function. Figure 2 shows the three steps for removing the c to the left of cursor. First, we remove the level 2 from the left of the cursor, making c the next element to the immediate left of the cursor (the second image). Next, since the c resides as a leaf in an unfocused tree, we *trim* this left tree by deconstructing its rightmost path (viz., the path to c). Section 3 explains the trim operation in detail. Finally, with c exposed in the left list, we remove it (fourth image).

After removing element c, the programmer unfocuses the RAZ. Beginning with the final state of Fig. 2, Fig. 3 illustrates the process of unfocusing the sequence. First, we add element y to one of the lists, storing its position in the sequence (second image). Next, we build trees from the left and right lists as follows: For each list, we fold its elements and trees, appending them into balanced trees; as with the initial tree, we use the levels to determine the height of internal nodes (third image). Having created two balanced trees from the left and right lists, we append them along their rightmost and leftmost paths, respectively; again, the append path compares the levels to determine the final appended tree (fourth image).

Finally, the programmer refocuses the RAZ. In Fig. 4 (as in Fig. 1), we descend the focus path to the desired element, this time z. As before, this path induces left and right lists that consist of levels and unfocused subtrees.

3   Technical Design

The full implementation of the RAZ in OCaml consists of about 170 lines. In this section, we tour much of this code, with type signatures for what we elide for space considerations.

Figure 5 lists the type definitions for the RAZ structure, which is stratified into three types: `tree`, `tlist`, and `zip`. The `tree` type consists of (unfocused) binary trees, where leaves hold data, and where internal binary nodes hold a level `lev` and total element count of their subtrees (an `int`). The `tlist` type consists of ordinary list structure, plus two `Cons`-like constructors that hold `levs` and `trees` instead of ordinary data. Finally, a (focused) `zip` consists of a left and right `tlist`, and a focused element that lies between them.

Levels for Probabilistically-Balanced Trees. As demonstrated in the code below for `append`, the levels associated with each `Bin` node are critical to maintaining balanced trees, in expectation. This property of balance is critical to the time

```
type lev = int    (* tree level *)
type dir = L | R (* directions for moving/editing *)

type 'a tree = (* binary tree of elements *)
               | Nil
               | Leaf of 'a
               | Bin  of lev * int * 'a tree * 'a tree

type 'a tlist = (* list of elements, levels and trees *)
               | Nil
               | Cons  of 'a      * 'a tlist
               | Level of lev     * 'a tlist
               | Tree  of 'a tree * 'a tlist
type 'a zip  = ('a tlist * 'a * 'a tlist) (* tlist zipper *)
```

Fig. 5. RAZ defined as a zipper of tree-lists.

complexity bounds given for many of the RAZ's operations, including focusing, unfocusing and many local edits.

The key insight is choosing these levels from a *negative binomial distribution*; intuitively, drawing random numbers from this distribution yields smaller numbers much more often (in expectation) than larger numbers. More precisely, drawing the level 1 is twice as likely as drawing the level 2, which is twice as likely as level 3, and so on. This means that, in expectation, a sequence of levels drawn from this distribution describes the sizes of subtrees in a perfectly-balanced binary tree. As described in Sect. 6, this insight comes from [12], who define the notion of level in a related context.

Fortunately, we can choose these levels very quickly, given a source of (uniformly) random numbers and a hash function. We do so by hashing a randomly-chosen number, and by counting the number of consecutive zeros in this hash value's least-significant bits.

```
let focus : 'a tree → int → 'a zip =
fun t p →
  let c = elm_count t in
  if p >= c || p < 0 then failwith "out of bounds" else
  let rec loop = fun t p (l,r) → match t with
  | Nil → failwith "internal Nil"
  | Leaf(elm) → assert (p == 0); (l,elm,r)
  | Bin(lv, _, bl, br) →
    let c = elm_count bl in
    if p < c then loop bl p       (l,Level(lv,Tree(br,r)))
    else            loop br (p - c) (Level(lv,Tree(bl,l)),r)
  in loop t p (Nil,Nil)
```

Fig. 6. The focus operation transforms a tree into a zip.

Focusing the RAZ. The `focus` operation in Fig. 6 transforms an unfocused tree to a focused zipper. Given an index in the sequence, p, and an $O(1)$-time `elm_count` operation on sub-trees, the inner `loop` recursively walks through one path of `Bin` nodes until it finds the desired `Leaf` element. At each recursive step of this walk, the `loop` accumulates un-walked subtrees in the pair `(1,r)`. In the base case, `focus` returns this accumulated `(1,r)` pair as a `zip` containing the located leaf element.

Proposition 31. *Given a tree t of depth d, and an $O(1)$-time implementation of* `elm_count`, *the operation* `focus t p` *runs in $O(d)$ time.*

```
let head_as_tree : 'a tlist → 'a tree
let tail : 'a tlist → 'a tlist

let grow : dir → 'a tlist → 'a tree =
 fun d t →
  let rec loop = fun h1 t1 →
    match t1 with Nil → h1 | _ →
    let h2 = head_as_tree t1 in
    match d with
    | L → loop (append h2 h1) (tail t1)
    | R → loop (append h1 h2) (tail t1)
  in grow (head_as_tree t) (tail t)

let unfocus : 'a zip → 'a tree =
  fun (l,e,r) → append (grow L l) (append (Leaf(e)) (grow R r))
```

Fig. 7. Unfocusing the RAZ using `append` and `grow`.

Unfocusing the RAZ. Figure 7 lists the `unfocus` operation, which transforms a focused `zipper` into an unfocused `tree`. To do so, `unfocus` uses auxiliary operations `grow` and `append` to construct and append trees for the `left` and `right` `tlist` sequences that comprise the zipper. The final steps of `unfocus` consists of appending the left tree, focused element e (as a singleton tree), and the right tree. We explain `append` in detail further below.

The `grow` operation uses `append`, and the simpler helper function `head_as_tree`, which transforms the head constructor of a `tlist` into a `tree`; conceptually, it extracts the next tree, leaf element or binary node level as `tree` structure. It also uses the function `tail`, which is standard. The `grow` operation loops over successive trees, each extracted by `head_as_tree`, and it combines these trees via `append`. The direction parameter d determines whether the accumulated tree grows from left-to-right (L case), or right-to-left (R case). When the `tlist` is `Nil`, the `loop` within `grow` completes, and yeilds the accumulated tree h1.

Under the conditions stated below, unfocus is efficient, running in polyloga-rithmic time for balanced trees with logarithmic depth:

Proposition 32. *Given a tree t of depth d, performing* unfocus *(*focus t p*) requires $O(d)$ time.*

We sketch the reasoning for this claim as follows. As stated above, the oper-ation focus t p runs in $O(d)$ time; we further observe that focus produces a zipper with left and right lists of length $O(d)$. Likewise, head_as_tree also runs in constant time. Next, the unfocus operation uses grow to produce left and right trees in $O(d)$ time. In general, grow makes d calls to append, combining trees of height approaching d, requiring $O(d^2)$ time. However, since these trees were placed *in order* by focus, each append here only takes constant time. Finally, it appends these trees in $O(d)$ time. None of these steps dominate asymptotically, so the composed operations run in $O(d)$ time.

```
let rec append : 'a tree → 'a tree → 'a tree =
  fun t1 t2 →
  let tot = (elm_count t1) + (elm_count t2) in
  match (t1, t2) with
  | Nil, _ → t2 | _, Nil → t1
  | Leaf(_), Leaf(_)      → failwith "leaf-leaf should not arise"
  | Leaf(_), Bin(lv,_,l,r) → Bin(lv, tot, append t1 l, r)
  | Bin(lv,_,l,r), Leaf(_) → Bin(lv, tot, l, append r t2)
  | Bin(lv1,_,t1l,t1r), Bin(lv2,_,t2l,t2r) →
            if lv1 >= lv2 then Bin(lv1, tot, t1l, append t1r t2)
                          else Bin(lv2, tot, append t1 t2l, t2r)
```

Fig. 8. Append the sequences of two trees into a single sequence, as a balanced tree.

Appending Trees. The append operation in Fig. 8 produces a tree whose ele-ments consist of the elements (and levels) of the two input trees, in order. That is, an in-order traversal of the tree result of append t1 t2 first visits the ele-ments (and levels) of tree t1, followed by the elements (and levels) of tree t2. The algorithm works by traversing a path in each of its two tree arguments, and producing an appended tree with the aforementioned in-order traversal prop-erty. In the last Bin node case, the computation chooses between descending into the sub-structure of argument t1 or argument t2 by comparing their levels and by choosing the tree named with the higher level. As depicted in the exam-ple in Fig. 4 (from Sect. 2), this choice preserves the property that Bin nodes with higher levels remain higher in the resulting tree. Below, we discuss further properties of this algorithm, and compare it to prior work.

```
let trim : dir → 'a tlist → 'a tlist =
  fun d tl → match tl with
  | Nil | Cons _ | Level _ → tl
  | Tree(t, rest) →
  let rec trim = fun hl t1 →
    match hl with
    | Nil → failwith "malformed tree"
    | Leaf(elm) → Cons(elm,t1)
    | Bin(lv,_,l,r) →
      match d with
      | L → trim r (Level(lv,Tree(l,t1)))
      | R → trim l (Level(lv,Tree(r,t1)))
  in trim t rest
```

Fig. 9. Function `trim` exposes the next sequence element.

Trimming a Tree into a List. The `trim` operation in Fig. 9 prepares a `tlist` for edits in the given direction `dir`. It returns the same, unchanged `tlist` if it does not contain a tree at its head. If the `tlist` does contain a tree at its head, `trim` deconstructs it recursively. Each recursive call eliminates a `Bin` node, pushing the branches into the `tlist`. The recursion ends when `trim` reaches a `Leaf` and pushes it into the `tlist` as a `Cons`.

The `trim` operation works most efficiently when it immediately follows a refocusing, since in this case, the cursor is surrounded by leaves or small subtrees, which each trim in constant time. If the cursor moves far through the zipper, however, it can encounter a node from high in the original tree, containing a significant proportion of the total elements of the sequence.

These facts suggest the following propositions:

Proposition 33. *Given a direction d, a position p, a tree t of size n, and a tlist l from one side of a zipper created by focus t p, trim d l runs in $O(1)$ time.*

Proposition 34. *Given a direction d, a position p, a tree t of size n, and a tlist l from one side of a zipper created by focus t p, a sequence of k calls to trim d l composed with move d runs in $O(k \log n)$ time.*

Figure 10 lists the code for inserting and removing elements from the zipper. The function `insert` uses `rnd_level` to generate a random level to accompany the newly-inserted element `ne`. Based on the removal direction, the function `remove` uses an internal helper `remove'` to remove the next sequence element in the given direction, possibly by looping. In particular, the `Cons` case is the base case that removes the element of the `Cons` cell; the `Nil` case is erroneous, since it means that there is no element to remove. The two remaining cases recur internally; specifically, the `Tree` case uses `trim`, explained above.

Figure 10 lists the type signatures of several other zipper-based editing functions: `view` accesses the next element to the right or left of the cursor, `replace`

```
let insert : dir → 'a → 'a zip → 'a zip =
  fun d ne (l,e,r) →
  match d with
  | L → (Level(rnd_level(),Cons(ne,l)),e,r)
  | R → (l,e,Level(rnd_level(),Cons(ne,r)))

let remove : dir → 'a zip → 'a zip =
  let rec remove' d s = match s with
    | Nil              → failwith "no elements"
    | Cons(_,rest)     → rest
    | Level(lv,rest)   → remove' d rest
    | Tree _           → remove' d (trim d s)
  in fun d (l,e,r) → match d with
  | L → (remove' L l,e,r)
  | R → (l,e,remove' R r)

let view    : dir → 'a zip → 'a
let replace : dir → 'a → 'a zip → 'a zip
let move    : dir → 'a zip → 'a zip

let view_cursor    : 'a zip → 'a
let replace_cursor : 'a → 'a zip → 'a zip
```

Fig. 10. Zipper edits: element insertion, element removal and several other variants.

replaces this element with another given one, and move moves the cursor to focus on an adjacent element. Finally, view_cursor and replace_cursor are similar to view and replace, respectively, except that they act on the element at the cursor, rather than an element that is adjacent to it.

4   Evaluation

In this section we evaluate the RAZ in comparison to a data structure with similar theoretic behavior, the finger tree [8], which we elaborate on in related work, Sect. 6. We demonstrate that the RAZ is comparable in performance with this more complex structure.

Experimental Setup. We present two experiments, each performed on both a RAZ and a finger tree. In the first experiment, we construct a sequence from scratch by inserting elements, each in a randomly chosen position. Insertion into the RAZ is by focusing, inserting a value, then unfocusing; insertion into the finger tree is by splitting, pushing a value, then appending. Upon reaching a target length, we record the total time taken. We use target lengths of 10k to 1M elements, and repeat the process for a total of five data points for each target. We plot the median of the results, shown in Fig. 11.

For the second experiment, we also insert elements into random positions in a sequence, but maintain a single sequence throughout the experiment. We measure the time taken for the first sequential group of 1M insertions, then the next group of 1M insertions, repeating until the sequence reaches 100M elements. We plot these measured times, shown in Fig. 12.

We compiled our code through opam with ocamlc verion 4.02 native mode, and ran it on a 2.8 GHz Thinkpad with 16 GB of RAM running Ubuntu 16.04. We use the "Batteries Included" [10] code for finger trees. The results in Fig. 11 were collected by using a separate process for each measurement, and those in Fig. 12 used one process per data structure. Ocaml's `min_heap_size` parameter was set to 800 MB. We report 100 values per data structure per plot.

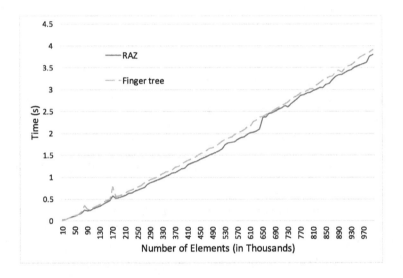

Fig. 11. Constructing sequences of different lengths from scratch

Results. Figure 11 shows the RAZ as slightly faster than a finger tree, but maintaining the same asymptotic behavior. We average the ratio of times, showing that the RAZ uses 5–6% less time on average. At 500k elements the RAZ takes 1.57 s vs the finger tree's 1.71 s, and at 950k elements the times are 3.54 s and 3.70 s, respectively. Figure 12 shows a great variance in times. Even with a million elements added for each measurement, the plot is not smooth. This is true for the RAZ with its probabilistic structure, but also for the more consistently structured finger trees. The average time in the last 20 entries plotted is 10.01 s for the RAZ and 9.77 s for the finger tree. We suspect that garbage collection effects may be (partly) responsible for this variance, but determining this with certainty is beyond the scope of this initial evaluation.

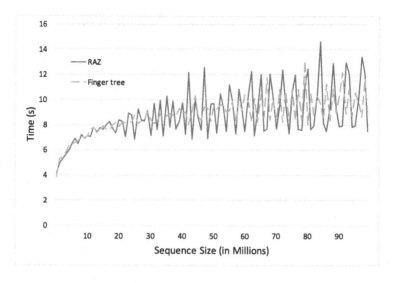

Fig. 12. Time taken to insert 1M elements into a sequence of varying size.

5   Discussion

A benefit of building a tree with specific heights is that of a stable form. The structure of the RAZ as a tree does not depend on the order of operations, but on the stored levels. This results in minimal changes, specifically, only the path from the adjusted elements to the root will be different. This is of great benefit for incremental computation, which is most effective for small changes. Early incremental structures by [12] used elements to determine heights, and had trouble with identical values. The RAZ sidesteps this issue with explicit stored levels for tree heights.

We struggled with the question of where to put the cursor when focusing into the RAZ. A RAZ may be focused on a element (as in the code described here), a level, or between the two. An early version of the RAZ placed the cursor between element and level, but the code was confusing and asymmetric. By focusing on an element, the code was reduced in length by about 25%, but may have made local edits a bit unintuitive. We have a rewrite that focuses onto a level, but it requires additional logic to deal with the ends of the sequence, which are bounded by elements.

There are two improvements we are considering as future work. One is to generalize the annotation of RAZ subtrees. The code presented here is annotated with size info to focus on a particular location. However, the RAZ could easily support arbitrary monoidal annotations of the kind described for finger trees in [8]. Another potential enhancement is to include arrays of elements in the leaves of the RAZ rather than a single element. Arrays may improve the speed of computations over the RAZ by allowing for better cache coherency. They may also reduce the effect of probabilistic imbalance, by cutting down on local seek time.

6   Related Work and Alternative Approaches

We review related work on representing purely-functional (persistent) sequences that undergo small (constant-sized) edits, supplementing the discussions from earlier sections. We also discuss hypothetical approaches based on (purely-functional) search trees, pointing out their differences and short-comings for representing sequences.

The "Chunky Decomposition Scheme". The tree structure of the RAZ is inspired by the so-called "chunky decomposition scheme" of sequences, from Pugh and Teiltelbaum's 1989 POPL paper on purely-functional incremental computing [12]. Similar to skip lists [11], this decomposition scheme hashes the sequence's elements to (uniquely) determine a probabilistically-balanced tree structure. The RAZ enhances this structure with a focal point, local edits at the focus, and a mechanism to overcome its inapplicability to sequences of repeated (non-unique) elements. In sum, the RAZ admits efficient random access for (persistent) *sequence editing*, to which the '89 paper alludes, but does not address.

Finger Trees. As introduced in Sect. 1, a finger tree represents a sequence and provides operations for a double-ended queue (aka, deque) that push and pop elements to and from its two ends, respectively. The 2–3 finger tree supports these operations in amortized constant time. Structurally, it consists of nodes with three branches: a left branch with 1–4 elements, a center for recursive nodes, and a right branch with 1–4 elements. Each center node consists of a *complete* 2–3 tree. This construction's shallow left and right (non-center) branches admit efficient, amortized constant-time access to the deque's ends. This construction also provides efficient (log-time) split and append operations, for exposing elements in the center of the tree, or merging two trees into a single 2–3 tree. The split operation is comparable to the focus operation of the RAZ; the append operation is comparable to that of the RAZ.

While similar in asymptotic costs, in settings that demand *canonical forms* and/or which employ *hash consing*, the 2–3 finger tree and RAZ are significantly different; this can impact the asymptotics of comparing sequences for equality. In the presence of hash-consing, structural identity coincides with physical identity, allowing for $O(1)$-time equality checks of arbitrarily long sequences. As a result of their approach, 2–3 finger trees are history dependent. This fact makes them unsuitable for settings such as memoization-based incremental computing [6, 7, 12].

Figure 13 depicts both a RAZ and a finger tree containing 15 elements, numbered sequentially. Elements are shown as circles, internal trees have a triangle around them, with diagonal lines denoting internal tree structure. Horizontal and vertical lines elide a simple structure for access to elements: a list in the RAZ case and an set of data types for the finger tree. Both these data structures provide access to the upper right element, labeled "15". We elide the current item and right side of the RAZ, as it is not important for this example.

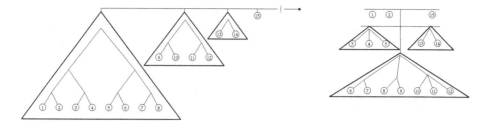

Fig. 13. A RAZ (left) and finger tree (right) representing the same sequence

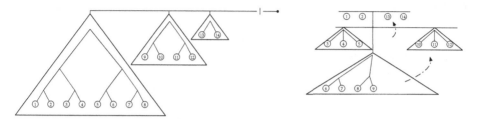

Fig. 14. Removing an element from a RAZ (left) and a finger tree (right), with structure maintenance on the finger tree

One major difference between the finger tree and RAZ is when they need to adjust their structure to maintain invariants. Figure 14 shows the result of deleting element 15 in both our example structures. They both expose this element, but the RAZ requires no maintenance at this point, while the finger tree does, since there are no elements left in the top finger. This is done by promoting a tree from the next deeper finger. In this case, the finger tree must promote another tree from even deeper. These promotions are indicated by the arrows in the figure.

RRB Vector. The *RRB-Vector* [14] uses a balanced tree to represent immutable vectors, focusing on practical issues such as parallel performance and cache locality. These performance considerations are outside the scope of our current work, but are interesting for future work.

Balanced Representations of Sets. Researchers have proposed many approaches for representing sets as balanced search trees, many of which are amenable to purely-functional representations (e.g., Treaps [2], Splay Trees [13], AVL Trees [1], and Red-Black Trees [3]). Additionally, skip lists [11] provide a structure that is tree-like, and which is closely related to the probabilistic approach of the RAZ. However, search trees (and skip lists) are *not* designed to represent sequences, but rather sets (or finite mappings).

Structures for sequences and sets are fundamentally different. Structures for sequences admit operations that alter the presence, absence and ordering of elements, and they permit elements to be duplicated in the sequence (e.g., a list of n repeated characters is different from the singleton list of one such character). By contrast, structures for sets (and finite maps) admit operations that alter the presence or absence of elements in the structure, but not *the order* of the elements in the structure—rather, this ordering is defined by the element's type, and is not represented by the set. Indeed, the set representation uses this (fixed) element ordering to efficiently search for elements. Moreover, set structures typically do not distinguish between the sets with duplicated elements—e.g., `add(elm, set)` and `add(elm, add(elm, set))` are the same set, whereas a sequence structure would clearly distinguish these cases.

Encoding Sequences with Sets. In spite of these differences between sets and sequences, one can *encode* a sequence using a finite map, similar to how one can represent a mutable array with an immutable mapping from natural numbers to the array's content; however, like an array, editing this sequence by element insertion and removal is generally problematic, since each insertion or removal (naively) requires an $O(n)$-time re-indexing of the mapping. Overcoming this efficiency problem in turn requires employing so-called *order maintenance data structures*, which admit (amortized) $O(1)$-time insertion, removal and comparison operations for a (mutable) total order [4,5]. Given such a structure, the elements of this order could be used eschew the aforementioned re-indexing problem that arises from the naive encoding of a sequence with a finite map. Alas, existing order maintenance data structures are *not* purely-functional, so additional accommodations are needed in settings that require persistent data structures. By contrast, the RAZ is simple, efficient and persistent.

7   Conclusion

We present the Random Access Zipper (RAZ), a novel data structure for representing a sequence. We show its simplicity by providing most of the code, which contains a minimal number of cases and helper functions. We describe some of the design decisions that increase simplicity. We evaluate the RAZ, demonstrating time bounds on par with far more complex data structures. Finally, we suggest multiple ways to enhance the RAZ to suit additional use cases.

References

1. AdelsonVelskii, M., Landis, E.M.: An algorithm for the organization of information. Technical report, DTIC Document (1963)
2. Aragon, C.R., Seidel, R.: Randomized search trees. In: 30th Annual Symposium on Foundations of Computer Science, Research Triangle Park, North Carolina, USA, 30 October–1 November 1989, pp. 540–545 (1989)
3. Bayer, R.: Symmetric binary B-trees: data structure and maintenance algorithms. Acta Inf. **1**, 290–306 (1972)
4. Bender, M.A., Cole, R., Demaine, E.D., Farach-Colton, M., Zito, J.: Two simplified algorithms for maintaining order in a list. In: Möhring, R., Raman, R. (eds.) ESA 2002. LNCS, vol. 2461, pp. 152–164. Springer, Heidelberg (2002). https://doi.org/10.1007/3-540-45749-6_17

5. Dietz, P.F., Sleator, D.D.: Two algorithms for maintaining order in a list. In: Proceedings of the 19th Annual ACM Symposium on Theory of Computing, New York, USA, pp. 365–372 (1987)
6. Hammer, M.A., et al.: Incremental computation with names. In: Proceedings of the 2015 ACM SIGPLAN International Conference on Object-Oriented Programming, Systems, Languages, and Applications, OOPSLA 2015, Part of SPLASH 2015, Pittsburgh, PA, USA, 25–30 October 2015, pp. 748–766 (2015)
7. Hammer, M.A., Khoo, Y.P., Hicks, M., Foster, J.S.: Adapton: composable, demand-driven incremental computation. In: ACM SIGPLAN Conference on Programming Language Design and Implementation, PLDI 2014, Edinburgh, United Kingdom, 09–11 June 2014, p. 18 (2014)
8. Hinze, R., Paterson, R.: Finger trees: a simple general-purpose data structure. J. Funct. Program. **16**(2), 197–217 (2006)
9. Huet, G.: The zipper. J. Funct. Program. **7**, 549–554 (1997)
10. OCaml Batteries Team: OCaml batteries included. https://github.com/ocaml-batteries-team/batteries-included. Accessed 12 July 2016
11. Pugh, W.: Skip lists: a probabilistic alternative to balanced trees. In: Dehne, F., Sack, J.-R., Santoro, N. (eds.) WADS 1989. LNCS, vol. 382, pp. 437–449. Springer, Heidelberg (1989). https://doi.org/10.1007/3-540-51542-9_36
12. Pugh, W., Teitelbaum, T.: Incremental computation via function caching. In: POPL (1989)
13. Sleator, D.D., Tarjan, R.E.: Self-adjusting binary trees. In: Proceedings of the 15th Annual ACM Symposium on Theory of Computing, Boston, Massachusetts, USA, 25–27 April 1983, pp. 235–245 (1983)
14. Stucki, N., Rompf, T., Ureche, V., Bagwell, P.: RRB vector: a practical general purpose immutable sequence. In: ICFP 2015 (2015)

Building a Generic Feedback System
for Rule-Based Problems

Nico Naus[1][(✉)] and Johan Jeuring[1,2]

[1] Utrecht University, Utrecht, The Netherlands
n.naus@uu.nl
[2] Faculty of Management, Science and Technology,
Open University of the Netherlands, Heerlen, The Netherlands

Abstract. We present a generic framework that provides hints on how to achieve a goal to users of software supporting rule-based problem solving from different domains. Our approach consists of two parts. First, we present a DSL that relates and unifies different rule-based problems. Second, we use generic search algorithms to solve various kinds of problems. This solution can then be used to calculate a hint for the user. We present three rule-based problem frameworks to illustrate our approach: the Ideas framework, PuzzleScript and iTasks. By taking real world examples from these three example frameworks and instantiating feedback systems for them, we validate our approach.

1 Introduction

Many software frameworks and systems support, model, or automate the process of human problem solving. With a problem we mean anything like a game or a puzzle, solving an exercise in physics, or search and rescue people in need. Typical examples of systems supporting problem solving are workflow management systems, intelligent tutoring systems, and expert systems.

A user of a system supporting problem solving sometimes needs help in making a decision or taking a step towards a particular goal. In the case of a game or a puzzle, a user might get stuck, and need a step in the right direction. For supporting a student solving an exercise in an intelligent tutoring system, hints are essential [24]. In search and rescue systems, hints can quickly give insight in the current situation, and can help a user in understanding why a next step has to be taken. A user has to take a decision under pressure of time and potential danger. Automatically suggesting and explaining the best option to perform may reduce the chance of human error, while still allowing intervention.

In all of the above examples a user follows a potentially flexible process, and needs information about where she is in the process, where she should go next, and why she should go there [5]. In this paper, we attempt to answer the question: how can we construct a generic framework that provides users of rule-based problem solving systems with feedback? To answer the question, we look at research performed in the intelligent tutoring community. In this community,

D. Van Horn and J. Hughes (Eds.): TFP 2016, LNCS 10447, pp. 172–191, 2019.
https://doi.org/10.1007/978-3-030-14805-8_10

a lot of research has been performed on how to build frameworks that provide the user with feedback on how to solve exercises [25], allows teachers to describe their exercises [17], and deals with different problem-domains [6]. The results are not directly applicable to the rule-based problems described above, but the central ideas inspire our approach.

There are many forms of hints and feedback possible. In this paper, we focus on next-step hints. This kind of hint indicates which of the steps that can currently be taken, is the best choice. For example, in an intelligent tutoring system, the next step that a student should apply is returned, for example "Eliminate constants" or "Remove double negation". In the case of a puzzle, we want to inform a player on what to do next, for example "Move left" or "Apply action x". In the case of a search and rescue system we want to report what immediate action needs to be taken, for example "Inform unit x" or "Escalate incident to level 2". The best sentence to use when presenting such a next-step hint is probably best determined by a teacher, but *which* next step to take is something we want to and can calculate automatically.

This paper proposes a unified framework to describe processes for problem solving. For this purpose, we use a domain specific language (DSL). Giving a hint in an intelligent tutoring system for solving equations often amounts to returning the next steps prescribed by the solving strategy, where providing a hint for a more complicated problem such as the traveling salesman problem requires more involved problem solving techniques. We obtain these different instances of problem solving processes by interpreting our DSL in different ways. Thus we have a unified framework for describing problem solving processes, which can be instantiated for different purposes by selecting different interpretations. The novelty of our framework is the way in which it relates rule-based problems, to make them tractable to standard, generic solving algorithms.

This paper is organized as follows. Section 2 discusses some examples for which problem-solving assistance is desirable. Section 3 introduces a DSL for describing the rule-based problem solving processes. Section 4 presents several methods for solving the various problems. In Sect. 5, we validate our approach and in Sect. 6 we compare our approach to previous work. Section 7 concludes.

2   Examples

This section illustrates and motivates our goal of providing help to people using a rule-based problem solving system by giving three examples: the Ideas framework [7], PuzzleScript [13], and the iTasks system [18]. Each of these frameworks can describe a variety of problems. We briefly introduce each framework, show an example problem described in the framework, and explain what kind of problem solving assistance is desired.

2.1   Ideas

The Ideas framework is used to develop services to support users when stepwise solving exercises in an intelligent tutoring system for a domain like mathematics

$$
\begin{aligned}
\mathit{dnfStrategy} \;=\;& \mathit{label}\ \texttt{"Constants"} && (\mathit{repeat}\ (\mathit{topDown}\ \mathit{constants})) \\
\mathrel{<*>}& \mathit{label}\ \texttt{"Definitions"} && (\mathit{repeat}\ (\mathit{bottomUp}\ \mathit{definitions})) \\
\mathrel{<*>}& \mathit{label}\ \texttt{"Negations"} && (\mathit{repeat}\ (\mathit{topDown}\ \mathit{negations})) \\
\mathrel{<*>}& \mathit{label}\ \texttt{"Distribution"} && (\mathit{repeat}\ (\mathit{somewhere}\ \mathit{distribution}))
\end{aligned}
$$

Fig. 1. A problem solving strategy in Ideas

or logic. It is a general framework used to construct the expert knowledge of an intelligent tutoring system (ITS). The framework has been applied in the domains of mathematics [7], programming [4], and communication skills [9].

The central component of the expert knowledge for an ITS is expressed as a so-called *strategy* in Ideas. For example, Fig. 1 gives part of a strategy for the problem of rewriting a logic expression to disjunctive normal form (for the complete strategy see Heeren et al. [7]). The framework offers various services based on this strategy, among which a service that diagnoses a step from a student, and a service that gives a next step to solve a problem. The student receives a logic expression, and stepwise rewrites this expression to disjunctive normal form using services based on the above strategy. At each step, the student can request a hint, like "Eliminate constants" or "Eliminate implications", or ask for feedback on her current expression. If no rules can be applied any more, the expression is in normal form.

The *dnfStrategy* Ideas strategy describes a rule-based process that solves the problem of converting an expression to disjunctive normal form. It is expressed in terms of combinators like $\mathrel{<*>}$ (sequence), *repeat* and *somewhere*, and further sub-strategies. Additionally, a *label* combinator is available, to label sub-strategies with a name.

2.2   PuzzleScript

PuzzleScript is an open source HTML5 Puzzle Game Engine [13]. It is a simple scripting language for specifying puzzle games. Its central component is a DSL for describing a game. PuzzleScript compiles a puzzle described in this DSL into an HTML5 puzzle game. Using the DSL, the game programmer describe a puzzle as a list of objects, rules that define the behavior of the game, a win condition, collision information, and one or more levels.

The hello-world example for PuzzleScript is given in Fig. 2. It describes a simple crate-pusher game, also called Sokoban. Objects are: background, walls, crates, the player and the targets for the crates. There is a single rule that states if a player moves into a crate, the crate moves with the player. Objects appearing on the same line in the collision layers are not allowed to pass trough each other. The winning condition is reached when all targets have a crate on them. Finally, a start-level is specified under *LEVELS*.

In a difficult game, we want to offer next-step hints to the player on how to proceed. Based on the state of the game, the *RULES*, *COLLISIONLAYERS* and *WINCONDITIONS*, an algorithm can calculate a hint for a user [14]. This

```
========    ======
OBJECTS     RULES
========    ======

Background   [>Player | Crate] → [ > Player | >Crate]
Green
             =============    ============    =======
Target       COLLISIONLAYERS  LEVELS          LEGEND
DarkBlue     =============    ============    =======

Wall         Background       #########       . = Background
Brown        Target           #......#        # = Wall
             Player, Wall, Crate  #.....@.#    P = Player
Player                        #.P.*.O.#       * = Crate
Blue         =============    #......#         @ = Crate and Target
             WINCONDITIONS    #......#         O = Target
Crate        =============    #########
Orange
             All Crate on Target
```

Fig. 2. Partial definition of the hello-world example of PuzzleScript

same information can also be used to check if a game can still be solved in the current state. For example, the game cannot be solved any more if a crate gets stuck in a corner.

2.3 iTasks

iTasks [18] supports task-oriented programming in the pure functional programming language Clean [19]. It allows for rapid workflow program development, by using the concept of task as an abstraction. Clean is very similar to Haskell, with a few exceptions. A data declaration starts with ::, types of function arguments are not separated by a function arrow (→) but by a space, and class contexts are written at the end of a type, starting with a |.

An iTasks program is composed out of base tasks, task combinators, and standard Clean functions. A task is a monadic structure. Its evaluation is driven by events and handling an event potentially changes a shared state. Tasks can be combined using combinators. The most common combinators are ⪢ (sequence), ⪢⋆ (step), −||− (parallel) and −&&− (choice). The step combinator can be seen as a combination of sequence and choice. It takes a task and attaches a list of actions to it, from which the user can choose. The chosen action receives a result value from the first task. The action, which is of type *TaskStep*, is a regular task combined with an action to trigger it, and a condition that must hold for the action to be available.

Figure 3 shows the partial source code of an iTasks program for a Command and Control (C2) system, as illustrated in Fig. 4. The illustration represents a ship with rooms and doors between them. Alice is a worker on the ship. This system is a simplified version of the C2 system built by the iTasks team in cooperation with the Royal Netherlands Navy [23].

The record type *ShipState* holds the state of the ship and the state of the worker. *shipTask* implements the C2 system. First, it uses the standard task for

shipStore :: *Shared ShipState*

shipTask :: *Task ShipState*
shipTask = *viewSharedInformation* "Ship" [] *shipStore*
        ≫⋆ [*OnAction* (*Action* "Move"   []) (*always moveTask*)
          , *OnAction* (*Action* "Pick up" []) (*ifValue hasInventory*
                    (*λst* → *set* (*applyPickup st*) *shipStore* ≫| *shipTask*))
          , *OnAction* (*Action* "Extinguish" []) (*ifValue canExtinguish*
                    (*λst* → *set* (*applyExtinguish st*) *shipStore* ≫| *shipTask*))]

moveTask :: *ShipState* → *Task ShipState*

hasInventory   :: *ShipState* → *Bool*
applyPickup   :: *ShipState* → *ShipState*
canExtinguish   :: *ShipState* → *Bool*
applyExtinguish :: *ShipState* → *ShipState*

Fig. 3. Example iTasks program, formulated by composing tasks

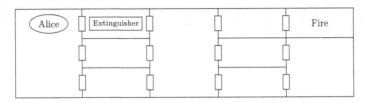

Fig. 4. Rendering of an example initial state for the simplified C2 system

viewing information, stored in the Shared Data Sources [18] (SDS), to display the current state. Then, it uses the step combinator ≫⋆ to combine the viewing task with the tasks offering the possible options.

When running *shipTask*, the iTasks system renders the *shipStore* together with three buttons that allow the worker to move, pick up an item, or extinguish a fire. If an action is not applicable (for example, an extinguish action when the worker does not hold an extinguisher), the button is disabled. When a user clicks an enabled button, the *shipStore* is updated accordingly.

The goal of this system is to extinguish a fire on the ship. We want to extend the functionality of our program to give a user a next-step hint if she does not know how to proceed. We could implement this in an ad-hoc fashion by developing hint functionality for each iTask program for which we want to give hints to the end user. Alternatively, we will use the same framework as we want to use in the previous examples. By using this framework, we do not have to reimplement the hint functionality for every iTask program from scratch.

$$
\begin{array}{ll}
:: \textit{Rule a} & = \textit{Rule Name (Effect a)} \\
:: \textit{Name} & :== \textit{String} \\
:: \textit{Effect a} & :== a \rightarrow a \\
:: \textit{Goal a} & :== \textit{Predicate a} \\
:: \textit{Predicate a} & :== a \rightarrow \textit{Bool}
\end{array}
$$

$$
\begin{array}{l}
:: \textit{RuleTree a} \\
= \textit{Seq} \, [\textit{RuleTree a}] \\
| \quad \textit{Choice} \, [\textit{RuleTree a}] \\
| \quad \textit{Parallel} \, [\textit{RuleTree a}] \\
| \quad \textit{Condition (Predicate a) (RuleTree a)} \\
| \quad \textit{Leaf (Rule a)} \\
| \quad \textit{Empty}
\end{array}
$$

Fig. 5. Types of the components of our DSL

3 Problem Formalization

Russell and Norvig [21] define a well-defined artificial intelligence (AI) problem as consisting of the following components:

Initial state. The state of the problem that you want to solve.
Operator set. The set of steps that can be taken, together with their effects.
Goal test. A predicate that is True if the problem is solved.
Path Cost function. A function that describes the cost of each operation.

We use a slightly simplified definition of an AI problem. If there is a cost associated with a certain operation, we encode this as an effect on the state. Therefore, we do not need a path cost function. We have an initial state, represented by a value of type a, and an operator set, represented by a *RuleTree*, and a goal test, represented by the predicate *Goal a*.

Figure 5 gives the types of the components of our DSL. A *Rule* consists of a *Name* and an *Effect*. The *Name* is used to identify the rule to the end user in a given hint. Therefore, these names should be informative and unambiguous. The *Goal* can be reached by performing one or more rules after each other to arrive at a state where the *Goal* condition is met. The solution depth is the number of rules that have to be applied to reach the *Goal*.

The components in the DSL follow naturally from the Russell and Norvig definition, except for the *RuleTree*. The design of the *RuleTree* is loosely based on strategy languages from the Ideas framework [7], iTask combinators [18], and the strategy language presented by Visser and others [26].

We implement the DSL as an embedded DSL in Clean. This allows us to use standard Clean functions to construct for example a rule tree. We chose not to implement recursion in our DSL, but instead make use of recursion in the host language. The advantage of this is that we can keep our DSL simple and small. Implementing recursion in the DSL requires adding abstraction and application, making the DSL significantly more complex. Another notable omission is support for multiple users, for example by means of an assign combinator. This restricts the set of rule-based problems that can be encoded to single-user problems. Apart from multi-user problems, any rule-based problem can be encoded in this DSL, and as long as there is an appropriate solving algorithm available, our framework can generate hints for it.

$shipSimulation :: RuleTree\ ShipState$
$shipSimulation = Seq$
$\quad [\,Choice\ [\,Choice\ (map\ (\lambda x \rightarrow Condition\ (isValidMove\ x)$
$\qquad\qquad\qquad\qquad\qquad\qquad (Leaf\ (Rule\ (toName\ x)$
$\qquad\qquad\qquad\qquad\qquad\qquad\qquad\quad (applyMove\ x))))$
$\qquad\qquad\qquad [1\,..\,maxRoomID])$
$\qquad , Condition\ hasInventory\ (Leaf\ (Rule\ \texttt{"Pickup"}\ applyPickup))$
$\qquad , Condition\ canExtinguish\ (Leaf\ (Rule\ \texttt{"Extinguish"}\ applyExtinguish))]$
$\quad , shipSimulation\,]$

$shipNotOnFire :: ShipState \rightarrow Bool$
$shipNotOnFire \quad \{ship\} \quad = (foldr\ (\wedge)\ True\ (map\ (notOnFire)\ (flatten\ ship)))$

Fig. 6. C2 in our DSL

3.1   C2 in Our DSL

To build intuition on how to translate a rule-based problem into our DSL, we have taken the iTasks example program from Sect. 2, listed in Fig. 3 and transformed it. First we build the *RuleTree* for our problem. We do this by using the constructors as combinators. At the top-level of the tree structure, we have two subtrees in sequence. The first subtree allows a choice between three options, namely the three actions the user can take: Move, Pick up, and Extinguish. In the case of Move, we construct the list of possible rooms that Alice can move to, by mapping a function that constructs a Condition over the list of rooms. This condition validates the move, before allowing this rule to be offered and applied. The Condition constructor is also used in the case of Pick up and Extinguish. The condition makes sure that there is something to pick up and something to extinguish, respectively. The second subtree is a recursive call to the whole tree. As mentioned earlier, we use the recursion from Clean here to construct recursive *RuleTrees*, recursion is not part of our DSL.

Now that we have our *RuleTree*, we need to construct the goal condition. This is simply a predicate over the state, which indicates if we have achieved our goal. In this case, we don't want the ship to be on fire, so we do a *foldr* over the rooms of the ship to check that none of the rooms are on fire.

4   Solving Implementations

The DSL introduced in the previous section offers a uniform approach to describe rule-based problems. Different classes of problems require different approaches to solving such problems. This section describes how we can view the DSL as an interface for which we can provide different interpretations to obtain different ways to approach a problem, and to obtain various services, in particular for providing hints.

$allFirsts :: (RuleTree\ a)\ a \rightarrow [Name]$
$allFirsts\quad t \qquad\qquad s\ =\ map\ toName\ (topRules\ s\ t)$

$topRules :: a\ (RuleTree\ a\quad) \rightarrow [Rule\ a]$
$topRules\quad \_\ Empty\qquad\quad =\ []$
$topRules\quad \_\ (Leaf\ r\quad) =\ [r]$
$topRules\quad \_\ (Seq\ []\quad) =\ []$
$topRules\quad s\ (Seq\ [rt:rts]\ ) =\ \textbf{case}\ rt\ \textbf{of}$
$$\qquad Condition\ c\ t \mid c\ s\qquad =\ topRules\ s\ (Seq\ [t:rt])$$
$$\qquad\qquad\qquad\quad \mid\ True\ \ =\ []$$
$$\qquad\qquad\qquad\_\qquad\quad =\ \textbf{case}\ topRules\ s\ rt\ \textbf{of}$$
$$\qquad\qquad\qquad\qquad\qquad []=\ topRules\ s\ (Seq\ rts)$$
$$\qquad\qquad\qquad\qquad\qquad x\ =\ x$$
$topRules\quad s\ (Choice\ rts\quad) =\ flatten\ (map\ (topRules\ s)\ rts)$
$topRules\quad s\ (Parallel\ rts\quad) =\ flatten\ (map\ (topRules\ s)\ rts)$
$topRules\quad s\ (Condition\ c\ rt) \mid\ \ c\ s\ \ =\ topRules\ d\ rt$
$$\qquad\qquad\qquad\qquad\quad \mid\ \ True\ =\ []$$

Fig. 7. Definition of the *allFirsts* hint service

This section shows the implementations of four services for giving hints for different classes of problems. All implementations take the strategy *RuleTree*, the current state in the form of a value of type *a* and the goal test *Goal*, and return the names of zero or more steps that can be taken at this point in solving the problem. As will become clear in the coming sections, not all implementations require a goal test. Some implementations require an additional scoring function like fitness or a heuristic. We also state what guarantees can be given for the implementation.

The implementations we give in this section all use Clean syntax.

4.1   All Firsts

allFirsts, listed in Fig. 7, returns the first steps that can be taken given a state and a *RuleTree* value. Since it does not take the goal into account, these steps are only relevant for problem domains where it is possible to precisely describe the next step to be taken in a solution towards a goal using a *RuleTree* value. Examples of such domains are mathematical and logic exercises. The *allFirsts* service is used if the tree describes only the steps that are always on a path to the goal. This is the case for example in the Ideas framework.

For the *allFirsts* algorithm, we cannot give any guarantee about the given hint. Since it simply returns all steps a user can take, it is completely up to the programmer to guarantee that only steps towards the goal can be taken.

$fitnessHint :: (a \rightarrow Int) \ (RuleTree \ a) \ a \rightarrow [Name]$
$fitnessHint \quad f \qquad\qquad rt \qquad\qquad s =$
$\quad map \ toName \ (findBest \ (map \ (\lambda(Rule \ n \ e) \rightarrow ((Rule \ n \ e), f \ (e \ s))) \ (topRules \ s \ rt)))$

$findBest :: [(Rule \ a, Int)] \rightarrow [Rule \ a]$
$findBest \quad [] \qquad\qquad\quad = []$
$findBest \quad [(r, n) : xs] \quad = fst \ (helper \ ([r], n) \ xs)$

$helper :: ([Rule \ a], Int) \ [(Rule \ a, Int)] \rightarrow ([Rule \ a], Int)$
$helper \quad a \qquad\qquad\quad [] \qquad\qquad\quad = a$
$helper \quad (rs, n) \qquad\quad [(r, n2) : xs] \quad | \ n \equiv n2 = helper \ (rs \mathbin{+\!\!+} [r], n) \ xs$
$\qquad\qquad\qquad\qquad\qquad\qquad\qquad\quad | \ n < n2 = helper \ (rs, n) \ xs$
$\qquad\qquad\qquad\qquad\qquad\qquad\qquad\quad | \ n > n2 = helper \ ([r], n2) \ xs$

Fig. 8. Definition of the fitness-based hint service

4.2   Fitness Scoring

Just as *allFirsts*, *fitnessHint*, listed in Fig. 8, only looks at the immediate next steps specified by the *RuleTree*. From these next steps, it selects the best by calculating the fitness of each step, and taking the step with maximum fitness. A fitness function is defined as a function from a to *Int*, where a lower score is better. The algorithm assumes that the fitness function ensures that a user gets closer to the goal if she follows the hints, but of course this depends on the relation between the fitness function and the goal. If a programmer passes a good fitness function as argument, that is, a step selected by the fitness function brings a user closer to the goal and not to a local optimum, then the step returned by *fitnessHint* is part of a sequence of steps that leads to the goal.

4.3   Brute Force

Figure 9 gives a brute force algorithm *bfHint*. It takes a *Goal*, a state a and a *RuleTree*, and returns a list of first steps that can be taken. It uses the function *bfStep*, which returns all paths that reach the goal. Since we only need the first step to produce a hint, we map the *traceToName* function over it. *bfStep* works recursively. It first takes the previous expansions, and checks if there are any states that fulfill the goal condition. If so, we return the traces of these expansions as a solution. If no expansions fulfill the goal, all states are expanded and *bfStep* is called recursively. This means that we search breadth-first. If multiple solutions are found at the same depth, all of these solutions are returned. Therefore, the return type of *bfHint* is a list of *Name*. We only give the type of *expand*.

If *bfHint* returns a hint, then by definition this is a step in a sequence of steps that achieves the goal. Not only that, but since it searches breadth-first for a solution, it is guaranteed to be the first step on the shortest path to the goal.

We have also implemented a special version of *bfHint* that allows the programmer to pass an additional pruning function called a *TraceFilter*. This special

$bfHint :: (Goal\ a)\ (RuleTree\ a)\ a \rightarrow [Name]$
$bfHint\quad g\qquad\quad rt\qquad\qquad s\ =\ map\ traceToName\ (bfStep\ g\ [([\,],rt,s)])$

$bfStep :: (Goal\ a)\ [([Name], RuleTree\ a, a)] \rightarrow [[Name]]$
$bfStep\quad g\qquad\quad items = \mathbf{case}\ [h \setminus\setminus (h,\_,d) \leftarrow items\ |\ g\ d]\ \mathbf{of}$
$\qquad\qquad\qquad\qquad\qquad\qquad\quad [\,] \rightarrow bfStep\ g\ (flatten\ (map\ expand\ items))$
$\qquad\qquad\qquad\qquad\qquad\qquad\quad x \rightarrow x$

$expand :: ([Name], RuleTree\ a, a) \rightarrow [([Name], RuleTree\ a, a)]$

$traceToName :: [Name] \rightarrow Name$
$traceToName\quad [\,]\qquad = ""$
$traceToName\quad [x,\_] \quad = x$

$bfHintFilter :: (TraceFilter\ a)\ (Goal\ a)\ (RTree\ a)\ a \rightarrow [Name]$

Fig. 9. Brute force algorithm

version, *bfHintFilter*, applies the filter to the list of expansions after every expansion to prune the search space. Some uses for this are limiting the search depth, pruning duplicate expansions or removing expansions that will never lead to a solution.

4.4 Heuristic Search

A potential problem with the brute force algorithm is that it expands every state until a state fulfills the goal predicate. This might be computationally very expensive. We can try to reach the goal using fewer resources by using a heuristic. A heuristic is a function $hr :: a \rightarrow Int$, with $\forall s : hr\ s \geqslant 0$, and $hr\ s \equiv 0$ if and only if s fulfills the goal condition. This heuristic function is used in the search algorithm to search for a solution in a more informed way. A heuristic function differs from a fitness function in the sense that it is no longer required that the function does not lead to a local optimum. The implementation takes this into account by keeping track of states that have already been observed. These states are considered to be closed, and will not be expanded twice.

Figure 10 gives our *heuristicHint* algorithm, which implements a best-first-search algorithm using a heuristic function.

heuristicHint initializes the arguments for *hDecide*.

hDecide looks at the highest scoring expansion. If it fulfills the goal condition, *hDecide* returns the trace of that expansion. If not, it checks if the *RuleTree* in the expansion is empty. If so, the expansion cannot be expanded further and is discarded. *hDecide* is called on the remaining list. If the expansion does not fulfill the goal and has a non-empty *RuleTree*, *hStep* is called to perform the next expansion.

hStep then performs an expansion step. It expands the states that have the lowest score. It then checks if any of the new states have already been observed before. If so, then they are discarded as the expansion is redundant. It adds the new states to the list of observed states, and scores them. Now, the whole list of scored states is sorted, and *hDecide* is called.

$heuristicHint :: (a \rightarrow Int)\ (Goal\ a)\ (RuleTree\ a)\ a \rightarrow Name$
$heuristicHint\ \ f\ \qquad g\ \qquad rt\ \qquad s\ =$
  $traceToName\ (hDecide\ f\ g\ [(0, ([\,], rt, s))])$

$hStep :: (a \rightarrow Int)\ \quad (Goal\ a)\ ([\,a\,], [(Int, ([Name], RuleTree\ a, a))]) \rightarrow [Name]$
$hStep\ \quad \_\ \qquad\qquad \_\ \qquad (\_\ ,[\,]\quad\ )\ \qquad\qquad\qquad\qquad = [\,]$
$hStep\ \quad h\ \qquad\qquad g\ \qquad (obs, [(n, t) : xs])\ \qquad\qquad\qquad =$
  $hDecide\ h\ g\ (obs \mathbin{+\!\!+} newObs, (sortScore\ ((map\ (\lambda(his, t, d) \rightarrow (h\ d, (his, t, d)))$
  $\qquad\qquad\qquad\qquad\qquad\qquad\qquad\qquad (filteredCnds)) \mathbin{+\!\!+} tail)))$

    where
        $candidates\ \ = [t : (map\ snd\ (takeWhile\ (\lambda(i, \_) \rightarrow i \equiv n)\ xs))]$
        $tail\ \qquad\quad = filter\ (\lambda(i, \_) \rightarrow i \not\equiv n)\ xs$
        $filteredCnds = filter\ (\lambda(\_, \_, d) \rightarrow \neg \circ (isMember\ d\ obs))\ (flatten\ (map\ expand\ candidates))$
        $newObs\ \quad = map\ (\lambda(\_, \_, d) \rightarrow d)\ closedExpansion$

$hDecide :: (a \rightarrow Int)\ (Goal\ a)\ ([\,a\,], [(Int, ([Name], RuleTree\ a, a))]) \rightarrow [Name]$
$hDecide\ \ h\ \qquad\quad g\ \qquad (\_,\ \ [(\_, (his, \_\qquad\quad, d)) : xns]\ \qquad)\ |\ g\ d = his$
$hDecide\ \ h\ \qquad\quad g\ \qquad (obs, [(\_, (\_\ \ , Empty, \_)) : xns]\ \quad)\ = hDecide\ h\ g\ (obs, xns)$
$hDecide\ \ h\ \qquad\quad g\ \qquad x\ \qquad\qquad\qquad\qquad\qquad\qquad\qquad = hStep\ h\ g\ x$

Fig. 10. The *heuristicHint* algorithm

When *hDecide* encounters an expansion that fulfills the goal condition, the trace of this expansion is returned, and *heuristic* takes the first step in the trace and returns it as a hint.

heuristicHint differs from *bfHint* in two ways. First, *heuristicHint* performs only one expansion at a time and does not do this in a breadth-first manner, but best-first. A consequence of using best-first search is that the result trace we get, is not guaranteed to be the shortest path to the goal.

Second, in order to be able to escape local optima, *heuristicHint* prunes away expansions that lead to states already observed. This prevents cyclic expansions, something *bfHint* does not take into account. However, this has no effect on the result of the algorithm since two states will have the same solution.

4.5   Other Algorithms

The algorithms described in this section have been implemented in our framework. There are many other algorithms that support solving problems of the kind described in Sect. 3. A programmer can implement these once, and then solve multiple problems using the same implementation in our framework. Some common algorithms not listed above are A*, Hill climbing, and probabilistic annealing.

$dnfRT :: RuleTree\ Expr$
$dnfRT = Seq\ [rptRule\ constantsR, rptRule\ definitionsR$
$\qquad\qquad\quad , rptRule\ negationsR, rptRule\ distributionR]$

$rptRule\ rule = Choice\ [Condition\ (canApply\ rule)\ (Seq\ [Leaf\ rule, rptRule\ rule])$
$\qquad\qquad\qquad\quad , Condition\ (\neg \circ (canApply\ rule))\ Empty]$

$canApply\ (Rule\ n\ e)\ s = (e\ s) \not\equiv s$

Fig. 11. DNF exercise in our DSL

5   Validation

Sections 3 and 4 fully describe our method for generating feedback systems. To summarize, we first describe the rule-based problem in our DSL. Once the problem is uniformly described, we get a hint function for free by means of the generic solving algorithms. In this section, we validate our approach.

We take real-world examples from each of the three rule-based problem frameworks introduced in Sect. 2, including the examples presented in that section and two new problems, and instantiate feedback systems for them using our proposed approach of first describing the problem using our DSL, and then applying a generic solving algorithm. By doing this, we validate that our approach indeed allows easy instantiation of a feedback system for different rule-based problems.

5.1   Ideas

The Ideas framework introduced in Sect. 2.1 is used to build intelligent tutoring systems. We have taken two examples, with different domains and problems, of actual systems implemented in Ideas: calculating the disjunctive normal form of a logic expression (see Fig. 11), and reducing a matrix to echelon form (see Fig. 12).

Disjunctive Normal Form. Figure 11 lists the description of the disjunctive normal form exercise in our DSL. This is almost a direct translation from the Ideas strategy listed in Sect. 2.1, Fig. 1.

Figure 11 lists the *RuleTree* for the DNF strategy. In order to encode it compactly, an additional combinator function is used called the *rptRule*. This function checks if the rule applies. If so, the rule can be applied, after which *rptRule rule* is called again. If not, the *Empty RuleTree* is returned and this will end the recursion. This means that the *rule* that *rptRule* is applied to, should have an effect on the condition, otherwise this recursion will never terminate.

The *RuleTree* is all that is required to build the hint-function. Since all steps offered by the *RuleTree* are on a path to the goal, we can just return them by using the *allFirsts* algorithm.

$toReducedEchelon = label$ "`Gaussian elimination`" ($forwardPass <*> backwardPass$)

$forwardPass = label$ "`Forward pass`" (
  $repeat$ ($label$ "`Find j-th column`" $ruleFindColumnJ$
      $<*> label$ "`Exchange rows`"   ($try\ ruleExchangeNonZero$)
      $<*> label$ "`Scale row`"   ($try\ ruleScaleToOne$)
      $<*> label$ "`Zeros in j-th column`" ($repeat\ ruleZerosFP$)
      $<*> label$ "`Cover up top row`" $ruleCoverRow$))

$backwardPass = label$ "`Backward pass`" (
  $repeat$ ($label$ "`Uncover row`" $ruleUncoverRow <*> label$ "`Sweep`" ($repeat\ ruleZerosBP$)))

Fig. 12. Gaussian elimination strategy in Ideas

The *hint* function below takes an expression in the domain, and returns steps that can be taken at this point. If no steps are returned, the exercise is solved.

$$hint :: Expr \rightarrow [Name]$$
$$hint = allFirsts\ dnfRT$$

Gaussian Elimination. Our second example is in the domain of linear algebra. The exercise at hand is to reduce a matrix to echelon form, using Gaussian elimination.

Figure 12 lists the strategy of Gaussian elimination that is used in the Ideas framework. It describes what steps must be applied to a matrix in order to transform it to the reduced echelon from, by means of Gaussian elimination.

The forward pass is applied to the matrix as often as possible. When this procedure no longer applies, the backwards pass is applied exhaustively. If no rules from either two phase apply, the matrix has been reduced. We leave out the exact details of what each rule in the passes does, they are available elsewhere [7].

In order to transform this description into our DSL, we need to introduce two new combinator-functions. Namely to deal with the *repeat* and the *try*. Figure 13 lists the complete description of Gaussian elimination in our DSL, together with these combinator-functions.

Since we are again dealing with a *RuleTree* where all the offered steps are on a path to the goal, no goaltest function is needed to build the hint-function.

$$hint :: Expr \rightarrow [Name]$$
$$hint = allFirsts\ toReducedEchelonRT$$

As with the DNF example, applying the *RuleTree* to the allFirsts algorithm instantiates the hint-function.

```
toReducedEchelonRT :: RuleTree Expr
toReducedEchelonRT = Seq [forwardPassRT, backwardsPassRT]

forwardPassRT = rptRT Seq [Leaf ruleFindColumnJ,  tryRule ruleExchangeNonZero
                         , tryRule ruleScaleToOne, rptRule ruleZerosFP
                         , Leaf ruleCoverRow]

backwardPassRT = rptRT Seq [Leaf ruleUncoverRow, rptRule ruleZerosBP]

rptRT rt = Choice [Condition (done rt) Empty
                 , Condition (¬ ∘ (done rt)) (Seq [rt, rptRT rt])]

tryRule rule = Choice  [Condition (canApply rule) (Leaf rule)
                      , Condition (¬ ∘ (canApply rule)) Empty]
```

Fig. 13. Gaussian elimination exercise in our DSL

5.2 PuzzleScript

PuzzleScript, as introduced in Sect. 2.2, is a puzzle game framework. We have taken the most well known puzzle game implemented in PuzzleScript, Sokoban, and built a hint system for it.

Sokoban. Figure 2 in Sect. 2.2 lists the source code for Sokoban, written in PuzzleScript. Since PuzzleScript is written in JavaScript and not in Clean, we cannot directly reuse auxiliary functions, like we did when transforming the C2 program.

Figure 14 lists the *RuleTree* for Sokoban. We first define *GameState* which models our state. It contains the *LevelState*, as well as the position of the player pX, pY. *sokobanRT* defines the *RuleTree*. In sequence, it offers choice from one of the four moves, and then recurses. All moves are conditional, they can only be chosen if they can actually be applied. We only supply the types of the functions *validMove* and *applyMove*.

On first attempt, we take the brute force algorithm, and use it to construct our hint-function. For trivial levels, this suffices, but once we have a solution depth of 15, we have to explore $3^{15} \approx 1.4 \times 10^7$ states, assuming that there are on average three valid moves per state.

Brute force clearly will not work. We have to come up with something a bit more clever. Literature on Sokoban [10] points to heuristics and search space pruning to help us order and restrict the search space, and construct a hint-function. Lim and Harrell have generalized these Sokoban heuristics to apply to most PuzzleScript games [14].

```
:: GameState = { lvl :: LevelState, pX :: Int, pY :: Int }
:: LevelState :== [[[ GameObject ]]]

sokobanRT :: RuleTree GameState
sokobanRT =
  Seq [ Choice [ Condition (validMove LeftMove)
                           (Leaf (Rule "Move Left"  (applyMove LeftMove  )))
               , Condition (validMove RightMove)
                           (Leaf (Rule "Move Right" (applyMove RightMove )))
               , Condition (validMove UpMove)
                           (Leaf (Rule "Move Up"    (applyMove UpMove    )))
               , Condition (validMove DownMove)
                           (Leaf (Rule "Move Down"  (applyMove DownMove)))]
      , sokobanRT ]

sokobanGoal :: GameState → Bool

validMove :: GameMove GameState → Bool
applyMove :: GameMove GameState → GameState
```

Fig. 14. Sokoban in our DSL

We implement a simple deadlock pruning filter to improve performance. A simple deadlock occurs when a crate is in an unsafe position, from where it will never reach a target. Removing these states reduces the search space.

Implementing heuristics for sokoban, like the mentioned work suggests, can be quite involved. This is beyond the scope of this paper, but could be implemented using the *heuristicHint* algorithm.

To perform simple deadlock detection, we first build a list of unsafe positions. To do this, we find all the corners in the game. After locating the corners, we generate a list of all horizontal and vertical paths from corner to corner. Paths that are not along a wall, or that have walls or targets on them, are removed. The cells on the remaining paths, together with the corners, form the list of unsafe positions. To determine if a state has a deadlock, we simply inspect all unsafe positions. If a state has a crate on an unsafe position, it is removed and thus not further expanded.

Below, the hint function is implemented. For the simple deadlock pruning function, we only provide the type.

$noDeadlock :: GameState \rightarrow Bool$

$hint :: GameState \rightarrow Name$
$hint = bfHintFilter\ (\lambda(\_,\_,b) \rightarrow noDeadlock\ b)\ sokobanGoal\ sokobanRT$

5.3   iTasks

The iTasks framework introduced in Sect. 2.3 is used to build workflow systems using a notion of task as an abstraction. We have taken two examples, with different domains, of actual systems implemented in iTasks: a C2 workflow system (see Fig. 3), and a sliding puzzle game (see Fig. 16).

```
:: GameState = { board :: [Int], dim :: Int, hole :: Int }
:: Dir = North | East | South | West
boardStore :: Shared GameState

slidePuzzle :: Task GameState
slidePuzzle =
    viewSharedInformation "Sliding Puzzle" [ViewWith viewBoard] boardStore
    ≫* map (λdir → OnAction (Action (toName dir) []) (ifValue (checkStep dir)
                            (λst → set (applyStep dir st) boardStore
                                                      ≫| slidePuzzle)))
        [North, East, South, West]

viewBoard :: GameState        → HtmlTag
checkStep :: Dir GameState → Bool
applyStep :: Dir GameState → GameState
```

Fig. 15. Sliding puzzle program written in iTasks

ShipAdventure. Figure 3 in Sect. 2.3 lists the partial source code of a C2 system written in iTasks. We already explored what this problem would look like in our DSL in Sect. 3.1. The *RuleTree* and *shipNotOnFire*-goal-test are listed in Fig. 6.

If we now want to build the hint-function that takes the state of the system and returns a hint for the user how to keep the ship from burning down, we can take the brute force algorithm from Fig. 9 and give it the *RuleTree* and goal-test as shown below.

$$hint :: (SimulationState \rightarrow [Name])$$
$$hint = bfHint\ shipNotOnFire\ shipSimulation$$

Sliding Puzzle. To demonstrate and experiment with iTasks, we implemented a simple sliding puzzle (also called n-puzzle). Figure 15 gives the (partial) source code of the iTasks program that we constructed. In this puzzle, the player arranges all tiles in order, by using the hole to slide the tiles over the board, as shown in Fig. 16.

The record type *GameState* holds the board configuration, the dimension of the puzzle, and the position of the hole. *Dir* defines the kind of moves a player can perform and *slidePuzzle* implements the puzzle.

As with the C2 system, *slidePuzzle* uses the standard task for viewing information to display the current state. Then, it uses the step combinator $\gg\star$ to combine the viewing task with the tasks offering the possible options. We use a *map* to generate the four options a player can choose from.

The goal of the puzzle is to move all tiles in positions so that they appear in order, as shown in Fig. 16b. We now want to add hints to the iTasks program. If the player gets stuck, we want to help out by providing a hint step.

Figure 17 lists the *RuleTree* and *goalTest* for the sliding puzzle. The functions *checkStep* and *applyStep* are the same Clean functions used by the iTasks implementation. The only additional function needed is the *goalTest*, that compares the current board to the solution-state.

(a) Initial state   (b) Goal state

Fig. 16. Instance of a block sliding puzzle, of dimension 3×3

$slidePuzzle :: RuleTree\ GameState$
$slidePuzzle = Seq$
$\quad [\ Choice\ [\ Condition\ (checkStep\ North)\ (Rule\ \texttt{"Move up"}\quad (applyStep\ North))$
$\quad\quad\quad , Condition\ (checkStep\ South)\ (Rule\ \texttt{"Move down"}\ (applyStep\ South))$
$\quad\quad\quad , Condition\ (checkStep\ West)\ (Rule\ \texttt{"Move left"}\ (applyStep\ West))$
$\quad\quad\quad , Condition\ (checkStep\ East)\ \ (Rule\ \texttt{"Move right"}\ (applyStep\ East))]$
$\quad , slidePuzzle\ ]$

$goalTest :: GameState \rightarrow Bool$
$goalTest\ \{board, dim\} = [0\mathinner{.\,.}((dim * dim) - 1)] \equiv board$

Fig. 17. Sliding puzzle in our DSL

The n-puzzle problem is too complex to apply a brute force algorithm. An 8-puzzle for example has an average branching factor of 2.67 [15], and an average solution length of 21.97 [20]. We can calculate that we have to visit $2.67^{21.97} \approx 3.39 \times 10^8$ states on average before a solution is found using brute force search.

This calls for a more informed algorithm. Russell and Norvig propose two heuristics for the n-puzzle problem [21]. The first, h_1, is the number of tiles out of place. h_2 is the sum of the (Manhattan) distances of the tiles from their goal positions. With help of h_1, we can construct the following hint function.

$hint :: GameState \rightarrow [Name]$
$hint = heuristicHint\ h1\ goalTest\ slidePuzzle$

$h1 :: GameState\quad \rightarrow Int$
$h1\quad \{board, dim\} = bDiff\ board\ [0\mathinner{.\,.}((dim * dim) - 1)]$
$\quad\quad\quad\quad\quad\quad\quad \textbf{where}$
$\quad\quad\quad\quad\quad\quad\quad\quad bDiff\ [\,]\quad\quad [\,]\quad\quad = 0$
$\quad\quad\quad\quad\quad\quad\quad\quad bDiff\ [x : xs]\ [y : ys]\ |\ x \not\equiv y = 1 + bDiff\ xs\ ys$
$\quad\quad\quad\quad\quad\quad\quad\quad\quad\quad\quad\quad\quad\quad |\ True\ = bDiff\ xs\ ys$

We use the heuristic search function instead of brute force. This expands the state space in an ordered way. When we now run the original program, in parallel with the hint function, we indeed get a hint for each possible state of the game.

6   Related Work

We follow in a long tradition of creating (domain specific) languages that allow uniform description of rule-based problems, such as planning problems. Some of the early languages written for this purpose are STRIPS [2], PLANNER [8] and SITPLAN [3]. Most of these are based on the same principles as our approach, namely to describe state, operator set and goal test. For example, a STRIPS problem is defined as $\langle P, O, I, G \rangle$, where P is the set of states the problem can be in, O the set of operators, I is the initial state, and G the goal state [1].

A more recent language is PDDL [16]. Version one of the language, from 1998, consists of a domain description, action set, goal description and effects. Again, these ideas coincide with our notion of a problem formalization. The PDDL standard has been updated several times [11], and there are many variants currently in use. These variants include MA-PDDL [12], which can deal with multiple agents, and PPDDL [27], which supports probabilistic effects.

The language we present is different from all of the aforementioned languages in several ways. Our language is a DSL, embedded in Clean. This means that the programmer can use the full power of Clean when constructing the problem description in our DSL. The languages mentioned above are not embedded in any language and therefore the programmer is limited to the syntax of the DSL in constructing the problem description. Another big difference is the fact that in all of the other languages mentioned, except PDDL, the state-space is finite. For example, in SITPLAN, part of the problem description is a finite set of possible situations, and in STRIPS, the set of states is defined as finite a set of conditions that can be either true or false. In our DSL, we do not limit the set of possible states. This allows us to describe many more problems in our DSL, but at the same time makes solving them harder.

The second part of our approach is to solve the problem described in our DSL. When comparing to other approaches, both SITPLAN and PDDL rely on general solvers, just like our approach. In fact, PDDL was initially designed as a uniform language to compare different planning algorithms in the AIPS-98 competition [16]. STRIPS and PLANNER however, do include a specific solving algorithm.

For each of the frameworks that we discussed in this work, there has been some research on generically solving problems. Lim and Harrell [14] present a generic algorithm for evaluating PuzzleScript that discovers solutions for different PuzzleScript games. From these solutions, one could take the first step in the sequence as a hint. The Ideas framework includes a set of feedback services to generate hints for the user. For example, the basic.allfirsts service generates all steps that can be taken at a certain point in the exercise [6]. For the iTasks framework, a system was developed to inspect current executions by using dynamic blueprints of tasks [22]. It can give additional insight in the current and future states, but does not act as a hint-system and does not take a goal into account.

7   Conclusions

With this paper, we set out to answer the question of how to construct a generic feedback framework for rule-based problems. Ideas from the intelligent tutoring community inspired our approach. We first construct a DSL that provides a uniform way to describe many different rule-based problems. Then we can use a generic algorithm to generate feedback, in the form of hints. In order to validate our approach, we have demonstrated that it is indeed possible to encode and instantiate a feedback system for many different problems.

7.1 Future Work

In the future we would like to extend our approach in several ways. First, we would like to extend our DSL to support multiple users. When dealing with for example workflow systems, it is almost always the case that there is more than one user. Secondly, we would like to extend the kind of feedback that we can give to the user. At this point, our system only returns one or more steps that serve as a hint. Other kinds of feedback could for example include a sequence of steps towards the goal or contextual information about where the user is in the greater system. When our DSL would support multiple users, we also need to offer other kinds of feedback. Imagine the situation where a user has to wait on a different user in order to reach her goal, or that a certain step has priority because other users are waiting on that step to be performed.

We are also very interested to see what questions and challenges would come up when our system would be integrated into one of the aforementioned rule-based frameworks. We think that the iTasks framework would be the most interesting candidate, since it allows for a vast amount of completely different problems to be encoded in it.

Acknowledgments. This research is supported by the Dutch Technology Foundation STW, which is part of the Netherlands Organization for Scientific Research (NWO), and which is partly funded by the Ministry of Economic Affairs.

References

1. Bylander, T.: The computational complexity of propositional STRIPS planning. Artif. Intell. **69**(1–2), 165–204 (1994)
2. Fikes, R., Nilsson, N.J.: STRIPS: a new approach to the application of theorem proving to problem solving. Artif. Intell. **2**(3–4), 189–208 (1971)
3. Galagan, N.I.: Problem description language SITPLAN. Cybern. Syst. Anal. **15**(2), 255–266 (1979)
4. Gerdes, A., Jeuring, J., Heeren, B.: An interactive functional programming tutor. In: Lapidot, T., Gal-Ezer, J., Caspersen, M.E., Hazzan, O. (eds) Proceedings of ITICSE 2012: The 17th Annual Conference on Innovation and Technology in Computer Science Education, pp. 250–255. ACM (2012)
5. Hattie, J., Timperley, H.: The power of feedback. Rev. Educ. Res. **77**(1), 81–112 (2007)
6. Heeren, B., Jeuring, J.: Feedback services for stepwise exercises. Sci. Comput. Program. **88**, 110–129 (2014)
7. Heeren, B., Jeuring, J., Gerdes, A.: Specifying rewrite strategies for interactive exercises. Math. Comput. Sci. **3**(3), 349–370 (2010)
8. Hewitt, C.: PLANNER: a language for proving theorems in robots. In: Proceedings of the 1st International Joint Conference on Artificial Intelligence, Washington, DC, May 1969, pp. 295–302 (1969)
9. Jeuring, J., et al.: Communicate!—A serious game for communication skills. In: Conole, G., Klobučar, T., Rensing, C., Konert, J., Lavoué, É. (eds.) EC-TEL 2015. LNCS, vol. 9307, pp. 513–517. Springer, Cham (2015). https://doi.org/10.1007/978-3-319-24258-3_49

10. Junghanns, A., Schaeffer, J., Sokoban: a challenging single-agent search problem. In: IJCAI Workshop on Using Games as an Experimental Testbed for AI Reasearch (1997)
11. Kovacs, D.L.: BNF definition of PDDL 3.1 (2011). http://www.plg.inf.uc3m.es/ipc2011-deterministic/attachments/OtherContributions/kovacs-pddl-3.1-2011.pdf
12. Kovacs, D.L.: A multi-agent extension of PDDL3. In: WS-IPC 2012, p. 19 (2012)
13. Lavelle, S.: PuzzleScript (2016). https://github.com/increpare/PuzzleScript
14. Lim, C.-U., Fox Harrell, D.: An approach to general videogame evaluation and automatic generation using a description language. In: Proceedings of IEEE CIG 2014: Conference on Computational Intelligence and Games, pp. 1–8 (2014)
15. Luger, G.F.: Artificial Intelligence: Structures and Strategies for Complex Problem Solving. Pearson Education, London (2005)
16. McDermott, D., et al.: PDDL-The Planning Domain Definition Language (1998)
17. Murray, T.: An overview of intelligent tutoring system authoring tools: updated analysis of the state of the art. In: Murray, T., Blessing, S.B., Ainsworth, S. (eds.) Authoring Tools for Advanced Technology Learning Environments, pp. 491–544. Springer, Dordrecht (2003). https://doi.org/10.1007/978-94-017-0819-7_17
18. Plasmeijer, R., Lijnse, B., Michels, S., Achten, P., Koopman, P.W.M.: Task-oriented programming in a pure functional language. In: Proceedings of PPDP 2012: Principles and Practice of Declarative Programming, pp. 195–206. ACM (2012)
19. Plasmeijer, R., van Eekelen, M.: Clean language report version 2.1 (2002)
20. Reinefeld, A.: Complete solution of the eight-puzzle and the benefit of node ordering in IDA. In: Proceedings of the 13th International Joint Conference on Artificial Intelligence, Chambéry, France, 28 August–3 September 1993, pp. 248–253 (1993)
21. Russell, S.J., Norvig, P.: Artificial Intelligence - A Modern Approach (3 International Edition). Pearson Education, London (2010)
22. Stutterheim, J., Achten, P., Plasmeijer, R.: Static and dynamic visualisations of monadic programs. In: Implementation and Application of Functional Languages, Koblenz, Germany, pp. 1–13, December 2015
23. Stutterheim, J., Achten, P., Plasmeijer, R.: C2 demo (2016). https://gitlab.science.ru.nl/clean-and-itasks/iTasks-SDK/tree/master/Examples/Applications/c2-demo
24. VanLehn, K.: The behavior of tutoring systems. Int. J. Artif. Intell. Educ. **16**(3), 227–265 (2006)
25. VanLehn, K., et al.: The Andes physics tutoring system: lessons learned. Int. J. Artif. Intell. Educ. **15**(3), 147–204 (2005)
26. Visser, E., Benaissa, Z.-E.-A., Tolmach, A.P.: Building program optimizers with rewriting strategies. In: Proceedings of the Third ACM SIGPLAN International Conference on Functional Programming (ICFP 1998), Baltimore, Maryland, USA, 27–29 September 1998, pp. 13–26 (1998)
27. Younes, H.L.S., Littman, M.L.: PPDDL1. 0: the language for the probabilistic part of IPC-4. In: Proceedings of the International Planning Competition (2004)

Author Index

Printed in the United States
By Bookmasters